Adirondack Trails
West-Central Region

Fourth Edition
Forest Preserve Series, Volume V

Editor, Norm Landis
Series Editor, Neal Burdick

Adirondack Mountain Club, Inc.
Lake George, NY

Cover photograph of South Inlet into Raquette Lake by Mark Bowie
Other photographs by James Appleyard, Mark Bowie, Eleanor Friend,
Norm Landis, Barbara McMartin, C. B. Moore, Richard Nowicki, Betsy
Tisdale
Page maps by Therese S. Brosseau
Overview maps by Forest Glen Enterprises
Design by Ann Hough
First edition published 1980. Second edition 1987. Third edition 1994.
Fourth edition 2006.

Published by the Adirondack Mountain Club, Inc.
814 Goggins Road, Lake George, NY 12845-4117
www.adk.org

The Adirondack Mountain Club is dedicated to the protection and responsible recreational use of the New York State Forest Preserve, and other parks,
wild lands, and waters vital to our members and chapters. The Club, found-
ed in 1922, is a member-directed organization committed to public service
and stewardship. ADK employs a balanced approach to outdoor recreation,
advocacy, environmental education, and natural resource conservation.

ADK encourages the involvement of all people in its mission and activities; its goal is to be a community that is comfortable, inviting, and accessible.

Library of Congress Cataloging-in-Publication Data

Adirondack trails : West-Central region / editor, Norm Landis. -- 4th ed.
    p. cm. -- (Forest preserve series ; v. V)
  Includes index.
  ISBN-13: 978-1-931951-16-6 (pbk.)
  ISBN-10: 1-931951-16-0 (pbk.)
 1. Hiking--New York (State)--Adirondack Park--Guidebooks. 2.
Trails--New York (State)--Adirondack Park--Guidebooks. 3. Adirondack
Park (N.Y.)--Guidebooks. I. Landis, Norm, 1949-

  GV199.42.N652A344 2006
  917.47'53--dc22

                           2006020180

ISBN 978-1-931951-16-6 $19.95 ISBN 1-931951-07-1 (set)

Printed in the United States of America
15 14 13 12 11 10 09 08 07 06   1 2 3 4 5 6 7 8 9 10

DEDICATION: OUTDOOR "HELPERS"

This edition of *Adirondack Trails: West-Central Region* is dedicated to forest rangers, assistants, foresters, and paid and volunteer trail and search crews.

Forest rangers and trail crews work on maintaining trails, which not only makes it easier for hikers to stay on their route but also protects plants and reduces erosion. For those who lose the route or are injured beyond their capacity to get themselves out, rangers and volunteer searchers stand ready to help.

To those who make the outdoors safer for us to enjoy, thank you.

—*Norm Landis*

WE WELCOME YOUR COMMENTS

Use of the information in this book is at the sole discretion and risk of the hiker. ADK and its authors make every effort to keep our guidebooks up-to-date; however, trail conditions are always changing.

In addition to reviewing the material in this book, hikers should assess their ability, physical condition, and preparation, as well as likely weather conditions, before a trip. For more information on preparation, equipment, and how to address emergencies, see the introduction.

If you note a discrepancy in this book or wish to forward a suggestion, we welcome your comments. Please cite book title, year of most recent copyright and printing (see copyright page), trail, page number, and date of your observation. Thanks for your help!

Please address your comments to:

Publications
Adirondack Mountain Club
814 Goggins Road
Lake George, NY 12845-4117
518-668-4447, ext. 23
pubs@adk.org

EMERGENCIES

For in-town or roadside emergencies call 911. For wilderness emergencies call DEC dispatch at 518-891-0235 (see p. 39).

Contents

Adirondack Park: West-Central

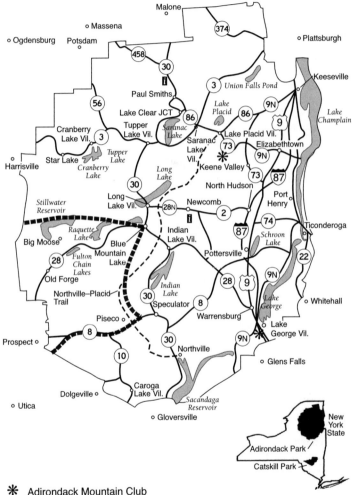

✳ Adirondack Mountain Club
ℹ Visitor Interpretive Center

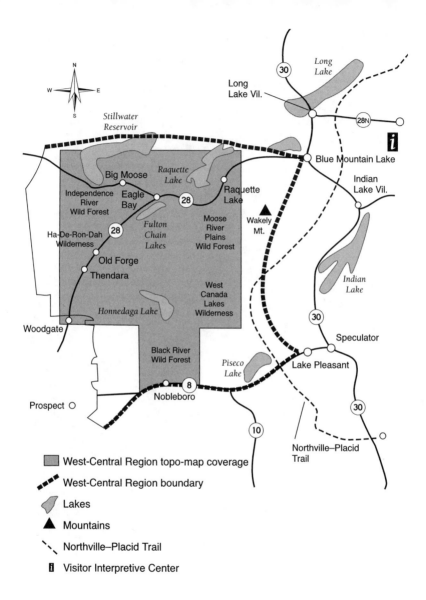

N
W — **E**
S

Long Lake

30

Long Lake Vil.

28N

Stillwater Reservoir

Blue Mountain Lake

i

Indian Lake Vil.

Big Moose

Raquette Lake

Independence River Wild Forest

Eagle Bay

28

Raquette Lake

▲ Wakely Mt.

Ha-De-Ron-Dah Wilderness

28

Fulton Chain Lakes

Moose River Plains Wild Forest

Indian Lake

Old Forge

Thendara

West Canada Lakes Wilderness

Honnedaga Lake

30

Speculator

Woodgate

Black River Wild Forest

Piseco Lake

Lake Pleasant

Prospect ○

8

Nobleboro

30

10

Northville–Placid Trail

West-Central Region topo-map coverage

West-Central Region boundary

Lakes

▲ Mountains

Northville–Placid Trail

i Visitor Interpretive Center

Browns's Tract inlet. MARK BOWIE

Preface

There are few mountains, but lots of wilderness in the West-Central Region of the Adirondacks, with many lakes and ponds where one can enjoy the outdoors. The region offers a variety of types of forests and wetlands, as well as some mountains with views and some overlooks, available free of charge.

Pushing a measuring wheel along the trails, I have sometimes gone for days seeing fewer than a handful of people, and have even had a lean-to to myself one holiday weekend and shared a lean-to with a sole companion, who was hiking with me, on another holiday weekend. So hiking in this area will likely provide solitude, although it also means you have to be more self-reliant and able to take care of yourself in an emergency, which is best done by taking along companions. The best ones are those who have first aid training as well as some practice with map and compass.

This book includes trails across vast amounts of territory—often out of cellular phone range—including the Ha-De-Ron-Dah, Pigeon Lake, and West Canada Lakes wilderness areas, where bicycles and things motorized are not allowed; and the Independence River, Black River, Moose River Plains, Fulton Chain, Sargent Ponds, and Blue Ridge wild forests, where bicycles are allowed. It also touches on the Pepperbox and Five Ponds wilderness areas.

Most people would not recognize these areas by name or be able to locate them immediately because they are more used to looking at road maps than Forest Preserve maps. That's why this guide continues to group trails according to how you can drive to them. For example, the Black River Wild Forest stretches from Old Forge south to NY 8, so access to trails in that one area could be from the Old Forge–Thendara area, the McKeever–Woodgate area, or the NY 8 area, and descriptions of trailheads and trails are listed in sections of the book with those headings.

If one had the time, it would be possible to hike from Stillwater Road through the Independence River Wild Forest across one remote dirt road into the Ha-De-Ron-Dah Wilderness Area, then out a dirt road and a mile and a half along back streets in Thendara into the Black

River Wild Forest, wade across the South Branch of the Moose River, and continue hiking all the way to Nobleboro on NY 8.

This book includes trails in the region south (and a couple north) of Stillwater Reservoir, east of (or close to) the Adirondack Park "Blue Line," north of NY 8, and west of the Northville–Placid Trail. Some trails along the fringes of the region are included even though they may also be in other volumes of the Forest Preserve Series.

To help you find these trails, in addition to the main map in the pocket in the back of this book, there are a number of page maps. Most trail descriptions start from one of four major routes: NY 12 from Utica to Lowville, NY 28 from Poland through Blue Mountain Lake, NY 8 from Utica through Lake Pleasant, and the Number Four–Stillwater (dirt) and Big Moose roads from Lowville to Eagle Bay.

Besides the state trails, this guide includes some other trails as well as information about unmarked/unmaintained routes, often old logging roads, but it would be best to save the latter until you've gained experience using map and compass since those extra skills would be needed in following them.

Most of the trails have been rechecked since the third edition, with some having new trailheads or other reroutes. Updates are a never-ending job, so make note of the address in the "We Welcome Your Comments" page in the front of the book (see p. 4) and help us keep descriptions as correct as possible.

Safe and happy trails,

—Norm Landis
Rome, NY
September 2006

Introduction

**The Adirondack Mountain Club
Forest Preserve Series**

The Forest Preserve Series of guides to Adirondack and Catskill trails covers hiking opportunities on the approximately 2.8 million acres of Forest Preserve (public) land within the Adirondack and Catskill parks. The Adirondack Mountain Club (ADK) published its first guidebook, covering the High Peaks and parts of the Northville–Placid Trail, in 1934. In the early 1980s, coinciding with the decade-long centennial celebration of the enactment of the Forest Preserve legislation in 1885, ADK set out to achieve its goal of completing a series of guides that would cover the two parks. Each guide in this series, listed below, is revised on a regular schedule.

Vol. I   *Adirondack Trails: High Peaks Region*
Vol. II   *Adirondack Trails: Northern Region*
Vol. III   *Adirondack Trails: Central Region*
Vol. IV   *Adirondack Trails: Northville–Placid Trail*
Vol. V   *Adirondack Trails: West-Central Region*
Vol. VI   *Adirondack Trails: Eastern Region*
Vol. VII   *Adirondack Trails: Southern Region*
Vol. VIII   *Catskill Trails*

The public lands that constitute the Forest Preserve are unique among all other wild public lands in the United States because they enjoy constitutional protection against sale or development. The story of this unique protection begins in the 1800s and continues today as groups such as ADK strive to guard it. This responsibility also rests with the public, who are expected not to degrade the Forest Preserve in any way while enjoying its wonders. The Forest Preserve Series of trail guides seeks not only to show hikers, skiers, and snowshoers where to enjoy their activities, but also to offer guidelines whereby users can minimize their impact on the land.

The Adirondacks

The Adirondack region of northern New York is unique in many ways. It contains the only mountains in the eastern United States that are not geologically Appalachian. In the late 1800s it was the first forested area in the nation to benefit from enlightened conservation measures. At roughly the same time it was also the most prestigious resort area in the country. In the twentieth century, the Adirondacks became the only place in the Western Hemisphere to host two winter Olympiads. In the 1970s the region was the first of significant size in the nation to be subjected to comprehensive land use controls. The Adirondack Forest Preserve (see below) is part of the only wild lands preserve in the nation whose fate lies in the hands of the voters of the entire state in which it is located.

Geologically, the Adirondacks are a southern appendage of the Canadian Shield. In the United States the Shield bedrock, which is over one billion years old, mostly lies concealed under younger rock, but it is well exposed in a few regions. Upward doming of the Adirondack mass in the past few million years—a process that is still going on, resulting in the mountains rising a few millimeters every century—is responsible for erosional stripping of the younger rock cover. The stream-carved topography has been extensively modified by the sculpting of glaciers, which, on at least four widely separated occasions during the Ice Age, completely covered the mountains.

Ecologically, the Adirondacks are part of a vegetation transition zone, with the northern, largely coniferous boreal forest (from the Greek god Boreas, owner of the north wind, whose name can be found on a mountain peak and series of ponds in the High Peaks region) and the southern deciduous forest, exemplified by beech-maple stands, intermingling to present a pleasing array of forest tree species. Different vegetation zones are also encountered as one ascends the higher mountains in the Adirondacks; the tops of the highest peaks are truly arctic, with mosses and lichens that are common hundreds of miles to the north.

A rugged and heavily forested region, the Adirondacks were generally not hospitable to Native Americans, who used the region principally for hunting. Remnants of ancient campgrounds have been found in some locations. The native legacy survives principally in place names.

The first European to see the Adirondacks was likely the French explorer Jacques Cartier, who on his first trip up the St. Lawrence River in 1535 stood on top of Mont Royal (now within the city of Montreal) and discerned high ground to the south. Closer looks were had by Samuel de Champlain and Henry Hudson, who came from the north and south, respectively, within a few weeks of each other in 1609.

For the next two centuries the Champlain Valley to the east of the Adirondacks was a battleground. Iroquois, Algonquin, French, British, and eventually American fighters struggled for control over the valley and with it supremacy over the continent. Settlers slowly filled the St. Lawrence Valley to the north, the Mohawk Valley to the south, and somewhat later, the Black River Valley to the west. Meanwhile the vast, rolling forests of the interior slumbered in virtual isolation, disturbed only by an occasional hunter, timber cruiser, or wanderer.

With the coming of the nineteenth century, people discovered the Adirondacks. Virtually unknown as late as the 1830s (the source of the Nile River was located before the source of the Hudson), by 1850 the Adirondacks made New York the leading timber-producing state in the nation. This distinction did not last for long, though, as the supply of timber was quickly brought close to extinction. Meanwhile, mineral resources, particularly iron, were being exploited.

After the Civil War, people began to look toward the Adirondacks for recreation. At the same time, resource conservation and wilderness preservation ideas began to take hold, sometimes conflicting with the newfound recreational interests. Conservation and preservation concepts were given legal standing in 1885, when the New York State legislature created the Adirondack Forest Preserve and directed that "the lands now or hereafter constituting the Forest Preserve shall be forever kept as wild forest lands." This action marked the first time a state government had set aside a significant piece of wilderness for reasons other than its scenic uniqueness.

In 1892, the legislature created the Adirondack State Park, consisting of Adirondack Forest Preserve land plus all privately owned land within a somewhat arbitrary boundary surrounding the Adirondacks, known as the "blue line" because it was drawn in blue on a large state map when it was first established. In 1894, in response to continuing abuses of the Forest Preserve law, the state's voters approved the inclusion of the "forever wild" portion of that law in the constitution of New York State, thus creating the only preserve in the nation that has constitutional protection. Today the Forest Preserve (the lands owned by the people of the State of New York) includes 2.5 million acres within the 6-million-acre Adirondack Park, the largest park in the nation outside of Alaska.

After World War I, tourism gradually took over as the primary industry in the Adirondacks. The growth of the second-home industry spurred implementation of land use plans and an Adirondack Park Agency to manage them. While the plans and the Agency have remained controversial, they indicate the need to address the issues facing the Adirondacks boldly and innovatively.

The West-Central Region

Trails in the west-central region often go to lakes, streams, rivers, or other heavily forested parts where there is no sweeping view. The region is mostly hilly, occasionally mountainous, but seldom open. The greatest attractions are the remote and wild forests, the lakes, and the waterways. With the exception of Blue Mt., West Mt., and a few lesser peaks such as Black Bear Mt., hiking in this region cannot be considered "mountain climbing." The highest mountain is Blue, which, although 3760 ft in elevation, ranks only 66th among the highest Adirondack peaks. Remote Blue Ridge is 3436 ft, and a few mountains over 3000 ft lie near the region on the E and N. The land slopes gently downward to the W, reaching about 1400 ft with hardly more than 100-ft hills.

Much of the region is public land, but several large tracts of posted private land are notable. The public should respect the owners' privacy, and avoid these regions. The largest tract of note is that of the Adirondack League Club (ALC) southeast of Old Forge. One ALC parcel includes Little Moose Lake, part of Woodhull Lake, and the Bisby Lakes; the other is centered about Honnedaga Lake. Few roads or public trails reach this land, so the hiker is unlikely to cross the boundary by accident. The Limekiln Creek–Third Lake Trail (trail 80) crosses a corner of this land on a public access route, and the J.P. Lewis Tract fits between the two ALC blocks of land. This tract was formerly leased to the ALC. Public access to the tract does not include the right to cross ALC boundaries. Another large tract is the International Paper Company holding south of Stillwater Reservoir. This land is crossed by the Number Four–Stillwater–Big Moose Rd. The property is leased to private sportsmen's groups, and is therefore off-limits to the public.

Geology

The west-central region was reduced to a peneplane (low hills) a hundred million years ago. Since then there has been some renewed uplift and dissection, producing today's topography. Major fault lines run NE-SW, determining the directional trend of the valleys and lake basins. Most streams of the region drain to the SW.

The last continental ice sheet receded from the Adirondacks 10,000 to 12,000 years ago and bequeathed to us the system of altered drainage and of lakes, ponds, and bogs that we see today. The western part of this region has a large amount of glacial sand and gravel. Eskers are more common in that area. These piles of gravel and boulders with steep sides and flat tops, which often seem to be manmade dams, were left at the sides and tips of glaciers when they melted.

Dams built at Forge Pond and Sixth Lake increased the original size of the Fulton Chain of Lakes. The dams are operated by the Hudson River-Black River Regulating District to control the water level of the Fulton Chain for purposes of recreation and to prevent floods of agricultural land along the Black River. The water level is kept up each year from late May through mid-September and lowered at other times.

Stillwater Reservoir is the largest body of water in the region at more than 10 square miles. Raquette Lake, at 8.4 square mi, is the second largest natural lake in the Adirondacks.

Along with lakes, ponds, and streams, the region is well endowed with swamps, marshes, and bogs—saturated areas, mostly open, where plant life predominates although open water may be present. A **swamp** is usually characterized by deciduous trees and shrubs, with a stream flowing through it; a **bog** by sphagnum moss floating over stagnant or semi-stagnant water, by other herbaceous (non-woody) plants, and by conifers, especially tamarack and black spruce, standing at its edge; and a **marsh** by grasses and other herbaceous plants. The term **vlei** or **vly** has also been used for a marshy or swampy meadow. It is sometimes difficult to determine from appearances which of these categories a wet area belongs to, and the use of these terms has been variable. Therefore, in this guide, the term "wetland" may be used for such areas.

Forests

The region is clothed primarily with a northern hardwood forest, with yellow birch, paper birch, sugar maple, red maple, and beech being the predominant species, although the beech are being decimated by a fungus disease. Other frequently seen species are the conifers—hemlock, red spruce, balsam fir, white pine, and northern white cedar—and the deciduous black cherry and white ash. On burned-over or recently logged areas, quaking aspen, big-toothed aspen, paper and gray birch, and fire (pin) cherry tend to dominate. Tamarack (larch) and black spruce are found in wet areas, as are red spruce and balsam fir. Spruce and fir, along with paper birch, predominate above 3000 ft (Blue Mt. Trail). The most common small-tree species is striped maple; in the higher areas, mountain maple and mountain ash are found.

Most of the region has been logged one or more times in the past, and there was considerable forest destruction by fires fed by slash left from logging operations in the early 1900s. Nevertheless, protected by the state constitution, majestic stands of forest on state land may be admired from along the trails. The largest of the deciduous species is yellow birch, followed by sugar maple; among the conifers it is white pine, followed by hemlock and red spruce. Most impressive of all the species encountered in the forest are the occasional great white pines, a common sight before logging started in the 19th century.

Fauna

The region has the usual array of Adirondack bird and animal life. The eerie cry of the loon at night on a remote lake is never to be forgotten by the backpacker, who also may occasionally find a raccoon or black bear intruding on his campsite in search of food. The plentiful white-tailed deer may sometimes be seen by the hiker or canoeist, and ample evidence of beaver work is found along streams and wetlands.

Each year the DEC stocks lakes, ponds, and streams of the region with fish, mostly trout. Acid rain, unfortunately, has depleted the fish population in many of the region's waters. (See section on hunting on page 36.)

History

Civilization in the west-central Adirondacks came to the Fulton Chain area from the Black River Valley on the SW and to the Blue Mountain Lake area from the Hudson Valley on the SE. The two currents met in the middle, one might say, at Raquette Lake. Early parcels, whose names appear on maps today, included the Black River Tract, the Brantingham Tract, John Brown's Tract, the Watson's Tract, the Great Tract Number Four, and others.

John Brown, a prominent businessman of Providence, Rhode Island, acquired title to one of the tracts, which came to be known as John Brown's Tract. In 1799 he launched a colonizing project by having a log dam erected at the site of the present Old Forge dam at the foot of the Fulton Chain, to power the saw and gristmills he had built. At the same time he had a road cut from the Forestport area NNE to the dam site. This was the old Remsen Road, 25 mi long, of which little remains. By 1800, twenty or so families had moved to the present Old Forge area to take up a rude agricultural existence. The colony failed, but it was revived in 1811 by John Brown's son-in-law, Charles Herreshoff. He moved into a house he built in the present-day village of Thendara, adjacent to Old Forge, repaired the dam and mills, and had a road cut from Moose River Settlement, located on that river W of present-day McKeever, NE to Thendara and Old Forge. This was the Brown's Tract Road. But the revived colony fared little better, and to bolster it Herreshoff opened a local iron mine and forge in 1817. That also was a failure, and Herreshoff committed suicide in 1819. The area was left to nature and a few hunters and trappers.

In 1822, John Brown Francis gave 100 acres each to ten families who settled at Number Four on Beaver Lake. Number Four had seventy-five settlers within ten years, but by 1847, only three families remained. The Fenton House at Number Four was built in 1826, became the resort of hunters and fishermen, and later expanded to become a notable summer resort.

Arthur Noble acquired title to a large block of land in the southern section, known as the Nobleboro patent of 1787. He established farming settlements at Nobleboro in 1790 and again in 1793, but the effort was soon abandoned. One can imagine how difficult it was to farm the poor soil. Lumbering became the principal activity of the region. Today, a scattering of homes and an occasional business are mostly what remain along NY 8.

On the W side, the Black River Valley and Tug Hill Plateau were settled early: the soil in the valley was apparently good enough to outweigh the disadvantage of very deep winter snows. Watson's tract, between Brantingham and Lowville, prospered well enough to be a cheese producer and a supplier of lumber brought from the Independence River basin. Permanent settlement never reached much farther into the Forest Preserve. Botchfordville on Otter Creek was a brief tannery and lumbermill town. Brantingham became a resort with the building of the first hotel in 1873. Chase Lake was already known in 1860 as "much visited by tourists." Number Four on Beaver River remains as a summer home area.

The rugged Brown's Tract Road provided the main access to the Fulton Chain area until 1892, when the railroad was pushed through. Steam navigation service from Old Forge to Fourth Lake started in 1883 and helped open the Fulton Chain and other lakes, such as Dart and Big Moose, to development. In 1896, a steam-launch service was established on Sixth, Seventh, and Eighth lakes and Brown's Tract Inlet, bringing passengers through the upper Fulton Chain and on to Raquette Lake. An interesting transportation feature was the "Pickle Boat," which plied the Old Forge-Fourth Lake route during 1905–1939, selling food and supplies at boat docks along the way. A full-fledged mail boat also operated on that route.

The Fulton Chain area was transformed by the highway and the automobile. Railroad travel declined. Public travel by steamboat has survived only in the form of modern excursion boats at Old Forge-Fourth Lake and on Raquette Lake, and tourist hotels and lodges have largely given way to motels and cottages. The Adirondack Scenic Railroad (www.adirondackrr.com) operates tourist excursions from Utica to the station at Thendara, as well as from Thendara north to Carter Station (and another section from Lake Placid to Saranac Lake), with longer trips proposed.

Logging on the W side became important by about 1875. There were log drives down the branches of the Independence, Black, and Moose rivers and their tributaries, those down the Moose River South Branch continuing as late as the 1940s. Forest products were shipped from Forestport on the Black River Canal from the first year it opened, 1850. Sites of former lumber camps are still to be seen in clearings in the forest, and one may see the remains of logging dams at the outlets of lakes and ponds. Thendara was a busy logging and lumber center from 1900 to 1922. As the timber gave out, and taxes had to be paid, large tracts were sold to New York State. Logging and development have continued on private land.

In winter, during the early 1900s before the days of modern refrigeration, ice was cut from Forge Pond and Raquette Lake and shipped by railroad to New York City and other population centers. Downhill skiing was developed at Old Forge, with snow trains arriving at Thendara in the 1930s and most of the 1940s. Since then, Old Forge and Inlet (on Fourth Lake) have become major Adirondack centers for ski touring and snowmobiling.

The most widely known event to have taken place in the region was, unfortunately, a murder. The vacationing Chester Gillette was convicted of drowning Grace Brown, who was carrying his unborn child, in South Bay of Big Moose Lake in July 1906. He was executed in 1908. This was fictionalized in Theodore Dreiser's celebrated book, *An American Tragedy*.

In the E part of the region, centering on Blue Mountain Lake, the initial inroads of civilization were in the form of logging operations undertaken in the 1840s and 1850s. The key event, however, came in 1871, when a railroad was built from Saratoga to North Creek. Thereupon a 30-mi route for buckboards and stagecoaches was established from North Creek to Blue Mountain Lake. Like the Brown's Tract Road, the ride was rough, but did not deter summer visitors from coming to the area.

Hotel building at Blue Mountain Lake began in the middle 1870s, so that by the early 1880s there were three large hotels: the Blue Mountain Lake Hotel, the Blue Mountain House (site of the present Adirondack Museum—www.adkmuseum.org), and, most grandiose of all, the Prospect House. The latter, completed in 1882, stood on Prospect Point near the SE end of the lake. It was the largest and most luxurious hotel of the Adirondacks and the world's first hotel to equip its rooms with electric lights. Harold Hochschild states in *Township 34* that during 1882–1890, with the three above-mentioned hotels operating to capacity, Blue Mountain Lake was probably the most fashionable mountain resort in the northern United States.

Blue Mountain Lake was a popular starting point for canoe and guideboat trips to Eagle, Utowana, and Raquette lakes and beyond; these trips often were conducted by Adirondack guides. The route to Raquette Lake was also served by public transportation established by

William West Durant, the leading developer of the area. Following an earlier rowboat system, he instituted a service in 1879 whereby passengers went by steamboat through Blue, Eagle, and Utowana lakes (once called the Eckford Chain), after which they walked along Bassett's Carry for the unnavigable upper section of the Marion River while baggage was hauled by horse and wagon, and then they embarked on a second steamer down the Marion River to Raquette Lake.

Hotels and private camps started being built in the Raquette Lake area during 1875–1880. Here Durant brought the construction of camps and lodges in the rustic mode to a new height of artistry and luxury, establishing a distinctive Adirondack camp architecture. Notable in this regard was Camp Pine Knot (www.cortland.edu/outdoor/raquette/huntington.html), which he built in 1879 on Long Point of Raquette Lake, and camps he built in the 1890s on Lake Mohegan and Sagamore Lake (www.sagamore.org), south of Raquette Lake, and subsequently sold to wealthy men. (The three camps are still in place, now owned by private institutions.)

In 1899–1900, as an addition to his public transportation service, Durant built the world's shortest standard-gauge railroad, the Marion River Carry Railroad. Three-quarters of a mile long, it operated over the former Bassett's Carry. Former Brooklyn street cars pulled by a steam engine carried passengers and baggage, guideboats and canoes between steamboat routes at either end of the line. (The engine and one of the cars are on exhibit at the Adirondack Museum.) The Raquette Lake Railroad was built at the same time; people could thereafter travel by connecting railroad and steamer between Blue Mountain Lake on the east and the Adirondack Railroad west of the Fulton Chain, including a transfer between boat and train at Raquette Lake village and a train stop at Eagle Bay on Fourth Lake. Besides passengers, baggage, and mail, freight cars were sometimes hauled over this route.

By the late 1890s, however, the era of big hotels was declining at Blue Mountain Lake. The Prospect House closed in 1903 as a financial loss (it was torn down in 1915). The Blue Mountain Lake House burned in 1886, was replaced, and burned again in 1904. The Blue Mountain House burned in 1880 but a replacement building continues as an exhibit at the Adirondack Museum.

With the coming of the modern highway between the Fulton Chain, Raquette Lake, and Blue Mountain Lake, the Marion River Carry

Railroad had its last year of operation in 1929.

Today the largest commercial and tourist center of the region is Old Forge. Other village centers are Brantingham, Forestport, Otter Lake, Thendara (adjacent to Old Forge), Eagle Bay and Inlet on Fourth Lake, Big Moose west of Big Moose Lake, Raquette Lake, and Blue Mountain Lake. Stillwater and Beaver River almost qualify as village centers; they each have a store and a restaurant. In addition to these centers, private camps and, in some places, tourist accommodations are located along the shorelines of much of the Fulton Chain, including almost all of Fourth Lake, and along considerable sections of Big Moose Lake, Raquette Lake, and Blue Mountain Lake.

The Black River Canal

In 1825, Governor Clinton proposed a Black River feeder canal to supply water to the top of the Erie Canal in Rome. Many dams were built to store water for summer use. The most notable of these reservoirs are Woodhull Lake, Sand Lake, North Lake, and South Lake. Several smaller reservoirs were created, such as Twin Lakes and Chub Pond, but these are now washed out and abandoned. The water was and is tapped off at Kayuta Lake, just beneath the NY 28 bridge at Forestport.

It is still possible to hike, bicycle, or ski portions of the towpath along the canal as it heads from Forestport to Boonville, and south from Boonville as it heads for Delta Reservoir. A section of the old canal route north of Boonville was used in the making of NY 12. One can still see portions of the old limestone block walls of the canal along the highway from Boonville to Lowville, and some of the old locks are still standing between the divided highway lanes. It is well worth the time to stop at one of these locks, which stand isolated after the canal walls upstream and downstream were torn away. One might imagine the locktenders walking out on top of the wooden doors to open the valves so that water would flow through, filling the lock.

State Land Units and Classifications

Since 1972, most Forest Preserve lands in the Adirondacks have been classified as either Wilderness, Primitive, or Wild Forest, depending on the size of the unit and the types of use thought to be desirable for that unit. The largest and most remote units are generally Wilderness, with only foot travel permitted and minimum facilities such as lean-tos.

Primitive areas are similar, but with a nonconforming "structure" such as a fire tower, road, or private inholding. Wild Forest areas are generally smaller but potentially more intensively used, with motorized travel or snowmobiles permitted on designated trails. Management of each unit is prescribed in a unit management plan (UMP), which determines what facilities, such as trails or shelters, will be built and maintained as well as any special regulations needed to manage each unit effectively.

Trails described in this volume are located in the following units:

◆ Wilderness Areas: Ha-De-Ron-Dah, Pigeon Lake, West Canada Lakes, Pepperbox, and Five Ponds

◆ Wild Forest Areas: Independence River, Black River, Moose River Plains, Fulton Chain, Sargent Ponds, and Blue Ridge

Using This Guidebook

The trails described in this book are all in the west-central region of the Adirondacks (see pp. 6–7 and folded map accompanying this guide), which includes the villages of Woodgate, Old Forge, and Raquette Lake. The private holdings and roads within this area divide the public Forest Preserve lands into separate areas or "units"; users must be aware that there are different regulations governing use of different land units. (See above for details.)

Like all the volumes in the Adirondack Mountain Club Forest Preserve Series of guides to Adirondack and Catskill trails, this book is intended to be both a reference tool for planning trips and a field guide to carry on the trail. All introductory material should be read carefully; it contains important information regarding current camping and hiking regulations as well as numerous suggestions for safe and proper travel by foot in the Adirondacks.

The guide is divided into eleven geographic sections, such as Indian River, Big Moose, and Blue Mt. The introduction to each of these sections gives hikers an idea of the opportunities available in that area as well as information on facilities and regulations common to that section. Each section's introduction also provides recommended hikes in the "short," "moderate," and "harder" categories. Many of these recommended hikes incorporate lesser-used trails in an attempt to make hikers aware of the many beautiful and seldom-visited places aside from the most popular hiking, climbing, and camping areas.

Abbreviations and Conventions

In each of the books in the Forest Preserve Series, R and L, with periods omitted, are used for right and left. The R and L banks of a stream are determined by looking downstream. Likewise, the R fork of a stream is on the R when one faces downstream. N, S, E, and W, again without periods, are used for north, south, east, and west. Compass bearings are given in degrees. N is 0 degrees, E is 90 degrees, S is 180 degrees, and W is 270 degrees.

The following abbreviations are used in the text and on the maps:

ADK	Adirondack Mountain Club
APA	Adirondack Park Agency
ATV	see 4WD
DEC	New York State Department of Environmental Conservation
MRPWF	Moose River Plains Wild Forest (formerly Moose River Recreation Area)
N–P	Northville–Placid (Trail)
PBM	Permanent Bench Mark
USGS	United States Geological Survey
4WD	Four-wheel-drive vehicle
ft	foot or feet
jct.	junction
km	kilometer or kilometers
m	meter or meters
mi	mile or miles
Rd.	Road
RR	railroad
yd	yard or yards

Maps

The folded map enclosed in the back pocket of this book is a composite of U.S. Geological Survey (USGS) quadrangles with updated overlays of trails, shelters, and private land lines. This map is especially valuable because of its combination of contour lines from the original base maps and recent trail information, updated with each printing of this guide. It covers most of the terrain described in this guidebook, but a few isolated trails not conveniently shown on it are shown on individual page maps located near the trail descriptions within the text. See the map legend on p. 26 for symbols used on the page maps.

All trails listed in this book are identified with a number correspon-ding to the number given the trail in the text. The folded map is letter-number coded, with letters running across the top and bottom of the map, and numbers running vertically on the sides (example: A4). Each trail's coordinate appears with the corresponding description in the book, and each trail is numbered on the map and in the book. These numbers are not used on any signs on the trails. A dead-end side trail is included under the number of the main trail. Extra copies of the two-sided West-Central map are available from many retailers or directly from the Adirondack Mountain Club, 814 Goggins Rd., Lake George, NY 12845-4117.

The ADK map of the west-central area is based on the USGS 15-minute series, now discontinued. These maps are excellent for their balance of size vs. detail, and they allow a single map to cover almost the entire west-central region. For hikers wishing to have the most detailed maps of the entire region, the USGS now produces only 7.5-minute x 15-minute metric topographic maps, which are excellent for their detail and accuracy, but leave the hiker with a need to own and carry many maps to cover the area (Beaver River, Blue Mt. Lake, Eagle Bay, Forked Lake, Honnedaga Lake, McKeever, Morehouseville, Number Four, Old Forge, Piseco Lake, Raquette Lake, Stillwater, Thendara, Wakely Mountain, West Canada Lakes). In a few cases along the periphery of the west-central region, the metric maps are not yet available, and older 7.5 x 7.5-minute USGS maps are still sold (Crystal Dale, Brantingham, Port Leyden, North Wilmurt); however, this last set of maps will not be of great interest to the hiker, because fewer public trails are to be found there.

New with this edition of the map are additional water features and names based on those shown on the metric series. Also new are junc-tions with major private roads that hikers might encounter on private land. Similar to the private trail junction symbols, these serve as land-marks with which to locate one's position as well as a reminder that hikers are not to use these roads or trails.

Trail Signs and Markers

Marked and maintained DEC trails for Adirondack hikers, cross-coun-try skiers, snowshoers, and snowmobilers tend to have signs posted at trailheads and major trail junctions. Trail signs give the distance to named locations on the trail. (See also Distance and Time, p. 29, for discrepancies regarding distances.)

Trail markers are metal or plastic disks found on the trails themselves and on trail signs. The color and type of marker used on a trail is included in the descriptions in this book. (Painted blazes on trees generally indicate property boundaries and should not be confused with marked trails.)

Differences in snowmobile marker colors do not mean different trails. Some trails are designated for both hiking and skiing, or hiking and snowmobiling, and have both types of markers. Those marked solely for snowmobiles should not be used by hikers in winter if the traffic is obviously heavy (Old Forge is a very active center for snowmobiling).

TRAIL MARKERS

It should go without saying that one should never remove any sign or marker. Hikers noticing damaged, missing, or incorrect signs should report this fact to DEC, Region 6 Headquarters, 317 Washington St., Watertown, NY 13601, serving Herkimer, Jefferson, Lewis, Oneida, and St. Lawrence counties. Region 5 Ray Brook Headquarters, P.O. Box 296, 1115 NYS Route 86, Ray Brook, NY 12977-0296.

With normal alertness to one's surroundings and exceptions made for lightly traveled trails, most Adirondack trails are easy to follow. Although this guidebook does mention particularly tricky turns or trails that might pose special difficulties, each hiker must remain alert at all times for changes of direction. Group leaders have a particular responsibility not to let inexperienced members of their party travel by themselves. A trail that seems obvious to a more experienced person may not be that way at all to an inexperienced member of the group.

All trails described in this guide are on public land or public rights of way that cross private land. The continued goodwill of public-spirited Adirondack landowners is directly dependent upon the manner in which the public uses this land. The "posted" signs occasionally found on rights of way are usually intended to remind hikers that they are on private land over which the owner has granted permission for hikers to pass. In most cases, leaving the trail, camping, fishing, and hunting are not permitted on these lands. Hikers should respect the owner's wishes.

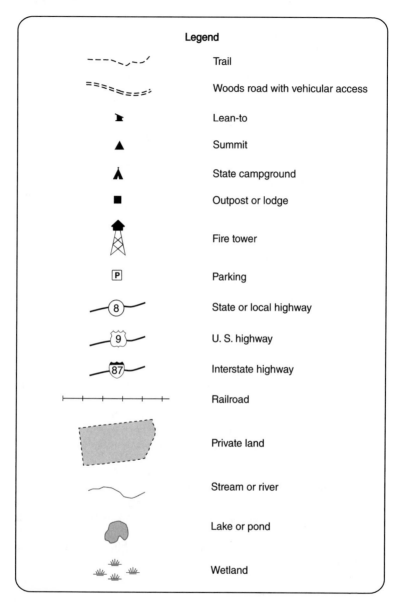

Legend

– – – ᐱ – – ⸍	Trail
≡≡≡≡≡≡≡⸗	Woods road with vehicular access
⯅ (flag)	Lean-to
▲	Summit
⛺	State campground
■	Outpost or lodge
🗼	Fire tower
P	Parking
⑧	State or local highway
⑨	U. S. highway
87	Interstate highway
├─┼─┼─┼─┤	Railroad
(shaded polygon)	Private land
(wavy line)	Stream or river
(blob)	Lake or pond
☙☙☙	Wetland

Ski Touring Trails

The following DEC trails, described in this guide, are marked with yellow ski touring markers or are listed as especially suitable for ski touring (cross-country skiing) in the DEC publication, "Nordic Skiing Trails in New York State:"

(27)	Cascade Lake Trail, E of Big Moose Rd.
(28)	Moss Lake Trail, W of Big Moose Rd.
(34-35-36)	Black Bear Mt. Trail Route, E of Fourth Lake
(52)	Tirrell Pond Trail, NE of Blue Mt. Lake, and Northville–Placid Trail, from NY 28N to Tirrell Pond and beyond
(55)	Cascade Pond Trail, SE of Blue Mt. Lake
(56)	Northville–Placid Trail, from NY 28 SW to Stephens Pond and beyond
(61)	Centennial Ski Trail, near Brantingham
(69)	Big Otter Lake East Trail, W of Old Forge (Novice)
(70)	Lost Lake Trail (Expert)
(72-73)	Middle Branch Lake Trail, from Big Otter Lake East Trail to Middle Settlement Lake (Intermediate)
(77-75-73)	Middle Settlement Lake, from the Scusa trailhead (steep climb at start) (Intermediate)
(80)	Limekiln Creek–Third Lake Trail, with connecting ski routes

Northville–Placid Trail, N from Piseco (see *Adirondack Trails: Northville–Placid Trail*, published by ADK)

Unless otherwise noted, the above trails are rated by DEC as suitable for intermediate-level skiers, except that the final ascent of Black Bear Mt. is for advanced skiers, and some trail sections are suitable for novice skiers. Other trails described in this guide that are marked as hiking trails are also open to ski touring and snowshoeing in winter, but they will tend to be narrower, rougher, or steeper than those listed.

The trail descriptions give general advice on use of the trails in winter. These descriptions are intended for experienced wilderness skiers and snowshoers. Twisting, hilly, remote trails are not for beginners.

Parking may be a problem for those wishing to ski some of these trails, as trailhead areas may not be snowplowed. Parking on the side of a plowed road is a sure way to prevent the plows from further keeping the route open. Be prepared to go some extra distance from your car to the start of your trip.

The leading locally-sponsored ski touring area is Fern Park, owned and maintained by the Town of Inlet on state and town land just SW of the community of Inlet. This network of trails for intermediate and advanced skiers is open to the public without charge. These trails connect with DEC ski touring trails between Limekiln Road and Third Lake. Access is from Inlet's South Shore Road, across from the Inlet Ski Touring Center, which has rental ski equipment. The accompanying map shows only one of the trails of the network, and its connection with a DEC ski trail.

The McCauley Mt. (downhill) Ski Area, located off Bisby Rd. just SE of Old Forge, has two ski touring trail loops appropriate for intermediate and advanced skiers. One is an attractive route of over 3 miles which passes Gray Lake and goes along Maple Ridge with a view over a ski slope. The other, 5 m in length, goes around McCauley Mt. and includes a 400-ft ascent. There is a charge for cross-country trail use.

Two golf courses are open to the public for ski touring without charge: the Thendara golf course north of NY 28 in Thendara, and the Inlet golf course on NY 28 SE of Inlet (just beyond Limekiln Rd.).

A well-established, privately operated ski touring center is that of the Adirondack Woodcraft Camps on Lake Kanacto, SW of Lake Rondaxe (access from Rondaxe Rd. N of Old Forge). There are trails around two ponds and by the North Branch of the Moose River (trails not shown on accompanying map), and a fee is charged. The center has rental equipment and provides instruction.

There are 10 km of trails at the Piseco Airport available for free.

Bicycling

Trails in the West-Central Region are more likely to be used by bicyclists than other regions. The basic DEC rule is that bicycles are not allowed in wilderness areas (such as Ha-de-ron-dah, Pigeon Lake, West Canada Lakes, and Blue Ridge wildernesses). Bicycles are allowed in wild forests (such as Independence River and Black River wild forests) EXCEPT where signs prohibit them. One trail where bicycles are prohibited, because it crosses private lands, is the Mt. Tom Trail (trail 3A). There is a network of bicycle trails in the Old Forge area. Maps are available at the Visitor Center, located on NY 28 next to Forge Pond in Old Forge.

Distance and Time

Trails in this guidebook have been measured with a measuring wheel. Distances are expressed to the nearest tenth of a mile. Shorter distances are expressed as yards, and the number of yards has usually been derived from a wheel measurement in the field. In cases where there is disagreement between a sign and the guide's stated distance, the latter can be assumed correct. DEC has been informed of these discrepancies.

At the start of each section of this guide, there is a list of trails in the region, the mileage unique to the trail, and the page on which the trail description begins. All mileages given in the trail description are cumulative, the beginning of the trail being the 0.0-mile point. A distance summary is given at the end of each description, with a total distance expressed in kilometers as well as in miles. If a trail has climbed significantly over its course, its total ascent in both feet and meters is provided.

To the inexperienced hiker, distances are likely to seem longer on the trail, depending on the weight of the pack, the time of day, and the frequency and degree of ascents and descents. He or she will quickly learn that there is a significant difference between "sidewalk miles" and "trail miles."

No attempt has been made to estimate travel time for these trails. A conservative rule to follow in estimating time is to allow an hour for every one and one-half miles, plus one half hour for each one thousand feet of ascent, letting experience indicate how close the individual hiker is to this standard. Most day hikers will probably go a little faster than this, but backpackers will probably find they go somewhat slower. Some quickening of pace usually occurs when descending, though this may not be true on steep descents.

Day Hiking and Wilderness Camping

It is not the purpose of this series to teach one how to hike or camp. The information below should, however, serve to make hikers aware of the differences and peculiarities of the Adirondacks while giving strong emphasis to currently recommended procedures for reducing environmental damage—particularly in heavily used areas. Users who intend to hike or camp for the first time are urged to consult a current book on the subject, attend one of the many workshops or training sessions available, or at least join a group led by someone with experience.

So What if it's Not Maintained?

A formal, DEC-marked trail and a bushwhack form the bookends of hiking possibilities in the Adirondacks—with lots more range in between than most hikers expect. Unmaintained trails, unmarked trails, "trailless" routes, or herd paths have two things in common: they are unmarked paths, lacking official DEC signs and markers, and they may necessitate advanced orientation skills.

Unmarked paths can range from reasonably well-trodden, well-defined routes with cairns to a whisper of a track with no discernable tread. A hiker's experience with one kind of unmarked path doesn't necessarily assist him or her on another. Hikers should carry a map and compass and know how to use them. They shouldn't let past experience inspire false confidence or tempt them to forego packing a map and compass.

Except for Johns Brook Lodge, 3.5 miles up the Marcy Trail from Keene Valley (see *Adirondack Trails: High Peaks Region*), there are no huts in the Adirondacks for public use, such as are common in the White Mountains of New Hampshire. There are many lean-tos at convenient locations along trails and also many possibilities for tenting. The regulations regarding tenting and the use of lean-tos are simple and unrestrictive compared to those of other popular backpacking areas in this country and Canada. It is important that every backpacker know and obey the restrictions that do exist because they are designed to promote the long-term enjoyment and protection of the resource.

Below are some of the most important Forest Preserve regulations, many of which pertain to day-hikers as well. These can also be found at: http://www.dec.state.ny.us/website/dlf/publands/bacrule.htm.

Complete regulations are available from the DEC and are posted at most trail access points.

• Except where marked by a "Camp Here" disk, camping is prohibited within 150 feet of roads, trails, lakes, ponds, streams, or other bodies of water.

• Groups of ten or more persons (nine in the High Peaks Region) or stays of more than three days in one place require a permit from the New York State Forest Ranger responsible for the area.

• Lean-tos are available in many areas on a first-come, first-served basis. Lean-tos cannot be used exclusively and must be shared with other campers. (See also below.)

• Use pit privies provided near popular camping areas and trailheads. If none are available, dispose of human waste by digging a hole six to eight inches deep at least 150 feet from water or campsites. Cover with leaves and soil.

• Do not use soap to wash yourself, clothing, or dishes within 150 feet of water.

• Fires should be built in existing fire pits or fireplaces if provided. Use only dead and down wood for fires. Cutting standing trees is prohibited. Extinguish all fires with water and stir ashes until they are cold to the touch. Do not build fires in areas marked by a "No Fires" disk. Camp stoves are safer, more efficient, and cleaner.

• Carry out what you carry in. Use Leave No Trace practices (see p. 34).

• Keep your pet under control. Restrain it on a leash when others approach. Collect and bury droppings away from water, trails, and campsites. Keep your pet away from drinking water sources.

• Observe and enjoy wildlife and plants but leave them undisturbed.

• Removing plants, rocks, fossils, or artifacts from state land without a permit is illegal.

• Do not feed any wild animals.

• Store food properly to keep it away from animals—particularly bears.

• No camping is permitted above 4000 feet (1219 meters) at any time of the year in the Adirondacks.

• Except in an emergency or between December 21 and March 21, camping is prohibited above an elevation of 3500 feet in the Catskills.

• At all times, only emergency fires are permitted above 4000 feet in the Adirondacks and 3500 feet in the Catskills.

Lean-tos

Lean-tos are available on a first-come, first-served basis up to the capacity of the shelter—usually about eight persons. Thus a small party

CELL PHONES

Cell phones should not be relied upon in case of emergency. Despite several highly publicized stories, their use in the backcountry is limited by terrain, distance from communication towers, and other factors. This is particularly true in the West-Central Region, where vast expanses of forest are out of reach of cellular coverage. These include, but are not limited to, the Moose River Plains Wild Forest and the Black River Wild Forests. Those who carry cell phones should, out of consideration for their fellow hikers, use them only when necessary—and should have alternative plans for handling emergencies in case they do not operate.

cannot claim exclusive use of a shelter and must allow late arrivals equal use. Most lean-tos have a fireplace in front (sometimes with a primitive grill) and sanitary facilities. Most are located near some source of water, but each camper must use his or her own judgment as to whether or not the water supply needs purification before drinking. It is in very poor taste to carve or write one's initials in a shelter. Please try to keep these rustic shelters in good condition and appearance.

Because reservations cannot be made for any of these shelters, it is best to carry a tent or other alternate shelter. Many shelters away from the standard routes, however, are seldom used, and a small party can often find a shelter open in the more remote areas.

The following regulations apply specifically to lean-tos, in addition to the general camping regulations listed above:

• No plastic may be used to close off the front of a shelter.
• No nails or other permanent fastener may be used to affix a tarp in a lean-to, but it is permissible to use rope to tie canvas or nylon tarps across the front.
• No tent may be pitched inside a lean-to.

Groups

Any group of ten or more persons or smaller groups intending to camp at one location three nights or longer must obtain a permit before camping on state land. This system is designed to prevent overuse of certain critical sites and also to encourage groups to split into smaller parties.

Permits can be obtained from the DEC forest ranger closest to the actual starting point of one's proposed trip. The local forest ranger can be contacted by writing directly; if in doubt about whom to write, send the letter to the DEC Lands and Forests Division Office address for the county in which your trip will take place (refer to DEC addresses in Trail Signs and Markers section). They will forward the letter to the proper ranger, but write early enough to permit a response before your trip date.

One can also make the initial contact with the forest ranger by telephone. Note that forest rangers' schedules during the busy summer season are often unpredictable. Forest rangers are listed in the white pages of local phone books under "New York, State of; Environmental Conservation, Department of; Forest Ranger." Bear in mind when calling that most rangers operate out of their private homes; observe the normal courtesy used when calling a private residence. Contact by letter is much preferred. Camping with a large group requires careful planning with a lead time of several weeks to ensure a happy, safe outing.

Forest Safety

The routes described in this guidebook vary from wide, well-marked DEC trails to narrow, unmarked footpaths that have become established through long use. With normal alertness and careful preparation the hiker should have few problems in land navigation. Nevertheless, careful map study and route planning are fundamental necessities. Hikers should never expect immediate help should an emergency occur. This is particularly true in winter, when fewer people are on the trails and weather is a more significant factor.

In addition to a map, all hikers should carry a compass and know at least the basics of its use. In some descriptions, the Forest Preserve Series uses compass bearings to differentiate trails at a junction or to indicate the direction of travel above timberline. More important, a compass can be an indispensable aid in the event that you lose your way.

Winter trips, especially, must be carefully planned. Travel over ice on ski and snowshoe trips must be done with caution. The possibility of freezing rain, snow, and cold temperatures should be considered from early September until late May. True winter conditions can commence as early as November and last well into April, particularly at higher altitudes. It is highly recommended that hikers travel in parties of at least

Leave No Trace

ADK supports the seven principles of the Leave No Trace program:

1. PLAN AHEAD AND PREPARE
   Know the regulations and special considerations for the area you'll visit. Prepare for extreme weather, hazards, and emergencies.
   Travel in groups of less than ten people to minimize impacts.
2. TRAVEL AND CAMP ON DURABLE SURFACES
   Hike in the middle of the trail; stay off of vegetation.
   Camp in designated sites where possible.
   In other areas, don't camp within 150 feet of water or a trail.
3. DISPOSE OF WASTE PROPERLY
   Pack out all trash (including toilet paper), leftover food, and litter.
   Use existing privies, or dig a cat hole five to six inches deep, then cover hole.
   Wash yourself and dishes at least 150 feet from water.
4. LEAVE WHAT YOU FIND
   Leave rocks, plants, and other natural objects as you find them.
   Let photos, drawings, or journals help to capture your memories.
   Do not build structures or furniture or dig trenches.
5. MINIMIZE CAMPFIRE IMPACTS
   Use a portable stove to avoid the lasting impact of a campfire.
   Where fires are permitted, use existing fire rings and only collect downed wood.
   Burn all fires to ash, put out campfires completely, then hide traces of fire.
6. RESPECT WILDLIFE
   Observe wildlife from a distance.
   Avoid wildlife during mating, nesting, and other sensitive times.
   Control pets at all times, and clean up after them.
7. BE CONSIDERATE OF OTHER VISITORS
   Respect other visitors and protect the quality of their experience.
   Let natural sounds prevail; avoid loud sounds and voices.
   Be courteous and yield to other users on the trail.

For further information on Leave No Trace principles, log on to www.lnt.org.

four people, be outfitted properly, rest when the need arises, and drink plenty of water. Leave trip plans with someone at home and then keep to your itinerary. For more information on winter travel, refer to the ADK publication *Winterwise* by John Dunn.

Drinking Water

For many years, hikers could trust almost any water source in the Adirondacks to be pure and safe to drink. Unfortunately, as in many other mountain areas, some Adirondack water sources have become contaminated with a parasite known as *Giardia lamblia*.

This intestinal parasite causes a disease known as giardiasis—often called "beaver fever." It can be spread by any warm-blooded mammal when infected feces wash into the water; beavers are prime agents in transferring this parasite because they spend so much of their time in and near water. Hikers themselves have also become primary agents in spreading this disease because some individuals appear to be unaffected carriers of the disease, and other recently infected individuals may inadvertently spread the parasite before their symptoms become apparent.

PREVENTION: Follow the guidelines for the disposal of human excrement as stated in Day Hiking and Wilderness Camping, above. Equally important, make sure that every member of your group is aware of the problem and follows the guidelines as well. The health of a fellow hiker may depend on your consideration.

WATER TREATMENT: No water source can be guaranteed to be safe. Boil all water for 2–3 minutes, utilize an iodine-based chemical purifier (available at camping supply stores and some drug and department stores), or use a commercial filter designed specifically for giardiasis prevention. If after returning from a trip you experience recurrent intestinal problems, consult your physician and explain your potential problem.

Hunting Seasons

Unlike the national park system, public lands within the Adirondack and Catskill state parks are open to sport hunting. There are separate rules and seasons for each type of hunting (small game, waterfowl, and big game), but it is the big-game season, i.e., deer and bear, that is most

BIG-GAME SEASONS IN THE ADIRONDACKS ARE USUALLY AS FOLLOWS:

EARLY BEAR SEASON: Begins the first Saturday after the second Monday in September and continues for four weeks.

ARCHERY SEASON (DEER AND BEAR): September 27 to opening of the regular season.

MUZZLE-LOADING SEASON (DEER AND BEAR): The seven days prior to the opening of regular season.

REGULAR SEASON: Next-to-last Saturday in October through the first Sunday in December.

On occasion, special situations require DEC to modify the usual dates of hunting seasons.

ADK does not promote hunting as one of its organized activities, but it does recognize that sport hunting, when carried out in compliance with the game laws administered by the DEC, is a legitimate sporting activity.

likely to concern hikers. Confrontations can occur when hikers and hunters are inconsiderate of the needs and rights of each other. Problems can be greatly reduced by careful planning.

It is advisable to avoid heavily hunted areas during big-game seasons. Because it is difficult to carry a deer or bear carcass long distances or over steep terrain, hikers will find few hunters more than a mile from a roadway or in rugged mountain country. Lower slopes of beech, maple, and hemlock have much more hunting pressure than cripplebush, spruce, and balsam fir on upper slopes. Motorized vehicles are not allowed in areas designated as Wilderness, so hike there; most areas designated as Wild Forest have woods roads where vehicles can be used, so avoid these areas, which are likely to be favored by hunters. Try to avoid the opening and closing day of regular deer season. For safety, wear a bright-colored outer garment; orange is recommended.

Bear Safety

Most wildlife in the Adirondacks and Catskills are little more than a minor nuisance around the campsite. Generally, the larger the animal the more timid it is in the presence of humans. Some animals are emboldened by the aroma of food, however, and bears, the most intimidating of these, quickly habituate to human food sources.

The following tips will reduce the likelihood of an encounter with a bear:

◆ Never keep food in your tent or lean-to.

◆ DEC now requires campers to use bear-resistant canisters in the Eastern Zone of the High Peaks Wilderness between April 1 and November 30.

◆ In other areas, use a canister or hang food at least fifteen feet off the ground from a rope strung between two trees that are at least fifteen feet apart and one hundred feet from the campsite. (Hangs using a branch have a high failure rate.) Using dark-colored rope tied off five or more feet above the ground makes it less likely that a foraging bear will see the line or find it while sniffing along the ground.

◆ Wrap aromatic foods well.

◆ Plan carefully to keep trash and leftovers to a minimum. Wrap in sealed containers such as large Ziploc bags, and hang or place in canister.

◆ Hang your pack, along with clothing worn during cooking.

◆ Keep a garbage-free fire pit away from your camping area.

BEAR CANISTERS

Bears in many wilderness areas have figured out the long-popular campers' technique of hanging food from a rope strung between two trees. Thus authorities are strongly encouraging—in some cases requiring—the use of bear-resistant, food-storage canisters.

These can be obtained from many outdoor retailers, borrowed from many ADK chapters, purchased from ADK's Member Services Center in Lake George, and rented or purchased at ADK's Heart Lake Program Center. The canisters also protect food from many smaller forest creatures.

The DEC's current management goal with respect to bears is to educate campers about proper food storage. Bears unable to get food from campers will, it is hoped, return to their natural diet. Thus campers play an important role in helping to restore the natural balance between bears and humans. Losing one's food to a bear should be recognized as a critical failure in achieving this goal.

◆ Should a bear appear, do not provoke it by throwing objects or approaching it. Bang pots, blow a whistle, shout, or otherwise try to drive it off with sharp noises. Should this fail, leave the scene.

◆ Report bear encounters to a forest ranger.

Rabies Alert

Rabies infestation has been moving north through New York State. Although it is most often associated with raccoons, any warm-blooded mammal can be a carrier.

Although direct contact with a rabid animal in the forest is not likely, some precautions are advisable:

• Do not feed or pet any wild animals, under any circumstances.

• Particularly avoid any wild animals that seem to be behaving strangely.

• If bitten by a wild animal, seek medical attention immediately.

Insect-Borne Diseases

Although not unique to the Adirondacks and Catskills, two insects found in these areas carry potentially lethal diseases. Deer ticks can spread Lyme disease, and mosquitos can transmit West Nile virus.

EMERGENCY PROCEDURES

For all emergencies, call the DEC 24-hour hotline: 518-891-0235.

All emergency assistance, including help from the local ranger, is dispatched from this number. Make sure the person going for help has the telephone number as well as a complete written description of the type and exact location of the accident. A location marked on the map can be very helpful. If possible, leave a call-back number in the event those responding to the incident require additional information.

Calling the above number is preferable to calling 911. At the DEC emergency number, the caller is usually able to speak directly with someone who is knowledgeable about the area where the accident has occurred. Cell phone callers are especially prone to problems because the call may be picked up by a distant tower in a neighboring jurisdiction (or even a different state) with the message then having to be relayed through several agencies.

This book includes Hamilton County in DEC Region 5, and Herkimer, Lewis, and Oneida counties in DEC Region 6.

DEC Region 5 (Ray Brook) contacts:
General information: 518-897-1200
Rangers: 518-897-1300
Environmental conservation officers: 518-897-1326
DEC Region 6 (Watertown) contacts:
General information: 315-785-2239
Rangers: 315-785-2263
Environmental conservation officers: 315-785-2231

These are issues of particular concern in the Catskills.

In both instances, protection is advisable. Wear long pants and long-sleeved shirts and apply an insect repellent with the recommended percentage of N, N-diethyl-meta-toluamide (commonly known as DEET). On returning home, thoroughly inspect yourself and wash yourself and your clothing immediately. Seek immediate attention if any early symptoms (rash, long-term fatigue, headache, fever) arise. ◆

The Independence River below Gleasmans Falls. RICHARD NOWICKI

Independence River Section

The land in this section does not have high relief; in fact, it is among the flattest areas in the entire Adirondack Park. Although the trails manage to have plenty of minor ups and downs, there are no peaks to scale. Trails in this section generally do not go to one particular hill or lake, but take the hiker on a meandering course through forests, past pretty ponds, and along fast-running water.

There are also a number of horse trails, which are popular with cross country skiers.

Those traveling through Lowville may want to take the time to visit the Lowville Demonstration Area NE of town on the W side of NY 812. (Parking can be found next to a fire tower just S of the DEC offices.) A nature trail there helps visitors learn how to identify trees. There is also a disabled fishing access site across the road on the Black River.

The trails of this section are accessible from various roads leading off Erie Canal Rd. (N–S along the Blue Line) or from Number Four Rd.–Stillwater Rd. between Lowville and Stillwater. In general, the available highway maps do not show the necessary rural roads along the Blue Line. A Lewis County highway map is a possible aid for people intending to hike in this section. These are $3 each (verify cost at 315-376-5350) with a check to Lewis County Highway Dept., 7660 State St., Lowville, NY 13367. The map shows state, county, and town roads, but not private roads, such as the continuation from the end of a town road on a "road" (single lane with bedrock outcroppings and sharp turns) to the Stony Lake trailhead, for example. Or, as another example, the drivable portion of the snowmobile trail of Steam Mill Rd. at Brantingham to Drunkard Creek trailhead. It does show the change between Erie Canal Rd. in the Town of Watson to Chases Lake Rd. in the Town of Greig, and the strange swing NE of the Beach Mill Rd. for the Beach Mill Pond (and Gleasmans Falls) trailhead.

SHORT HIKES:
◆ Payne Lake Horse Trail—1.8 mi (2.9 km) round trip. Interesting pine hills and sandy flats above and beyond Payne Lake. See trail 2B.
◆ Panther Pond—2.6 mi (4.2 km) round trip. Panther Pond and

lean-to are an excellent setting for a quiet summer day of lounging. See trail 6.

◆ Sunday Lake—0.8 mi (1.3 km) round trip. Nice lake. Easy walk except for some rutted spots in the old road. See trail 7.

MODERATE HIKE:

◆ Gleasmans Falls—5.8 mi (9.4 km) round trip on Beach Mill Pond Trail (2). 10- and 5-ft thundering falls in a narrow gorge, with views straight down, if you wish. Be sure to step out for a look on the boulder-strewn riverbed below the falls at the crossing of Second Creek.

HARDER HIKE:

◆ Panther Pond, Independence River loop—17.8 mi (28.7 km) round trip. This loop, with only the 0.3-mi start duplicated at the end, leads past the Panther Pond lean-to and crosses the Independence River twice, uses the Panther Pond–Independence River, Fish, Mt. Tom, and Independence River Trails, which may include wading the river. The East Bridge is closed to snowmobilers but can still be accessed with caution by hikers. The Unit Management Plan calls for its removal, however. A portion of a support beam on the N end is damaged. (A shorter loop, all N of the Independence River, is no longer possible on trails because a section has been abandoned.) See trails 6, 3, 3A, and 5.

(1) Halfmoon Lake Trail

Map: pp. 44–45

This was once a private camp. Traces of the homesite and other improvements are still visible. Halfmoon Lake is small, and surrounded by white pines. The stream crossing requires worrisome wading or good athletic ability.

▶ Trailhead: From Lowville, turn E on River Rd. and go 4.1 mi to Watson. Turn L on Number Four Rd., and go 8.9 mi to a small dirt road on the R (S) with posted land on either side (1.0 mi past the Adirondack Park boundary). The road is not marked and is easy to miss. The posted signs are placed so that it appears that the road is also posted; it is not. Coming from the E, it is 4.5 mi from the Stillwater Rd.-Number Four Rd. jct. Turn S on the dirt road, and pass some private dirt roads on the R. Go 1.4 mi to a Y jct., turn R, and go another 0.1 mi. Park in the small unmarked space on the R. There are no trail markers. ◀

FROM THE TRAILHEAD (0.0 mi), the old road goes slightly downhill to a bulldozed barrier at Burnt Creek. The washed-out bridge beyond left a hole in the trail only partly covered by boulders, which will probably require wading. The bridge will not be replaced. Following the creek crossing, a small climb uphill is followed by level terrain through white pines. There's another crossing at Tuttle Creek.

After the second creek, the route turns more E and meets the outlet of Halfmoon Lake at 0.9 mi. Following around the shore, the route

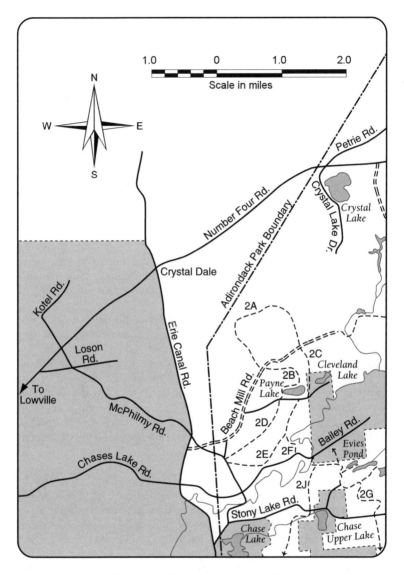

Halfmoon Lake to Stony Lake Rd.

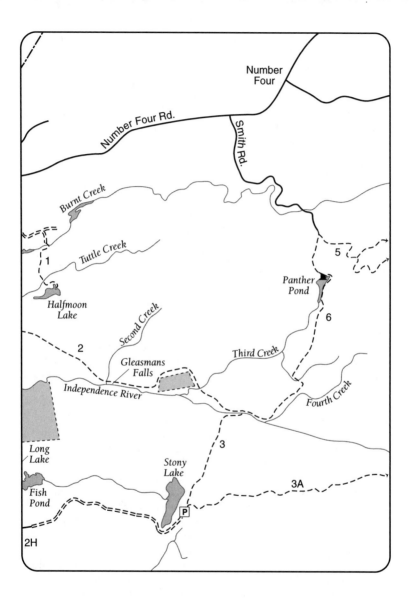

Number Four

Number Four Rd.

Smith Rd.

Burnt Creek

Tuttle Creek

1

Halfmoon Lake

Second Creek

2

Gleasmans Falls

Independence River

Long Lake

Fish Pond

Stony Lake

P

3

3A

2H

Third Creek

Panther Pond

5

6

Fourth Creek

ends on a peninsula at 1.0 mi at the site of a former summer home. This spot is beautiful and peaceful.

❊ Trail in winter: Suitable for snowshoeing or backcountry skiing, but the creek crossing may be treacherous if not fully crusted over. Winter parking along Number Four Rd.

𝕸 Distances: Number Four Rd. to trailhead, by car, 1.5 mi; from trailhead to Halfmoon Lake, 1.0 mi (1.6 km).

(2) Beach Mill Pond Trail

Map: pp. 44–45

The trail starts near the outlet of a wetland that was once Beach Mill Pond. The dam and mill are long gone. This route connects the Blue Line region with the interior of the Independence River Wild Forest, but is more notable for the fact that it passes Gleasmans Falls on the Independence River. The falls are of modest height, but pass through a narrow gorge, with the trail offering views from 50 ft straight above. They are well worth the trip.

▶ Trailhead: From Lowville, turn E on River Rd. and go 4.1 mi to Watson. Turn L on Number Four Rd., go 2.7 mi and turn R on Loson Rd., going 0.4 mi to McPhilmy Rd. Turn R, go 2.5 mi, crossing Erie Canal Rd., and continue on a dirt road to unmarked Beach Mill Rd., L (dirt). Turn L and go 3.0 mi on Beach Mill Rd., keeping L at a split in the road where Cleveland Lake Rd. goes R, to the barrier and trailhead parking. ◀

FROM THE PARKING LOT (0.0 mi), the yellow-marked trail turns S and descends the creek bank, then crosses the creek headed E. After a trail register, the old road climbs very gently NE toward the remains of Beach Mill Pond, then turns more E and climbs to easy hilltop walking. Watch for a marvelous white pine beside the trail in these uplands.

A gradual turn to the SE leads eventually back to the lowlands and the Independence River at 2.5 mi, at the point where Second Creek reaches the river. The wide, boulder-strewn riverbed to the R is worth a side trip for the view looking up toward the falls.

Not long after the trail crosses Second Creek, the falls can be heard ahead. The trail reaches solid rock and approaches the gorge at an informal campsite at 2.9 mi, then follows in and out along the cliffs above, finally approaching the top of the highest falls (10 ft) at 3.1 mi.

Beyond the falls, the trail is almost unused, but is generally well marked. An exception to this mostly easy trail occurs soon after the falls.

At 3.4 mi, the route approaches the riverbank, but bypasses this wetland by turning L and skirting the beaver pond. It turns E to go along the side of an embankment which dams yet another beaver pond above. The high bank seems out of place and man-made, but is no doubt natural. The trail goes below the short beaver dam at its E end and crosses the creek. It may take a little searching to recognize the trail. Continue L (E) on the trail through another short wetland, and you will be clear of the beaver area.

Once out of the area of beaver activity, the trail goes E for a short way, then turns N to go around a private parcel of land. The route is obscure due to the lack of foot traffic necessary to keep a foot trail obvious. Watch carefully for the yellow trail markers.

The route goes N for 0.4 mi, then turns E into another large beaver pond. Cross on the 200-ft-long beaver dam, then go L for about 50 ft to regain the trail. The next 0.4 mi E is decently marked, but the footpath is obscure and on very uneven ground (with thin soil that barely covers an enormous field of boulders). The route crosses Pine Creek on a fine bridge at 5.3 mi and turns S on the hillside beyond. Be careful to follow the yellow-marked route S and not the well-worn unmarked trail, which goes R onto private land at about the same location.

Continuing S along the hillside, the path curves E as it approaches Third Creek, then turns S to cross it. After another small hill, the route finally approaches the Independence River after joining with an old road to the private land just bypassed (turn L when you reach this road). This road crosses the river at a fording place, while the trail goes L and continues along the N bank for another 0.4 mi.

Finally, at 7.1 mi, the trail reaches a jct. at the Independence River West Bridge. Across the river, the Fish Trail (trail 3) goes 2.2 mi to Stony Lake Rd., roughly accessible by car. Eastward and then northward, the Panther Pond–Independence River Trail (trail 6) goes to a trailhead at Smith Rd. in 5.0 mi. By following this last route to the Independence River Trail (trail 5), connections can be made by the Silvermine Trail (trail 63) to the Partridgeville Rd. trailhead out of Brantingham, and from that trailhead, connections can be made to the Ha-De-Ron-Dah Wilderness trails (see Brantingham and Old Forge-Thendara sections).

❋ Trail in winter: Suitable for snowshoeing and backcountry skiing, but Beach Mill Rd. is not plowed in winter. This adds 3.0 mi to the trip from Erie Canal Rd. Snowmobiles use Beach Mill Rd.

🐾 Distances: From Beach Mill Rd. trailhead to Gleasmans Falls, 2.9 mi; to Independence River West Bridge, 7.1 mi (11.5 km); to Smith Rd. trailhead, 12.1 mi; to Stony Lake Rd. trailhead, 9.3 mi (15 km).

(2A) Beach Mill Horse Trail

Map: pp. 44–45

The trail goes through semi-open pine plains with sandy soil. Its major attraction is the pleasant, easy walking and the interesting plant life which survives on rather infertile sandy soil. It is short enough to allow an easy loop trip, including the soft, sandy road walk back to the car.

▶ Trailhead: From Lowville, turn E on River Rd. Go 4.1 mi to Watson. Turn L on Number Four Rd., go 2.7 mi, and turn R on Loson Rd., going 0.4 mi to McPhilmy Rd. Turn R, go 2.5 mi, crossing Erie Canal Rd., and continue on a dirt road to unmarked Beach Mill Rd., L (dirt). Turning L, go 2.0 mi on Beach Mill Rd. to the first trailhead or 2.5 mi to the second trailhead, both on the L side. ◀

STARTING FROM THE W trailhead (0.0 mi), the blue-marked horse trail goes almost straight N from the road, turns E at 0.4 mi, turns S at 1.0 mi, and reaches the second trailhead at 1.2 mi. The terrain is remarkably level and pleasant going.

❋ Trail in winter: Suitable for snowshoeing or skiing, but snowmobiles may be active. Beach Mill Rd. is not plowed in the winter.

🐾 Distances: Trailhead to trailhead, 1.2 mi (1.9 km).

(2B) Payne Lake Horse Trail

Map: pp. 44–45

Payne Lake is quiet and scenic, with sandy soil and surrounding evergreens. The high sand bank on the N of the lake gives the trail some elevation, with one small scenic vista.

▶ Trailheads: To reach the N end, from Lowville, turn E on River Rd., go 4.1 mi to Watson, and turn L on Number Four Rd. Go 2.7 mi, and turn R on Loson Rd., going 0.4 mi to McPhilmy Rd. Turn R, go 2.5 mi, crossing Erie Canal Rd., and continue on a dirt road to unmarked

Beach Mill Rd., L (dirt). Turn L and go 2.0 mi on Beach Mill Rd. to the trailhead on the R.

To reach the S end proceed from Lowville, as above to unmarked Beach Mill Rd., L (dirt). Turn L and go 1.0 mi on Beach Mill Rd. to Cleveland Lake Rd. Turn R and go 0.6 mi to an unmarked fork in the road. The trail is on the L at the fork. It is a blue-marked horse trail. ◀

STARTING AT THE N TRAILHEAD (0.0 mi), the blue-marked horse trail goes through open scrub, briefly joins an old road, and finally plunges into white pine forest at 0.5 mi. A short climb brings the trail to the long, narrow ridge above Payne Lake. The pines almost mask the lake, allowing just a hint of a view. The vista is somewhat better at a rail and bench placed near the W end of the lake at 0.7 mi. From here, the trail slowly descends through an open forest of large pines to Cleveland Rd. near the W end of the lake at 0.9 mi.

❊ Trail in winter: Suitable for snowshoeing or skiing, but snowmobiles may be active. Beach Mill Rd. is not plowed in the winter.

⚹ Distances: N trailhead to Payne Lake ridge, 0.5 mi; to S trailhead, 0.9 mi (1.5 km).

(2C) Cleveland Lake Horse Trail

Map: pp. 44–45

▶ Trailheads: To reach the N trailhead, turn E from Lowville, on River Rd., go 4.1 mi to Watson, and turn L on Number Four Rd. Go 2.7 mi, and turn R on Loson Rd., going 0.4 mi to McPhilmy Rd. Turn R, go 2.5 mi, crossing Erie Canal Rd., and continuing on a dirt road to unmarked Beach Mill Rd., L (dirt). Turn L, go 2.5 mi on Beach Mill Rd. to the trail on the R.

To reach the S trailhead, proceed as above to unmarked Beach Mill Rd., L (dirt). Turn L and go 1.0 mi on Beach Mill Rd. to Cleveland Lake Rd. Turn R and go 0.6 mi to an unmarked fork in the road. Take the R fork and continue for 0.5 mi. The trail is on the L, just inside private land. The prudent course is to park about 0.1 mi W along the road, on state land. ◀

THE BLUE-MARKED HORSE TRAIL goes on almost level terrain covered with pines for 0.8 mi. The S half passes through private land; be sure to stay on the trail.

❋ Trail in winter: Suitable for snowshoeing or skiing, but snowmobiles may be active. Beach Mill Rd. is not plowed in the winter.

🚶 Distance: 0.8 mi (1.3 km).

(2D) **Frost Pocket Horse Trail**

Map: pp. 44–45

▶ Trailheads: To reach the N trailhead, from Lowville, turn E on River Rd., go 4.1 mi to Watson, and turn L on Number Four Rd. Go 2.7 mi, and turn R on Loson Rd., going 0.4 mi to McPhilmy Rd. Turn R, go 2.5 mi, crossing Erie Canal Rd., and continue on a dirt road to unmarked Beach Mill Rd., L (dirt). Turn L and go 1.0 mi on Beach Mill Rd. to Cleveland Lake Rd. Turn R and go 0.6 mi to an unmarked fork in the road. The trail is on the R at the fork.

To reach the S trailhead, proceed from Lowville, as above to McPhilmy Rd. Turn R, go 2.9 mi, crossing Erie Canal Rd., and continuing on a dirt road past unmarked Beach Mill Rd., L (dirt), to a minor unmarked road, L. The trail is on the L just after the road. (The Proceeding Trail, not listed separately in this guide, also starts at this trailhead and connects in 0.7 mi to Old Number Four Horse Trail, trail 2E.) ◀

LIKE ALL THE TRAILS in this region, the path of this blue-marked horse trail is through pine forest with pleasant sandy soil and little change in elevation.

❋ Trail in winter: Suitable for snowshoeing or skiing, but snowmobiles may be active.

🚶 Distance: 1.3 mi (2.1 km).

(2E) **Old Number Four Horse Trail**

Map: pp. 44–45

▶ Trailheads: To reach the N trailhead, turn E from Lowville, on River Rd., go 4.1 mi to Watson, and turn L on Number Four Rd. Go 2.7 mi, and turn R on Loson Rd., going 0.4 mi to McPhilmy Rd. Turn R, go 2.5 mi, crossing Erie Canal Rd. and continuing on a dirt road to unmarked Beach Mill Rd., L (dirt). Turn L and go 1.0 mi on Beach Mill Rd. to Cleveland Lake Rd. Turn R and go 0.6 mi to an unmarked fork in the road. Take the R fork and continue for 0.3 mi. The trail is on the R.

To reach the S trailhead from Lowville, turn E on River Rd., go 4.1

mi to Watson, and turn L on Number Four Rd. Go 2.7 mi, turn R on Loson Rd., going 0.4 mi to McPhilmy Rd. Turn R, go 3.5 mi, crossing Erie Canal Rd. and continuing on a dirt road to paved Bailey Rd. on the L. Turn L and go 0.6 mi to the trailhead on the L. ◀

THIS OLD JEEP ROAD (a blue-marked horse trail) offers easy going through level but somewhat varied terrain. At the S end, another old road goes W. Called the Proceeding Trail, and not separately listed in this guide, it connects to the Frost Pocket Horse Trail (trail 2D). These connections close a loop, allowing one to park at Payne Lake and take a pleasant 3.3-mi circuit starting on the Frost Pocket Horse Trail and returning W to Payne Lake from the N trailhead of Old Number Four Horse Trail. The Elbow Horse Trail (trail 2F) connects to this trail 0.4 mi from the S trailhead. It is worth the side trip to go 0.1 mi to The Elbow on the Independence River. The banks are undercut by the river. Do not stand on the very edge; the bank could easily collapse from your weight, and you would plunge down the steep slope into the river.

✳ Trail in winter: Suitable for snowshoeing or skiing, but snowmobiles may be active.

🚶 Distance: 1.1 mi (1.8 km).

(2F) Elbow Horse Trail

Map: pp. 44–45

▶ Trailhead: From Lowville, turn E on River Rd. Go 4.1 mi to Watson and turn L on Number Four Rd. Go 2.7 mi, and turn R on Loson Rd., going 0.4 mi to McPhilmy Rd. Turn R, and go 3.5 mi, crossing Erie Canal Rd., and continue on a dirt road to paved Bailey Rd. on the L. Turn L, go 1.1 mi to the trailhead (a two-track road) on the L. ◀

THIS SHORT BLUE-MARKED HORSE TRAIL connects Bailey Rd. on the S to Old Number Four Horse Trail (2E) on the N. Its chief attraction is The Elbow, an oxbow on the meandering Independence River. The trail approaches the high bank, giving a good view. The banks are undercut by the river. Do not stand on the very edge; the bank could easily collapse from your weight, and you would plunge down the steep slope into the river.

✳ Trail in winter: Suitable for snowshoeing or skiing, but snowmobiles may be active.

✖ Distances: Trailhead to The Elbow, 0.2 mi; to Old Number Four Horse Trail (2E), 0.4 mi (0.6 km).

(2G) **Dragline–Evies Pond–Gumdrop Horse Trail**

Map: pp. 44–45, 138–139

This path is actually labeled by the DEC as four short trails: the Dragline Trail, Evies Pond Trail, Fish Pond Trail, and Gumdrop Trail. They use pieces of old roads which start on private land. Although the route described does not go to any of the named ponds, one can easily make side trips on the old roads to reach these ponds. The Chase Creek Horse Trail (trail 2J) connects to the present route 0.3 mi from the N trailhead.

▶ Trailheads: To reach the N trailhead, turn E from Lowville, on River Rd., go 4.1 mi to Watson, and turn L on Number Four Rd. Go 2.7 mi, and turn R on Loson Rd., going 0.4 mi to McPhilmy Rd. Turn R, go 3.5 mi, crossing Erie Canal Rd., and continue on a dirt road to paved Bailey Rd. on the L. Turn L and go 1.4 mi to the bridge over the Independence River. The trailhead is on the R just across the bridge. Park back from the bridge on the W side or at the old gravel pit on the E side; the rest of the land E of the bridge is private.

To reach the middle trailhead, follow Lovers Lane Rd., 1.0 mi W of the S trailhead.

To reach the S trailhead, turn E from Lowville, on River Rd., go 4.1 mi to Watson, and turn L on Number Four Rd. Go 2.7 mi, turn R on Loson Rd., going 0.4 mi to McPhilmy Rd. Turn R, go 2.3 mi to Erie Canal Rd. Turn R. Go 1.9 mi to Stony Lake Rd. Turn L and go 2.7 mi to the trailhead on the L. ◀

STARTING FROM THE N TRAILHEAD (0.0 mi), the blue-marked horse trail goes along the riverbank for 0.2 mi until it passes private land, then turns L (E) to meet Chase Creek Horse Trail (trail 2J) at 0.3 mi and Evies Pond Trail at 0.7 mi. The road L at the corner leads to private land. Turning R, the route passes the end of Evies Pond, then zigzags. At 0.8 mi, a road leads L for 0.3 mi to a turnaround (the middle trailhead) on the beautiful ridge between Evies Pond and Long Pond. Continuing S on Evies Pond Rd., the trail soon turns E to Fish Pond Rd. That road continues on to the N shore of Fish Pond, but the trail leaves it at 1.3 mi to go S around Mahan Pond and on to the S trailhead on

Stony Lake Rd. (1.9 mi).

❋ Trail in winter: Suitable for snowshoeing or skiing, but snowmobiles may be active.

⚞ Distances: N trailhead to Chase Creek Horse Trail jct., 0.3 mi; to Evies Pond side road, 0.8 mi; to Fish Pond jct., 1.3 mi; to S trailhead, 1.9 mi (3.1 km).

(2H) Hinchings Pond Horse Trail

Map: pp. 44–45, 138–139

▶ Trailheads: To reach the N trailhead, turn E from Lowville, on River Rd., go 4.1 mi to Watson, and turn L on Number Four Rd. Go 2.7 mi, and turn R on Loson Rd., going 0.4 mi to McPhilmy Rd. Turn R and go 2.3 mi to Erie Canal Rd. Turn R. Go 1.9 mi to Stony Lake Rd. Turn L and go 2.7 mi to the trailhead on the R.

To reach the S trailhead, proceed from Lowville, as above to Erie Canal Rd. Turn R. Go 2.3 mi to Sand Pond Rd. Turn L and go 1.2 mi (passing a private Chase Lake road) to a fork in the road. Take the narrow L fork (Bull Pond Rd.). Go another 1.5 mi, crossing a section of private land and continuing to another jct. The better road to the R leads to private land. The Fletcher Horse Trail (trail 57B) comes in on the R at this jct. Continue straight ahead a short distance to the end. The trail turns L off the end of the road. ◀

THE BLUE-MARKED HORSE TRAIL leads through scrub and pine plain, with two creek crossings. There is no convenient circuit route. One must return by the same route to the starting point.

❋ Trail in winter: Suitable for snowshoeing or skiing, but snowmobiles may be active.

⚞ Distance: 1.1 mi (1.8 km).

(2J) Chase Creek Horse Trail

Map: pp. 44–45, 138–139

This trail leads from the Confusion Flats parking lot, across Stony Lake Rd. (the N trailhead), to end on trail 2G. It passes Parsons Pond and makes one creek crossing in the S section, while the N section is more varied, with ups and downs and no water to wade. This is a pleasantly interesting route to Evies Pond, but is not the shortest way to get there (see trail 2G).

▶ Trailheads: To reach the N trailhead, turn E from Lowville, on River Rd., go 4.1 mi to Watson, and turn L on Number Four Rd. Go 2.7 mi, and turn R on Loson Rd., going 0.4 mi to McPhilmy Rd. Turn R and go 2.3 mi to Erie Canal Rd. Turn R. Go 1.9 mi to Stony Lake Rd. Turn L and go 1.6 mi to the trailheads on both sides of the road.

To reach the S trailhead, from Lowville, proceed as above to Erie Canal Rd. Turn R. Go 2.3 mi to Sand Pond Rd. Turn L and go 0.8 mi to the Confusion Flats parking area on the R. The trail starts across the road from Confusion Flats Rd. ◀

Starting at the S trailhead (0.0 mi), the red-marked horse trail heads NE through level scrub pine, crossing a dirt road from Chase Lake at 0.6 mi. Turning N, the trail passes Parson Pond at 0.7 mi. After a few ups and downs, the path is even until it approaches Chase Creek. The creek must be waded at 1.5 mi. The trail regains 40 ft of elevation to meet the N trailhead at Stony Lake Rd. (1.6 mi). The N section has considerably more ups and downs and a 50-ft notch to cross at 2.0 mi. It joins trail 2G at 2.5 mi. To the L, it is another 0.3 mi to the Bailey Rd. trailhead.

❋ Trail in winter: Suitable for snowshoeing or skiing, but snowmobiles may be active.

🐾 Distances: S trailhead to Chase Creek, 1.5 mi; to N trailhead, 1.6 mi; to trail 2G, 2.5 mi (4 km).

(2K) Independence River and Shady Horse Trails

Map: p. 138–139

This is an especially pleasant trail, which drops 270 ft on fairly gentle slopes to reach the meandering Independence River. Of course, what goes down must come up, and the climb is equally interesting.

▶ Trailheads: To reach the N trailhead, turn E from Lowville, on River Rd., go 4.1 mi to Watson, and turn L on Number Four Rd. Go 2.7 mi, and turn R on Loson Rd., going 0.4 mi to McPhilmy Rd. Turn R and go 2.3 mi to Erie Canal Rd. Turn R. Go 2.3 mi to Sand Pond Rd. The trail is 0.4 mi farther down Erie Canal Rd. on the R, but the best foot access is a two-track dirt road just 300 ft S of the Sand Pond Rd. jct. This horse trail is blue-marked at both ends, and yellow in the middle.

To reach the W trailhead, go 2.0 mi S from Sand Pond Rd. (N trailhead). Turn R on Donnatburg Rd. and go to the end at a closed bridge over the river. An old road goes N for 0.1 mi to meet the trail.

To reach the S trailhead, go 0.5 mi farther S on Erie Canal Rd. from the N trailhead. ◄

STARTING ON THE TWO-TRACK ROAD near the N trailhead (0.0 mi), it is only 250 ft to a jct. where the official trail comes in from the L. Continuing on the old road, the descent begins at 0.2 mi and continues on an old road until leveling out near a bend in the cascading river at 0.6 mi. The next bend of the river is much more peaceful. The old road follows the riverbank, then takes a sharp L at 1.1 mi. At this corner, the old road continues 0.1 mi down the river to the W trailhead off Donnatburg Rd.

After the turn, the trail ascends an old road, then leaves it to wiggle gently upward, sometimes along property lines and sometimes through rounded notches. After a final spurt of somewhat steeper climbing, the path reaches Shady Trail at 1.8 mi. Up the ridge to the R, it is 0.3 mi on the blue-marked trail to the S trailhead. To the L, the blue-marked Shady Trail follows easy ground to a jct. with the yellow trail from farther up the road. Shady Trail turns R and crosses the trail heading to the horse Assembly Area. Continuing ahead (N) on that trail, the jct. with the two-track road is at 2.6 mi. The N trailhead is 250 ft to the R.

❋ Trail in winter: Suitable for snowshoeing or skiing, but snowmobiles may be active.

❦ Distances: Two-track road near N trailhead to start of descent, 0.2 mi; to bottom, 0.6 mi; to S trailhead, 2.2 mi (3.5 km).

(3) Fish Trail

Map: A2, pp. 44–45, 138–139

The Fish Trail, heavily used by ATVs, can be used as part of a loop hike from Panther Pond across the West Bridge and the East Bridge (as long as the latter remains; see trail 5) over the Independence River and back to Smith Rd. Or it could be used with trails E and S beyond Pine Lake, through the Ha-De-Ron-Dah Wilderness Area. There is also a trailhead on the S end of the trail on state land accessible over a private road by rugged vehicles.

▶ Trailhead: One end of this trail is found at the West Bridge over the Independence River, reachable from the Beach Mill Pond Trail

(trail 2) or the Panther Pond–Independence River Trail (trail 6). Although this trail is probably more often used as an interior trail, there is a trailhead on its S end, E of Stony Lake. From Lowville, turn E on River Rd., go 4.1 mi to Watson, and turn L on Number Four Rd. Go 2.7 mi, turn R on Loson Rd., and go 0.4 mi to McPhilmy Rd. Turn R, go 2.2 mi to Erie Canal Rd., turn R, and go 1.9 mi to Stony Lake Rd. (gravel). Turn L (NE). (If you go too far on Erie Canal Rd., North Shore Rd. is just beyond the jct., and the outlet of Chase Lake is just beyond that.) Head E on Stony Lake Rd., entering the Adirondack Park at 0.2 mi. Stony Lake Rd. is paved for 0.7 mi, then drops to one lane, passes the Chase Creek horse trail at 1.7 mi, passes N of Upper Chase Lake L on a short stretch of paving, and then again on dirt passes the Gumdrop (L) and Hinchings Pond (R) horse trails at 2.9 mi. From here on, the "road," with sharp bends and occasional bedrock outcroppings, is passable by passenger car, but is not for faint-hearted drivers.

Private land starts at 5.4 mi from Erie Canal Rd. There is sufficient space for three cars on the R, next to a DEC sign announcing that the next 0.9 mi is a public easement across private land. Hikers may walk the road for another 0.9 mi, but those who have pickups or 4WD vehicles can drive past cabins—cautiously, as some are immediately adjacent to the road—to the state land boundary at 6.3 mi. There is a parking lot 200 ft beyond the boundary sign. Those last 200 ft are very muddy and rough. (The impassable road continues as the Mt. Tom Trail to Balsam Flats, trail 3A.) ◀

ASSUMING THAT MOST HIKERS will avoid the rough road to the trailhead and will use this as part of a loop, the following description is S from the West Bridge to the grassy parking lot (where the Mt. Tom Trail and Independence River Trail can be used to loop E and back N).

From the West Bridge (0.0 mi), the yellow-marked trail—a dirt road—enters a clearing and turns R (W), paralleling the river for a ways, reaching a jct. at 0.25 mi. The route R (NW) goes to an informal campsite overlooking the river and fording place, used to supply a private camp across the river.

The trail turns L (S) on the generally level woods road, bypassing road-width mudholes from time to time. At 0.8 mi it reaches the end of a beaver meadow/pond L; at 0.9 mi the wetland is also on the R. At 1.0 mi the beaver ponds connect on top of the road, where hikers will probably wade whether they want to or not, as the clumps of vegetation on the sides are apparently bog plants that sink when stepped on.

At 1.3 mi there is an arrow as the trail moves from the road onto a lightly used foot path L, which crosses a bridge below the main beaver pond (and above another) at 1.4 mi. Passing through ferns, the trail goes over a small rise, bends R, and reaches the grassy parking lot at the Stony Lake trailhead at 1.7 mi (2.7 km). From there it is 6.3 mi R to Erie Canal Rd. The truck road L is the Mt. Tom Trail (trail 3A).

❀ Trail in winter: Suitable for snowshoeing or backcountry skiing, but the trail is 6.3 mi from the plowed Erie Canal Rd.

🐾 Distances: West Bridge to jct., 0.25 mi; to crossing at beaver ponds, 1.0 mi; to foot trail, 1.3 mi; to Stony Lake trailhead, 1.7 mi (2.7 km).

(3A) Mt. Tom Trail

Map: A2, pp. 44–45, 138–139

This trail does not go to nearby Mt. Tom, but acquired its name because it goes over lands owned by the Mt. Tom Club. This is the shortest route to reach Balsam Flats, and at one time it was known as Balsam Flats Rd. It crosses private land, on which the state has a trail easement for hiking, snowmobiling, and horse travel, but bicycles are not allowed. Travelers must remain on the trail when passing through the private land.

▶ Trailhead: See trail 3. ◀

FROM THE STONY LAKE TRAILHEAD (0.0 mi), the rocky old road heads E with snowmobile markers, rising rather steeply about 185 ft over a small hill. Shortly after crossing the next creek beyond this hill, the trail reaches private land (stay on the trail) at 0.9 mi. After the next creek crossing, at 1.5 mi, the route ascends gently 260 ft over a more significant hill. At 2.2 mi, a private road enters R, but the trail continues ahead, bending L. As the path levels out at the top, the trail is again on state land at 2.7 mi. The descent is a little steeper down to the jct. with the Silvermine Trail (trail 63) at 3.3 mi. To the L, Smith Rd. is 7.9 mi. Ahead, it is 0.2 mi to an access point on the river, and 7.4 mi to Partridgeville Rd.

❀ Trail in winter: Snowmobile trail. Suitable for snowshoers and intermediate skiers, but very far from any parking place.

✻ Distance: Trailhead to private land, 0.9 mi; to state land, 2.7 mi; to Silvermine Trail, 3.3 mi (5.3 km).

(4) Francis Lake Trail

Map: A1

Francis Lake is close to the road and has two good sites for picnicking (no facilities), both of them on paths that are not the main trail (see below, "W Access" and "E Access"). There are two private holdings on the lake.

▶ Trailhead: From the jct. of Number Four Rd. and Stillwater Rd. at Number Four settlement, go 0.9 mi W on Number Four Rd. Turn L (S) on Smith Rd. and go 1.5 mi. Park in a former gravel pit on the L (E). The trail is an old road starting at the R rear of the gravel pit. Because this is an unofficial trail, there are no markers. ◀

FROM THE GRAVEL PIT (0.0 mi), the route is an unmarked old road, easy to follow, leading NE through open woods. At 0.5 mi, the SW end of the lake is visible through open forest L.

The old road soon passes within 50 ft of a tiny inlet of the lake, then curves away and becomes more overgrown. It eventually returns to Smith Rd., but is probably not of interest to hikers past this point. The lake edge on this S side is somewhat boggy and the forest floor is too uneven for camping. Camping is reported to be easier on a point of land farther around the lake to the E.

Two other paths lead to points on the NE end of Francis Lake:

For the *W access*, from the jct. of Number Four Rd. and Stillwater Rd. at Number Four settlement, go 0.6 mi E on Stillwater Rd. There is parking on the R (S) for one car at a turn-in for a barricaded former private road. The route, for foot traffic only, follows this road past the barricade for 500 ft along the outlet stream, then turns L and goes another 300 ft to the cleared site of a former summer home. This site is on a point of land, with nice views and a pleasant open area suitable for camping.

For the *E access*, go 0.3 mi farther E on Stillwater Rd. Park off the road on the S side just before a bend, and slightly beyond a barricaded former access road on the R (S). The route goes between two wooden posts at the roadside and reaches the lake in a few paces. In the fall of 2004, this route was hardened to allow wheelchair access. A floating dock will be available during summer for canoe, kayak, and car-top boat launching. No trailers are allowed. To the R, on a slight hill, a beautiful grove of large white pines has been somewhat degraded by attempts to build fires on the forest floor; that practice could prove disastrous for these fine old trees. A very short road section just E of this access is also on state land for the first 0.1 mi, and is worth the short walk to get the view.

※ Trail in Winter: Suitable for snowshoers and skiers.

𝕸 Distance: Gravel pit to closest approach to lake, 0.5 mi (0.8 km)

(4A) Bills Pond Trail

Map: A1

▶ Trailhead: On Number Four Rd., go 0.9 mi W of the jct. with Stillwater Rd. at Number Four settlement. Turn L (S) on Smith Rd., identified by a DEC trailhead sign. Drive S past the location of the former Number Four fire tower at 0.1 mi (R). Continuing S, the parking spot is at the end of the drivable road, 3.8 mi from Number Four Rd. ◀

FROM THE BACK END OF THE PARKING AREA (0.0 mi), the old Bills Pond Rd. heads NE. Although unmarked, the trail on this road shows some use, and the road is obvious. (Trail 6 starts on a good road to the R [S], past a roadblock.)

The old road beyond the parking lot continues its gentle climb, weaving a bit, but aiming generally NE. Near the top, at a jct. at about 0.6 mi, the route turns onto a faint road L (N)—the Bills Pond Rd. It shows no obvious use, and has not been cleared for several years. (If you miss the turn at this jct., the main road starts down, with a noticeable hillside up to the L. If you enter a clearing, you have gone too far.) Attempt to follow this faint road through blowdowns. It continues N to Bills Pond, keeping about 50 ft above a notch (L).

As the pond comes into view at 0.8 mi, the old road turns R and goes parallel to the pond, reaching a wetland at the E end. The hiker should leave the old road when the pond first comes into view and head for the pond. There are no trails. If you go L to the outlet, and cross on the beaver dam, you can reach an open rock slab at water's edge on the N side for a nice stopping place and a good view of the pond.

※ Trail in winter: Suitable for snowshoeing or backcountry skiing.

Because Smith Rd. is not plowed, distance to the pond in winter is 4.6 mi from Number Four Rd.

🚶 Distances: Trailhead to jct., 0.6 mi; to Bills Pond, 0.8 mi (1.3 km).

(5) Independence River Trail

Map: A1, pp. 44–45

This is an interior trail, although only 0.3 mi from the Smith Rd. trailhead for the Panther Pond–Independence River Trail (trail 6). It is marked as a snowmobile trail, although snowmobiles can no longer use the East Bridge over the Independence (it has a split beam under the N end), but hikers should be able to use it for a while. A section of trail from the Panther Pond–Independence River Trail easterly to N of Fourth Creek has been abandoned, so a loop hike using these two trails now totals 17.8 mi. The section N of the river has mudholes with ATV tracks, as well as sections with easy walking. The description is from the S end as part of the loop.

▶ Locator: For the N end, from the trailhead for the Panther Pond–Independence River Trail (trail 6), go S 0.3 mi to a jct. and register. The S end is at the E end of the Mt. Tom Trail (trail 3A) and the N end of the Silvermine Trail (trail 63). ◀

FROM THE JCT. of the Mt. Tom and Silvermine trails (0.0 mi), the trail heads N, dropping to the East Bridge over the Independence River at 0.4 mi. There is an informal campsite R, upstream about 20 yd from the bridge. The bridge, which has damage to a beam on the N end, is closed to snowmobilers but should be usable by cautious hikers. If it is removed, then wading will be required.

Rising slightly on a brief stretch of muddy ground, the trail bends L (W) and goes along the river, sometimes out of sight and sometimes near, eventually turning R (N) away from the river at 1.1 mi. There are ups and downs as the trail heads generally N until crossing Fourth Creek on a bridge at 2.6 mi. Bending NE, it passes a number of mudholes and at 3.7 mi clings to the edge next to a cliff rising L, passing a beaver pond R for nearly 75 yd, passing more mudholes, and reaching a jct. at 4.0 mi. Trail R is the Emmet Hill Rd. Snowmobile Trail (trail 10), which heads NE 1.75 mi to the drivable McCarthy Rd. (trail 11), 2.9 mi S of Stillwater Rd.

Bending L at the jct., the trail heads generally NW with minor ups and downs, crossing a small beaver dam at 4.2 mi and a mudhole at 4.7 mi on a section of otherwise decent road-width. It reaches a jct. at 7.0 mi. The trail R is the North Crossover Snowmobile Trail (trail 9), which goes E 3.0 mi to the drivable McCarthy Rd., 1.9 mi S of Stillwater Rd.

From the jct., the wide trail bends L (W), generally on a gravel truck road over a rise and down to end at a jct. with a register at 7.5 mi (12.1 km). The trail R goes 0.3 mi N to the Smith Rd. trailhead. The yellow-marked Panther Pond–Independence River Trail L (trail 6) goes 1.0 mi to the Panther Pond lean-to.

❋ Trail in winter: Snowmobile trail, although the closure of the East Bridge to snowmobilers may reduce the traffic S of the Emmet Hill Rd. Snowmobile Trail (trail 10). Otherwise suitable for snowshoeing and backcountry skiing, but remote. The winter trailhead may be at Number Four Rd.

🐾 Distances: Mt. Tom and Silvermine trails to Independence River, 0.4 mi; to bend N away from river, 1.1; to Fourth Creek bridge, 2.6 mi; to jct. with Emmet Hill Rd. Snowmobile Trail, 4.0 mi; to jct. with North Crossover Snowmobile Trail, 7.0 mi; to register on Panther Pond–Independence River Trail, 7.5 mi (12.1 km).

(6) Panther Pond–Independence River Trail

Map: A1, pp. 44–45

Panther Pond and its lean-to are reason enough to make this trip, but the pleasant additional hike to the Independence River is also worth the effort. Smith Rd. twists SE through hardwood forest, past the private gate to Trout Pond, and ends at a barricade by Pine Creek. Foot and snowmobile trails extend from here in many directions, such as the unmarked one straight ahead (E), which goes to Bills Pond (trail 4A). The yellow foot trail R goes S to Panther Pond lean-to, then over a hill with an open rock ridge (no view) and joins with snowmobile trails leading S to the Independence River.

▶ Trailhead: On Number Four Rd., go E 16.2 mi from NY 26 in Lowville or go 1.0 mi W from the jct. with Stillwater Rd. at Number Four settlement. Turn S on Smith Rd., identified by a DEC trailhead sign opposite a "Number 4 Business District" sign. Pass the Trout Lake private gate R at 2.1 mi, continuing to the end of the drivable road, 3.8 mi from Number Four Rd. ◀

HEADING S past the barricade (0.0 mi), the trail follows an old road over Pine Creek and continues on this road past an unmarked L fork, reaching a marked fork at the trail register at 0.3 mi. To the L is the Independence River Trail (trail 5).

Continuing ahead on the R fork, the yellow-marked Panther Pond Trail goes 90 yd on an old woods road, then turns L into the woods and along a hillside on a footpath. Watch for that turnoff as the wider path continues ahead with snowmobile markers. It goes through a couple of low sections with corduroy, then up a hill and around a magnificent white pine at 1.25 mi, and reaches the lean-to and Panther Pond at 1.3 mi. This setting is beautiful, perfect for a lazy summer day.

Going L around the pond, the yellow trail continues near the shore, past a beaver pond on the L, and finally leaves Panther Pond at some notable cliffs on the L side at 1.9 mi. The trail follows along Third Creek for a ways, then goes into the woods and across Snake Creek. The trail continues away from this creek, past a swampy region, and then ascends a ragged little hill with open rock along the summit ridge starting at 2.7 mi and continuing to beyond 2.8 mi. The open regions are not large enough for distant views, but the openings are pleasant, with many white pines in the area. This hill has a gently descending ridge on the S side, with the trail following the ridge nearly to the bottom.

When the flats of a vlei feeding Third Creek come into view, the trail descends a short way. Watch for a turn L where another trail, now abandoned, goes ahead at 4.2 mi. The route follows an old woods road through easy terrain, with an occasional wet spot. At 4.4 mi, a noisy cascading creek signals a gentle turn to the R. The trail follows this creek (Fourth Creek) for several minutes, until reaching the Independence River. Here it turns R and follows the bank of this busy river to end at the West Bridge at 5.0 mi. The Beach Mill Pond Trail (trail 2) continues W along the N bank of the river, past Gleasmans Falls, to a trailhead on Beach Mill Rd. Across the bridge, the Fish Trail (trail 3) continues a loop.

✸ Trail in winter: Trailhead at Number Four Rd. Snowmobile territory. Easy for snowshoes, generally easy for skis, but the trip can be a long one with trailbreaking in deep snow. The section just S of Panther Pond is for experienced skiers.

𑫷 Distances: Trailhead to Independence River Trail (trail 5), 0.3 mi; to Panther Pond and lean-to, 1.3 mi; to Fourth Creek, 4.4 mi; to West Bridge on the Independence River, 5.0 mi (8.1 km).

(7) Sunday Lake Road and Trail

▶ Trailhead: From the jct. at Stillwater, go W on Stillwater Rd. 4.0 mi to McCarthy Rd. (3.6 mi E of Number Four Rd.). Turn L (S) onto McCarthy Rd. Go 0.4 mi to a road L (E). Park here and walk. The road looks good, but gets very difficult in a short distance, suitable only for high-center vehicles. There are no trail markers, but the route is unmistakable. ◀

FROM MCCARTHY RD. (0.0 mi), head E 0.4 mi to the shore of Sunday Lake at an informal campsite. It is a very pretty lake.

❋ Trail in winter: Suitable for snowshoe or ski access to Sunday Lake. McCarthy Rd. is not plowed.

🐾 Distances: McCarthy Rd. to Sunday Lake, 0.4 mi. Winter access from Number Four Rd., 0.8 mi (0.6 km).

A typical trail along the Independence River. BARBARA MCMARTIN

Miscellaneous Trails

The following trails are S of Stillwater Rd. starting from the drivable McCarthy Rd. and Snowmobile Trail (trail 11) and are convenient for further exploration in the region, possibly by mountain bike.

(8) Sunday Lake Link Trail

Map: A1

THIS 0.6-MI TRAIL allows snowmobiles and hikers to connect all the trails of the area without going onto Stillwater Rd. See trail 11 for the W trailhead and trail 12 for the E trailhead. The trail is on the L at 0.2 mi on McCarthy Rd. and on the R at 0.1 mi on Basket Factory Rd., and is marked with DEC snowmobile markers.

(9) North Crossover Snowmobile Trail

Map: A1

CONNECTS THE INDEPENDENCE RIVER TRAIL (trail 5) and McCarthy Rd. and Snowmobile Trail (trail 11), S of Stillwater Rd. It is an easy-to-follow route 3.0 mi long, perhaps usable for extended loop travel, and marked with DEC snowmobile markers. Although there are signs cautioning that the trail may not be passable due to high water, there is a path around the flooded area on the S side of the trail 0.8 mi from the W end. There is another beaver pond at 2.3 mi from the W end opposite an 8 to 10 ft high rock wall. The trail crosses the Lewis-Herkimer County line but no sign indicates the boundary.

(10) Emmet Hill Rd. Snowmobile Trail

Map: A1

THIS TRAIL connects the Independence River Trail (trail 5) and McCarthy Rd. and Snowmobile Trail (trail 11) S of Stillwater Rd. and S of the North Crossover Snowmobile Trail (trail 9), and so can be used for a loop, possibly by bicycle. This is an old road past a log cabin, now tumbled down, located on a pond in Fifth Creek, 1.5 mi from the E end. The cabin belonged to Emmet Hill, former forest ranger at Stillwater.

McCarthy Rd. and this trail might be usable for a shorter trail access to the East Bridge on the Independence River, closed to snowmobilers but usable by cautious hikers. The trail shows damage from ATVs, but is mostly easy grades. A beaver pond can be crossed on a dam at the Herkimer-Lewis County line 1.6 mi from the E end. Trail length is 1.75 mi (2.8 km). The trail is marked with DEC snowmobile markers and yellow foot trail markers.

(11) McCarthy Rd. and Snowmobile Trail

Map: A1

THIS OLD ROAD connects with Stillwater Rd. 3.5 mi E of its intersection with Number Four Rd. (4.0 mi W of Stillwater). It leads S past the Sunday Lake Link Trail (trail 8) at 0.3 mi, the Sunday Lake Road and Trail (trail 7) at 0.4 mi, the North Crossover Snowmobile Trail (trail 9) at 1.9 mi, and the Emmet Hill Rd. Trail (trail 10) at 2.9 mi, and ends at a private land boundary at 5.0 mi. The road is easily drivable for the first four miles, but the last mile is in poor shape, although according to the Unit Management Plan it is due for rehabilitation. A pickup or 4WD vehicle would be best used here. The road is a snowmobile trail, but markers are not likely to be seen. The state has acquired a recreational easement on a block of private land 0.2 mi E of the end of the road. Sportsmen can now park off the road before the gate and bushwhack to reach the area, which includes Blue, Hitchcock, Grass, and Moose ponds.

(12) Basket Factory Rd. and Snowmobile Trail

Map: B1

BASKET FACTORY RD. connects with Stillwater Rd. 4.0 mi E of the jct. with Number Four Rd. and 3.5 mi W of the jct. at Stillwater. It is a good gravel road extending 3.3 mi to a turnaround. Trail 8 connects on the R at 0.1 mi. The trail going L at the end-of-road turnaround leads 0.4 mi to private land. At 2.3 mi from Stillwater Rd., a two-track road forks R and goes down a short distance to an unofficial campsite at Sunday Creek. There is a small bridge over the creek, and an old, unofficial trail continues S.   ◆

Fourth Lake from Black Bear Mt. MARK BOWIE

Big Moose Section

This network affords a variety of circuit and through hikes that visit one or more wild lakes and ponds: Cascade Lake, Chain Ponds, Windfall Pond, Queer Lake, Mays Pond, Chub Lake, Constable Pond, Pigeon Lake, and Otter Pond.

There are several ascents to viewpoints: Billys Bald Spot, West Mt., Cork Mt., Onondaga Mt., Eagle Cliff, Rocky Mt., Black Bear Mt., and Bald (Rondaxe) Mt. The trail to Rocky Mt. is most notable because of its shortness and the quality of the scenery.

The trails of this section are reached from Big Moose Rd. between the communities of Eagle Bay and Big Moose, or from NY 28 in the region of Eagle Bay and Inlet, all within nine miles from the jct. in Eagle Bay. Many of the trails form a network extending E and NE of Big Moose Rd. and originating at trailheads on that road and on Higby Rd. S of Big Moose Lake. Together with the trails reached by boat, they lie in the Pigeon Lake Wilderness Area of the Forest Preserve. These are foot trails only; bicycles are not allowed in Wilderness Areas.

TRAILS REACHED BY BOAT:
Three DEC trails to lakes, and a side trail to a stream, are accessible only by boat going to the E end of Big Moose Lake. Each of the four trails ends at a lean-to. See boat launch information for trail 18 and descriptions for trails 18, 19, and 20.

SHORT HIKES:
◆ Cathedral Pines—0.1 mi (0.2 km) round trip. A very short route to see a small grove of beautiful large white pines. See trail 40.
◆ Moss Lake Circuit Trail—2.5 mi (4.0 km) loop. Easy walking through woods around the lake, with access routes to the lake on the N side. See trail 28.
◆ Eagle Cliff Trail—0.5 mi (0.8 km) round trip. Climbs to a good view of Fourth Lake and Eagle Bay. See trail 32.

MODERATE HIKES:
◆ Cascade Lake Trail—6.0 mi (9.7 km) round trip. Gentle grades past

waterfalls and nice picnic areas as well as a great ski. See trail 27.

◆ Rocky Mt. Trail—1.2 mi (1.9 km) round trip. Climbs to a great view of Fourth Lake, Eagle Bay, and Inlet. The trail is short, but the climb is vigorous. See trail 33.

HARDER HIKE:

◆ Queer Lake Loop (using trails 21, 24, and 22)—8.7 mi (14.0 km) round trip. Visit Constable Pond, Chub Lake, and Queer Lake using the Constable Pond–West Mt. trailhead.

(14) **Razorback Pond Trail**

Map: C1, p. 281

▶ Trailhead: From Eagle Bay, drive 7.3 mi NW on Big Moose Rd. to the hamlet of Big Moose. Just before the RR crossing, turn R onto Twitchell Rd., paved for the first mile, and drive 2.0 mi to a parking lot on the lake at the end of the road. The lake is 1.5 mi long and has private camps around it. There is a boat landing at the parking area. ◀

THE PATH STARTS L (W) at the edge of Twitchell Lake (0.0 mi), crossing the gravel boat handling area. It follows an old logging road with yellow markers and is wet and muddy in places.

At 0.3 mi, it turns L at a fork; the R fork goes to a private camp on the lake. At 0.7 mi, the Beaver River–Twitchell Trail (trail 128) starts on the hillside R.

At 0.8 mi, as the trail enters private land, the trail curves R and starts to climb. Shortly beyond the curve, an obscure unmarked trail goes L 150 ft to Silver Lake. This is a private lake, with limited access except at this trail point.

Continuing on past the jct., the path follows the old road, climbing and skirting the E side of the lake. As the route turns W, it leaves the old road and starts climbing the hillside N of the lake. After bumping over another hillside, the trail heads N on level ground, crosses an inlet of Razorback Pond at 1.7 mi, leaves private land, and meets the Pigeon Lake Wilderness Area at the NE corner of the pond. Climbing a hillside just a little, and staying back in the thick woods, the trail follows along the pond to its midpoint, then turns S and ends at a small camping area at the edge of Razorback Pond, 2.0 mi from the trailhead.

❋ Trail in winter: Easily skied as far as Silver Lake. The hillside section just beyond Silver Lake is best left to experienced skiers. Easy snowshoeing.

❧ Distances: Twitchell Lake to Silver Lake, 0.8 mi; to Razorback Pond, 2.0 mi (3.2 km).

(15) **Snake Pond**

Map: C1, p. 281

This short trail extends NW down from Twitchell Rd. to Twitchell Creek, adjacent to Snake Pond, for a round trip hike of 1.4 mi. It passes impressive timber and attractive conifers. It descends 200 ft, although it may seem like more, in just over two thirds of a mile. Its main attraction seems to be access to the water.

▶ Trailhead: From Eagle Bay, drive 7.3 mi NW on Big Moose Rd. to the hamlet of Big Moose. Just before the RR crossing, turn R onto Twitchell Rd. and drive 1.1 mi to where the trail starts on the L after the Post camp. Parking is on the wide shoulder. ◀

FROM THE ROAD (0.0 mi), the blue-marked trail descends gradually to a register, bends L for nearly 300 yd, and then turns R and heads generally NW the rest of the way. A dense stand of small balsam and spruce surrounds the trail, with mature spruce towering above, at 0.5 mi.

The trail ends at 0.7 mi at Twitchell Creek, fringed by a brushy wetland and conifers, including balsam and tamarack. The creek, the outlet of Twitchell Lake, runs W and then N to the Stillwater Reservoir in the Beaver River–Black River watershed.

On the other side of the creek is a narrow point of land separating it from Snake Pond, with conifers that obscure a view of the pond. If you ford the creek and cross the point of land you will be at the edge of this conifer-lined, mucky-bottomed pond. As an alternative, a path downstream a few steps from the end of the trail on mostly dry land and a couple of mossy wet areas leads 85 yd back to the boggy Twitchell Creek streamside where a view of the pond, perhaps including a loon, is possible.

❋ Trail in winter: Of no obvious interest, but done easily with snowshoes.

❀ Distances: Trailhead to Twitchell Creek, 0.7 mi (1.1 km).

(16) Billys Bald Spot–Squash Pond Trail

Map: C1

This trail climbs 340 ft from Martin Rd. on the N shore of western Big Moose Lake to "Billy's Bald Spot," where there is a view over the lake, and continues to Squash Pond to the W. This is a private trail on private land, but for many years the owners have permitted the public to use the trail.

▶ Trailhead: From NY 28 in Eagle Bay, drive 5.6 mi NW on Big Moose Rd., turn R on Martin Rd. (no road sign), and follow it parallel to the N shore of Big Moose Lake for 0.6 mi to where the trail starts at some gravel over a culvert on the L, opposite Camp Vetti. Park along the road; do not block driveways. In addition to yellow and orange metal markers, there is also flagging. ◀

FROM THE ROAD (0.0 mi), the trail, worn into the hillside, immediately ascends and within yards angles R (nearly N) and upward (despite a large log that might divert hikers L) for 0.1 mi, then bends L, rising farther W to reach "Billy's Bald Spot" near the top at 0.4 mi. The last two thirds of the trip is up the slope at an angle, with the uphill side on the R. At the site of a privately built lean-to covered with names, there is an open ledge at the edge of a steep slope, offering a nice view over much of Big Moose Lake, more than three miles long. Forested hills are seen beyond the lake.

The trail continues slightly upwards NW from the W back corner of the lean-to (avoid path going down to the side), marked by flagging and some orange metal disks. It goes over a hill above the viewpoint, reaching 2250 ft and passing impressive red spruce, among other tall trees. It descends to approach a stream at 0.9 mi, turns R, and reaches the end of Squash Pond at a beaver dam at 1.0 mi. There are a couple of islands, one of which may be reached via a blowdown, but otherwise it has a mostly boggy shoreline.

❀ Trail in winter: Steep hill suitable for vigorous snowshoeing, although roadside parking could be difficult.

🐾 Distances: Martin Rd. to viewpoint, 0.4 mi; to Squash Pond, 1.0 mi (1.6 km). Ascent to viewpoint, 340 ft (104 m).

(17) Safford Pond Trail

Map: C2

This is both a DEC blue-marked hiking trail (on the N half) and a DEC-marked snowmobile trail. It leads from Big Moose Rd. near the W end of Big Moose Lake SW past West Pond, Safford Pond, and Goose Pond to the second trailhead just N of Lake Rondaxe. The S half is marked only as a snowmobile trail, but is a good hiking trail, except for a 50-yd spot below a beaver dam. High water coming up the trail may limit side trip access to Goose Pond. The hike, including side trips, totals 6.4 mi, while the driving distance is 12.7 mi between trailheads.

▶ Trailheads: To reach the N trailhead from NY 28 in Eagle Bay, drive 5.5 mi on Big Moose Rd. to the Orvis Schoolhouse trailhead parking lot on the L. This is about 100 ft from the jct. where Big Moose

Rd. goes L and Martin Rd. (unmarked) goes R to the N shore of Big Moose Lake.

To reach the trailhead on the S end from the Tourist Information Center in Old Forge, drive 4.4 mi NE on NY 28. Turn L (W) on Rondaxe Rd. Go 1.4 mi to a crossover jct. between two parallel roads. Turn R, then immediately L, continuing NW parallel to the previous route. You will be on the bed of the old Raquette Lake Railroad. Go 0.5 mi farther to a bridge, and turn R at the next corner (North Rondaxe Rd.). Go 0.7 mi to the snowmobile trail on the L. Park on the N edge of the road near the trailhead. ◄

AT THE N END (0.0 mi), this route is broad, easy, and mostly used for access to West Pond. A short red-marked side trail at 0.4 mi leads 70 yd to a waterfall among huge rocks on the outlet of West Pond. Water is sometimes hidden behind the rocks. This side trail goes L just as the trail turns R and begins a short, steep climb.

Some 100 yd beyond this jct., a red-marked side trail goes L (S and E) 300 yd to a clearing on the W shore of West Pond next to its outlet. The pond is very scenic, although much of the shoreline is boggy.

From the jct. with the West Pond side trail, the Safford Pond Trail (R) continues with ups and downs, crossing some snowmobile bridges.

At 2.3 mi, a blue-marked side trail goes R (SW) 190 yd to an informal campsite on the inlet to Safford Pond. It lies in a spruce-fir setting. Downstream a short way, the stream enters a large open wetland at the end of Safford Pond. This side trail can be somewhat obscure.

The main trail continues to another jct. at 2.4 mi, where the main route continues L as a snowmobile trail. The jct. may be noticeable only by the trail signs high on the trees.

Continuing R (S), toward the pond, the blue trail goes through scrub evergreens, crosses a wetland with many tamaracks, reenters woods, and climbs over a ridge. Turning L for 100 yd, the trail ends in a small spot near the pond where campfires have been made at 2.7 mi from the trailhead, and 0.3 mi from the jct. The clearing is set in pines and tamaracks and has a pebbly beach. To the R lies the bog-lined N arm and inlet of the pond. The pond is nicely surrounded by spruce, white pine, and fir. Too narrow and right on the shoreline, this is not a suitable place to camp, but it is a nice place to stop for a rest. Viburnum undergrowth is especially dense and tall near Safford Pond, then seems to get shorter and shorter as one goes S.

Continuing from the jct., the snowmobile trail goes SE and then S. It turns SW while crossing a marsh and creek, eventually turning SE again to approach Goose Pond at 3.7 mi. The pond is visible in the distance (the sign says 0.1 mi), but high water comes within about 15 yd of the main trail. Slide Off Mt. is across the pond.

Continuing S, the main trail, now generally level and smooth, reaches a wide wetland at 4.5 mi on old corduroy and a misplaced bridge that may look like an island. The trail then swings around the base of a hill and heads E toward the road, passing on the L a snowmobile trail that leads to private land at Dart Lake. The trail is smooth and easy to the North Rondaxe Rd. trailhead at 5.2 mi.

✸ Trail in winter: The S half is suitable for beginning skiers at least as far as Goose Pond, and easy intermediate skiing to Safford Pond. The N half is better left to the intermediate to expert skier.

🐾 Distances: N trailhead to West Pond, 0.7 mi; to Safford Pond campsite, 2.5 mi; to Safford Pond, 2.7 mi; to Goose Pond, 3.7 mi; to S trailhead, 5.2 mi (8.3 km). From the S trailhead to Goose Pond, 1.5 mi; to Safford Pond, 3.1 mi (5 km).

(18) Gull Lakes Trail

Map: D1

The two small Gull Lakes (Gull Ponds) lie N of the E end of Big Moose Lake. The trail passes Lower Gull Lake and ends at a lean-to on Upper Gull Lake, where there is good swimming.

▶ Trailhead: This trail is accessible only by boat on Big Moose Lake. A launching site (without ramp) near the E end of the lake is at the bay on the SE shore of the lake. This is reached by driving almost to the end of Higby Rd. (which goes NE off Big Moose Rd. S of the lake, 3.7 mi from NY 28 at Eagle Bay) and then returning R at the fork and proceeding less than 0.2 mi to the bay. The parking area here is maintained by the Town of Webb. Canoes and motorboats may be rented and launched at Dunn's Boat Service, located on Big Moose Rd. on the S shore at the W end of Big Moose Lake 5.2 mi from NY 28 at Eagle Bay. Parking is available. This adds two miles or more each way to the boat distance along with the larger, W part of Big Moose Lake, which can be especially choppy on windy days. ◀

GO BY BOAT, roughly 35 degrees magnetic from the launch site at the end of Higby Rd., about 1.1 mi to the marshy inlet at the NE end of Big Moose Lake. Continue NE along the N side of the inlet for 0.4 mi. Past a stream L emptying into the inlet, about 150 yd beyond, is a landing with a sign for the Gull Lake lean-to.

From the lake (0.0 mi), the trail heads NE, gradually gaining ground to approach the Gull Lakes outlet stream, paralleling the stream to the S shore of Lower Gull Lake, 208 ft higher than the inlet. After crossing the outlet, the marked trail turns W and becomes narrow and muddy around the lower lake between cliffs L and the lake R, then heads N to the lean-to on the S shore of Upper Gull Lake (1.2 mi). There is a Herkimer-Hamilton County line marker about 15 ft from the trail on the L, just 20 yd before the lean-to.

❄ Trail in winter: May be suitable for snowshoeing or backcountry skiing from Higby Rd. over the ice, when Big Moose Lake is frozen solid. Watch for bad ice at the narrows on the long arm known as "the Inlet."

🐾 Distances: Higby Rd. launch to landing, 1.5 mi; W end of Big Moose Lake to landing, 3.7 mi; landing to lean-to, 1.2 mi (1.9 km).

(19) Sister Lake Trail (and Andys Creek)

Map: D1

Lower Sister Lake, remote and pristine, lies NE of Big Moose Lake and is connected by a narrow waterway with Upper Sister Lake on the NE. Bushwhacking to the Upper Lake from the trail's end is reported to be very messy.

▶ Trailhead: This trail is accessible only by boat on Big Moose Lake. Refer to the trailhead and launching site for the Gull Lakes Trail (18), but also note that the E end of the inlet gets very shallow, so getting through to the stream may be possible only with a canoe or kayak. ◀

TRAVEL BY BOAT to the NE corner of Big Moose Lake (NW of East Bay, heading roughly 35 degrees magnetic), about 1.1 mi from the launch site at the end of Higby Rd. Proceed NE and E to the shallow end of a marshy waterway (called "the Inlet") at about 2.3 mi, where a canoe or kayak would be desirable, trying to find your way into the stream, and about one third of a mile up a winding stream, staying L, to a landing at about 2.6 mi from Higby Rd.

The trail begins (0.0 mi) with an elevated bog bridge of nearly 70 yd, then is on mostly dry land with few markers. At 0.2 mi, a spur leads

L to Andys Creek lean-to. This blue-marked trail goes N from the main trail, crosses Andys Creek at 0.15 mi (0.35 mi from the landing) on an impressive bridge with six steps up to the top of a crib. The steps allow the bridge to line up with the higher bank on the other side, and decrease the danger of it being swept away like its predecessors. The trail then turns NE to the lean-to at 0.3 mi (0.5 mi from the landing). The stream, which flows S to "the Inlet," has attractive rapids near the lean-to. The round-trip hiking distance from the boat landing to the lean-to and back is 1.0 mi.

From the Andys Creek spur jct., the main Lower Sister Lake Trail goes NE, first along the level for nearly a mile, then ascending nearly 200 ft. The trail contours around a sharp hill, turns R (E) as it approaches Lower Sister Lake, and continues on the contour to reach the lean-to at 3.3 mi. It has a fine location on a point along the E shore of Lower Sister Lake. There is a nice ledge at the shoreline, and a beach nearby.

❋ Trail in winter: 2.3 mi from Higby Rd. over the ice, when Big Moose Lake is frozen solid, to the start of the trail. Watch for bad ice at the narrows on the inlet, and get off the lake on either side at the end to avoid the thin ice marsh at the inlet creek.

𝕸 Distances: Higby Rd. launch to landing, 2.3 mi; W end of Big Moose Lake to landing, 5.0 mi; landing to Andys Creek lean-to via spur, 0.5 mi; landing to Lower Sister Lake lean-to, 3.3 mi (5.3 km).

(20) Russian Lake Trail

Map: D1

▶ Trailhead: This trail is accessible only by boat on Big Moose Lake. Refer to the trailhead for the Gull Lakes Trail (18). ◀

GO BY BOAT to the end of East Bay on Big Moose Lake. From the Higby Rd. boat launch, this is reached by following the shore R. At the end of East Bay there is a dock on the L (N) side.

From the dock (0.0 mi), the trail goes slightly N of E to a lean-to, which is nicely located by a ledge at the edge of Russian Lake, at 0.7 mi.

❋ Trail in winter: Smooth 1.3 mi trip over Big Moose Lake from Higby Rd., when the lake is frozen solid. Watch for thin ice when approaching the shore on East Bay.

𝕸 Distances: Higby Rd. launch to landing, 1.3 mi; W end of Big Moose Lake to landing, 3.5 mi; landing to lean-to, 0.7 mi (1.1 km).

(21) Constable Pond–West Mt. Trail

Map: D1

This long wilderness trail extends from Higby Rd. just S of Big Moose Lake NE past Constable Pond, Pigeon Lake, and Otter Pond to the summit of West Mt., W of the northern part of Raquette Lake. There it meets the end of the Raquette Lake–West Mt. Trail (trail 43). The part of the trail beyond Constable Pond is one of the most remote from any road or development in the whole region. It has wet areas, blow-downs, and wet stream crossings, passes several magnificent specimens of white pine between Constable Pond and the end of Pigeon Lake, and makes an 800-ft ascent of West Mt., the last 600 ft being steep or moderately steep. The view from the summit is mostly over Raquette Lake, the fire tower having been removed.

Branching SE off the trail are the Hermitage Trail, the Mays Pond Trail, and the Queer Lake Trail (trails 22, 23, and 24), permitting various circuit and through hikes. A round-trip hike of the network involves backpacking, but the lack of lean-tos or informal campsites along the way is a limiting factor. Because this trail is in a designated Wilderness Area (Pigeon Lake), bicycles are not allowed.

▶ Trailhead: From NY 28 in Eagle Bay, drive 3.7 mi on Big Moose Rd. Turn R on Higby Rd. for 1.3 mi to Judson Rd. (R), and park along the road (without blocking Judson Rd.). If necessary, park along the boat landing road on the R, a little farther down Higby Rd. The trail starts on Judson Rd., a private unpaved road with a barrier (on the E). There are state symbols on a sign, but it may not be evident that that is the trail, and there are no markers along Judson Rd. The rest of the trail is marked with DEC blue markers, with additional red markers near West Mt. ◀

FROM HIGBY RD. (0.0 mi), the route follows Judson Rd. for the first 0.2 mi, then turns R just before the road turns L to cross Constable Brook. After about 20 yd there is a vehicle barrier, a large map sign, and a trail register. The blue trail follows an old road along the S side of broad, rocky Constable Brook.

At 0.5 mi the red-marked Hermitage Trail (trail 22) goes R (SSE) toward Queer Lake. Some 25 yd beyond this jct. the path turns L, crosses Constable Brook on a bridge, and goes E, now on a footpath, on the N side of the brook, reentering private land.

The trail meets another old road at 0.9 mi and follows it R. In 100 yd, the trail recrosses Constable Brook on a logging bridge and within 20 yd turns L on the other side, leaving the old road. This footpath soon enters the state Forest Preserve and the Pigeon Lake Wilderness Area. Another jct. on the R at 1.3 mi is for the yellow-marked Mays Pond Trail (trail 23), which goes to that pond and on to the Queer Lake area.

The trail parallels Constable Brook and its open wetland L. At 2.2 mi the path nears Constable Pond, visible through tall spruce and hemlock, and goes parallel to its S shore. At just before 2.6 mi a spur path goes L a few yards to the edge of the pond. 55 yd beyond, the yellow-marked Queer Lake Trail (trail 24) goes R (SE) 0.6 mi to Chub Lake and the Queer Lake region. 70 yd beyond the jct., with a brook on the L, an informal campsite is on the R, the only one to be found along this trail.

Some streams and wet spots alternate with sections of nice woodland path. Pigeon Lake's outlet stream crosses the trail at 3.9 mi. The trail then turns R, going through messy undergrowth and across a bog. The water of Pigeon Lake becomes visible through the trees on the R by a sign at 4.9 mi, and in less than 100 yd the trail comes closer to the lake at its narrow N section and a sign.

This lake is about the size of Constable Pond, 0.7 mi long, with a boggy shoreline fringed by white pine and spruce. Some red markers start to appear near the lake. Both blue and red markers are found on the rest of the trail.

At 5.4 mi, about opposite the end of the lake, the trail passes a magnificent white pine on the L as Pigeon Lake passes from the scene. At 5.6 and 5.8 mi, in a spruce forest, there are two crossings of the outlet of Otter Pond, which includes another pond well out of sight to the R. For the rest of the way the trail is on higher, drier ground in a forest of hardwoods and scattered spruce and fir.

After paralleling Otter Pond's outlet for a considerable distance,

Pigeon Lake Wilderness
JAMES APPLEYARD

the route crosses it a third time and then a small pond appears on the R just below Otter Pond. Otter Pond may be detected through the trees R after the trail passes the small pond, at 6.7 mi.

At 7.6 mi, having already gradually ascended 1280 ft, the trail begins the final, steeper 620-ft ascent of West Mt. At 8.0 mi the trail levels near the summit, crosses a saddle between the N peak and summit, and then turns R (S) to climb slightly before reaching a jct. with the Raquette Lake–West Mt. Trail (trail 43) at 8.1 mi. Turn R on that trail and reach the open summit of West Mt. in 50 yd. A fair section of Raquette Lake can be seen, but trees fringing the top limit views in other directions.

One may continue the trip down the Raquette Lake–West Mt. Trail to Brown's Tract Rd., but the two trailheads are far apart and there are no trails to complete a loop. Thus two cars are required.

❋ Trail in winter: Suitable for snowshoeing. West Mt. would require excellent skiing ability. Only groups with good winter experience should attempt the full distance on unbroken trail.

🦌 Distances: Higby Rd. to Hermitage Trail (trail 22), 0.5 mi; to Mays Pond Trail (trail 23), 1.3 mi; to Constable Pond and Queer Lake Trail (trail 24), 2.6 mi; to Pigeon Lake outlet crossing, 3.9 mi; to Pigeon Lake, 4.9 mi; to Otter Pond, 6.7 mi; to summit of West Mt., 8.1 mi (13.1 km). Continuation to Brown's Tract Rd., via trail 43, 13.0 mi (20.9 km). West Mt. ascent (from Higby Rd.), 1073 ft (327 m). Summit elevation, 2902 ft (885 m).

(22) Hermitage Trail

Map: D1

The trail is named after a private camp located near the end of the trail. It provides some pleasant walking, although the S end tends to be rough and wet. The route has moderate ups and downs and in part goes through a mixed forest with large specimens of yellow birch.

▶ Locator: This is an interior trail from the Constable Pond–West Mt. Trail (trail 21), 0.5 mi from the trailhead, to the Queer Lake Trail (trail 24), 2.2 mi from the Windfall Pond trailhead. ◀

FROM THE START, 0.5 mi E of the trailhead on the Constable Pond–West Mt. Trail (trail 21) (0.0 mi), the red-marked route goes SE. At 0.1 mi, a private trail comes in on the L at an acute angle and at 0.3

mi the wetland of the Mays Pond outlet appears on the L.

At 1.0 mi the route forks R, crosses an intermittent stream in a wetland at 1.2 mi, and ascends to a jct. at 1.3 mi. Here, 1.8 mi from the Higby Rd. trailhead, the Hermitage Trail ends at the yellow-marked Queer Lake Trail (trail 24). To the R, the latter trail goes WSW 2.1 mi to Big Moose Rd. via Windfall Pond. Avoid the path going immediately L at this jct.; it goes to a private camp. Straight ahead, the Queer Lake Trail goes 1.3 mi to the lean-to on Queer Lake via a final side trail.

❉ Trail in winter: Easy backcountry skiing or snowshoeing.

𒀭 Distances: Higby Rd. trailhead of Constable Pond–West Mt. Trail to start of Hermitage Trail, 0.5 mi; Hermitage Trail to Queer Lake Trail, 1.3 mi (2.1 km). Higby Rd. to Queer Lake Lean-to (a likely use for this trail), 3.1 mi (5.0 km).

(23) Mays Pond Trail

Map: D1

▶ Locator: This is an interior trail. The N end is on the Constable Pond–West Mt. Trail (trail 21), 1.3 mi from its trailhead. The S end is on the Queer Lake Trail (trail 24), 2.6 mi from its trailhead. ◀

FROM ITS N END on the Constable Pond–West Mt. Trail (0.0 mi), the yellow-marked path ascends gradually through a tall forest, levels off, and descends 100 ft past lofty red spruce to Mays Pond. At 0.4 mi, where the trail forks L, a short R fork drops down to the edge of the pond near the E end of its N shore. The towering white pines around this pond add to its beauty.

The yellow trail continues beyond the side trail and along the NE shore of Mays Pond, past majestic pines and through dense spruce. An inlet to the pond passes underfoot at 0.6 mi. Beyond it, the narrow trail goes up somewhat steeply almost 300 ft, and at 1.1 mi the trail reaches height of land and crosses the divide between the Moose–Black River and Raquette River watersheds. Finally, there is a descent. At the bottom, at 1.3 mi, the trail ends on the yellow-marked Queer Lake Trail (trail 24). This point is 2.6 mi from the Higby Rd. trailhead. To the L on the yellow trail, it is 0.5 mi to the Queer Lake lean-to. A loop trip to Queer Lake lean-to and return by the Hermitage Trail equals 6.2 mi.

❉ Trail in winter: Easy snowshoeing. Due to steepness, this trail is for good backcountry skiers only.

🚹 Distances: Higby Rd. trailhead of Constable Pond–West Mt. Trail to start of Mays Pond Trail, 1.3 mi; Mays Pond Trail to Queer Lake Trail, 1.3 mi (2.1 km). Higby Rd. to Queer Lake Lean-to (a likely use for this trail), 3.0 mi (4.8 km). Return to start via Hermitage Trail (trail 22), 6.2 mi (including Queer Lake Lean-to).

(24) Queer Lake Trail

Map: D1, 2

▶ Trailhead: From NY 28 in Eagle Bay, drive 3.2 mi N on Big Moose Rd. and turn R into the Windfall Pond Trailhead. The other end of the trail is on the Constable Pond–West Mt. Trail (21). ◀

FROM THE REGISTER (0.0 mi), the yellow-marked trail goes E on the S side of a stream in an easy stretch. At 0.1 mi it forks L and crosses the stream on a bridge. Be careful here not to continue on the path straight ahead which, in a few yards, has an informal campsite on the L by the stream.

The trail goes E on the N side of the stream. At 0.7 mi, the trail recrosses the stream on a bridge with a flume on the R. It climbs SE along Windfall Pond's outlet, reaching a jct. at 1.1 mi, just W of the pond. The blue-marked Chain Ponds Trail (trail 25) goes R here, while the yellow trail turns L to go toward Queer Lake. The trail promptly crosses the outlet of Windfall Pond after which, with an informal campsite on the R under the hemlocks, a side trail goes R a few yards to the edge of Windfall Pond. This is a small body of water partly lined by fallen trees.

Continuing ENE along the N side of the pond and beyond, the route goes through stands of towering hardwoods and along a slope that drops off L. At 1.9 mi there is a short, moderately steep descent, partly on bedrock outcropping. In an area of tall timber, the red-marked Hermitage Trail (trail 22) connects on the L at 2.2 mi. The yellow-marked Queer Lake Trail turns R (SE), climbs a ridge, and in 200 yd turns N and descends moderately. This bypass up and down the hillside avoids a crossing of private land at the Hermitage.

After a brook crossing at the bottom, another jct. appears at 2.4 mi. An unmarked trail leads L (W) 60 yd to the Hermitage, a private camp. The marked trail goes R at this jct. and travels ENE along the level, crossing a wetland at 2.5 mi, and at 2.7 mi reaches a jct. where the blue-marked Chain Ponds Trail rejoins on the R (trail 25). 13 yd beyond, the yellow trail turns L (NW) and a side trail goes straight ahead, reaching the muddy edge of the NW bay of Queer Lake at 2.7 mi. There is an informal campsite set in the spruce with a view of the enclosed bay and a red-marked spur trail to a suggested campsite.

From the jct., the yellow trail crosses a wetland at the corner of the bay, climbs steeply, and parallels the N shore of the bay. At 3.0 mi the yellow-marked Mays Pond Trail (trail 23) comes in from the L (N).

Following the lakeshore, the trail passes a red-marked spur R to the Queer Lake lean-to at 3.3 mi. This side trail goes S and SE to the beginning of the peninsula projecting from Queer Lake's N shore. It then crosses the narrow wetland on split logs at the base of the peninsula, follows the edge of the lake's NW bay a short ways, and crosses the peninsula at its narrowest section to reach the lean-to on its other side 0.2 mi from the main trail. The spur route here is lent primeval charm by tall hemlocks, white pines, and red spruce. The lean-to is nicely situated on the NW shore of the main body of Queer Lake, with some large rocks at the water's edge. The distance from the trailhead on Big Moose Rd. is 3.5 mi. There is an unmarked path from the log planks at the base of the peninsula to its tip, ending at a large boulder on the tip after a massive blowdown.

From the lean-to spur jct., the yellow trail continues E along a hillside, turns N at 4.7 mi, and crosses the divide between the Raquette River and Moose–Black River watersheds. Descending, the trail weaves a bit, then reaches a brook with beaver activity at 5.0 mi.

At 5.2 mi, Chub Lake is partly visible through the trees on the R, the trail passing above its S shore. The path crosses an inlet at 5.4 mi on a plank bridge in a spruce-fringed wetland, with the pond visible on the R.

The trail reaches a jct. at 5.6 mi, where it turns L toward Constable Pond. A yellow-marked side trail to Chub Lake continues straight (NE) and then turns E for 0.2 mi to the NW shore of conifer-lined Chub Lake. There is an attractive informal camping area under a stand of spruce, as well as a nice rock ledge at the shoreline extending underwater.

From the jct. with the side trail, the Queer Lake Trail continues NW, through stands of spruce and with further small ups and downs, to end at 6.0 mi at the blue-marked Constable Pond–West Mt. Trail (trail 21) on the SE shore of Constable Pond. To the L, it is 2.6 mi to the Higby Rd. trailhead. To the R, it is 5.5 mi to West Mt. and 10.5 mi to the Uncas Rd. trailhead (see trails 42, 43).

❊ Trail in winter: For intermediate backcountry skiers. Easy snowshoeing.

⚸ Distances: Big Moose Rd. to Windfall Pond and Chain Ponds Trail (trail 25), 1.1 mi; to Hermitage Trail (trail 22), 2.2 mi; to Chain Ponds Trail E end, 2.7 mi; to Queer Lake, 2.7 mi; to Mays Pond Trail (trail 23), 3.1 mi; to Queer Lake Lean-to spur, 3.3 mi; to turn N, 4.7 mi; to Chub Lake, 5.2 mi; to Constable Pond–West Mt. Trail (21), 6.0 mi (9.7 km).

(25) Chain Ponds Trail

Map: D2

This overall V-shaped trail starts from the yellow Queer Lake Trail (trail 24) at Windfall Pond, goes SE to a jct. with the red Cascade Lake Link Trail (trail 26), and then proceeds N past Chain Ponds to rejoin the Queer Lake Trail just W of Queer Lake, forming a triangle with the Queer Lake Trail. The trail has considerable ascents and descents. It passes areas of rugged rock formations and cliffs. The E section tends to be narrow and overgrown. For scenery, this is the more interesting route from the road to the Queer Lake area.

▶ Locator: The Chain Ponds Trail joins the Queer Lake Trail (trail 24) on both ends, by Windfall Pond at 1.1 mi from Big Moose Rd. (W end) and at 2.7 mi near the W bay of Queer Lake (E end). Access is usually from the latter. The trail also meets the Cascade Lake Link Trail (trail 26), and thus is accessible from the Cascade Lake Trail (trail 27) trailhead. ◀

FROM WINDFALL POND (0.0 mi), the blue-marked Chain Ponds Trail heads SE. After a few yards, a short side trail goes L to the edge of small Windfall Pond.

Passing S of the pond, the main trail ascends SE through stately hardwoods. At 0.4 mi a faint path leads R a short way to the edge of a boggy pond.

The trail makes a further ascent at 0.5 mi near an imposing rock wall on the L with rock going up through the treetops and out of sight, and then descends, going through ferns and muddy spots. At 1.0 mi, an interesting area of cliffs, crevasses, caves, and large boulders begins on the L. At a jct. at 1.4 mi, the blue trail turns L (N) toward Chain Ponds, and the red Cascade Lake Link Trail (trail 26) comes in from the R.

Continuing N, the blue-marked trail crosses the outlet of Chain Ponds at 1.8 mi. L is the S section of Chain Ponds lined by fallen timber, and to the R a wetland through which the outlet runs. Chain Ponds is one body of water divided into three sections by two necks of land. It has a predominantly wetland shoreline with some dead standing timber.

A side trail at 1.9 mi goes L to the end of the pond. The trail goes N above the E side of the S section of Chain Ponds and through a mixed hardwood-coniferous forest.

The trail ascends, Chain Ponds being no longer visible, but then starts to drop with a glimpse of the N end of the ponds at 2.5 mi. At 2.8 mi, it ends at the yellow-marked Queer Lake Trail (trail 24). To the L on the yellow trail it is 1.6 mi to Windfall Pond and the other end of the Chain Ponds Trail, and 2.7 mi to the trailhead on Big Moose Rd. To the R, the NW bay of Queer Lake is almost at hand.

❄ Trail in winter: For good skiers only, owing to the hills. Easy snowshoeing.

🐾 Distances: Big Moose Rd. via Queer Lake Trail (trail 24) to start of trail, 1.1 mi; Queer Lake Trail to Cascade Lake Link Trail, 1.4 mi; to Chain Ponds, 1.8 mi; to E jct. with Queer Lake Trail near Queer Lake, 2.8 mi (4.5 km).

(26) Cascade Lake Link Trail

Map: D2

This route goes N from the Cascade Lake Trail (trail 27) at a point just W of the lake to the blue-marked Chain Ponds Trail (trail 25). It ascends 275 ft and crosses the divide between the Moose–Black River and Raquette River watersheds, providing a link between Cascade Lake on the S and Windfall Pond, Chain Ponds, and Queer Lake on the N. It allows for longer trips from lake to lake within the wilderness area.

▶ Locator: This is an interior trail linking the Cascade Lake Trail (1.4 mi from the Cascade trailhead) with the Chain Ponds trail, leading to the rest of the Pigeon Lake Wilderness Area trails. ◀

FROM THE JCT. with the Cascade Lake Trail (27) just W of Cascade Lake (0.0 mi), the red-marked trail goes W on level ground, skirting a hill. At 0.2 mi, the trail turns N and climbs up a ridge. It begins to level off at 0.5 mi, but further small ascents follow. It bends NE and then curves back N through a couple of gullies to meet a jct. with the blue-marked Chain Ponds Trail (trail 25) on the level at a high point at 1.1 mi. To the L are Windfall Pond via the Chain Ponds Trail (trail 25) and the Big Moose Rd. trailhead via the Queer Lake Trail (trail 24). R leads to Chain Ponds, Queer Lake, and other trails of the Pigeon Lake Wilderness Area.

❊ Trail in winter: For good wilderness skiers only, owing to the fairly steep ascents and descents. Easy snowshoeing.

🐾 Distances: Cascade Lake Trail (trail 27) to Chain Ponds Trail (trail 25), 1.1 mi (1.8 km).

(27) **Cascade Lake Trail**

Map: D2

This is a 6.0-mi ski touring circuit and hiking trail from Big Moose Rd. E to Cascade Lake, then around the lake and back to the road over the initial route. The high points of the trip are a camping area halfway along the N side, and the falls at the E end of the lake.

This description covers the trail as a circuit hike clockwise around the lake, but the hiker headed for the falls should use the S shore trail, because it is much drier than the trail segment past the E end beyond the falls. Trail connections on the W end of the lake allow for a trip to the interior of the Pigeon Lake Wilderness Area, a loop trip to trailheads farther W on Big Moose Rd., or access to the lake by hikers from the Big Moose Lake area.

Cascade Lake Camp, now the camping area, was a summer camp for girls, with a clientele of 50 girls and a stable of 25 horses in 1947. The camp's original building was previously the summer home of Charles Snyder, an attorney who bought the land when Dr. William Seward Webb first subdivided his vast holdings.

▶ Trailhead: From NY 28 in Eagle Bay, drive NW on Big Moose Rd. for 1.2 mi (avoiding an old trailhead on a dangerous S curve at 0.8 mi), and park in the DEC parking lot on the R. There are DEC yellow ski trail markers around the lake. This is also a designated horse trail. ◀

FROM THE BACK R CORNER of the parking lot (0.0 mi), the trail goes 0.4 mi SE to join an old woods road, which it follows with yellow ski markers (there may also be red hiking trail markers) NE through a hardwood forest. The rocky road goes gradually up and down, passing the Herkimer-Hamilton County line (marker R) soon before reaching a Y jct. at 1.1 mi. Here the S section of the circuit around Cascade Lake diverges. Hikers headed for the falls should turn R here, and follow a good route—possibly a little wet just before the end—E to the falls at 2.9 mi.

Continuing on the clockwise route, the trail turns L and descends to level ground as it approaches the outlet. At 1.3 mi, a field on the R, lying just W of the lake, is the site of a nineteenth-century lumber camp. Those hauling a canoe can enter this clearing and look for an opening through trees about 30 yd L from the back R corner for access to the end of the lake just over 0.1 mi from the trail. In another 150 yd a bridge crosses the lake's outlet with a wetland on the L.

At 1.4 mi, the red-marked Cascade Lake Link Trail (trail 26) goes L (N) to the blue-marked Chain Ponds Trail (trail 25). Straight ahead on a broad, pleasant route E on the N side of Cascade Lake, the route passes an informal campsite on the R. At 1.9 mi, an inviting open area R is an obvious and pleasant site for camping. This rounded point of land has grass, white pines, a beach, and a sandy lake bottom. This was the site of the summer camp for girls. Returning from here makes a pleasant hike of 3.8 mi round trip.

Beyond the open area, this wide road passes other open areas that were sports fields for the camp, including a tennis court R at 2.1 mi. Beyond them, the trail passes side paths R to campsites near the lake, then descends to a wet, muddy section and across the marshy end of the lake, then climbs gradually to a 90-degree turn R (may be tricky for skiers coming down from the falls). Drier terrain follows; the trail crosses a stream at 3.0 mi, within earshot of the falls. This is Cascade Lake's main inlet, and approximately 25 yd farther up is the high, narrow waterfall that gives the lake its name.

After the waterfall, the route turns W and goes parallel to the lake shore, but at some distance, so the lake is not visible. The old road passes a safe (without a door or any money in it) L, climbs a hillside above the lake, then follows along the contours to reach a jct. that completes the circuit of the lake at 4.9 mi. Ahead, it is 1.1 mi to the trailhead, for a total distance of 6.0 mi.

❋ Trail in winter: This is a DEC ski route, gentle and suitable for novice skiers, with one 90-degree turn on a gentle slope NW of the falls of any concern. Before the snow is thick enough, the creeks and wetlands on the E end of the lake may be messy for novices. Ski the route counterclockwise, starting on the S trail. If the creek crossing is messy, you can still see the falls and then turn back.

🐾 Distances: Trailhead to loop jct., 1.1 mi; to falls by S route, 2.9 mi; to campsite on N side, 1.9 mi; to falls by N route, 3.0 mi; to return to trailhead after complete circuit, 6.0 mi (9.7 km).

(28) Moss Lake Circuit Trail

Map: C, D2

Moss Lake (a later simplification of Morse Lake), on the SW side of Big Moose Rd., was for 50 years the site of a girls' camp. The State of New York acquired the property in 1973, and whatever structures remained were removed. The area now has no facilities other than privies at campsites, some reachable only by water, and the trail, which makes a circuit of the lake. There is a descriptive photo board at the trailhead showing many aspects of the former camp. After the state acquired the land, the camp was, for a time, occupied by Mohawk settlers, whose confrontation with New York State was very much in the news at the time.

The trail has DEC yellow markers of both the hiking and ski touring variety, and it provides an easy and attractive hike along a mostly level woods road. This is also a designated horse trail.

The Bubb Lake Trail (29) joins the Circuit Trail near the SE corner of Moss Lake, so that all or part of each trail may be covered in one hike.

▶ Trailheads: Drive 2.1 mi NW on Big Moose Rd. from its beginning at Eagle Bay and park in the area outlined by posts on the L. A small shelter contains two registers, one for those choosing a campsite (by sliding a site number over into the "Occupied" column) and one for those visiting for the day. 0.1 mi NW up the road, there is another trailhead for disabled access. Paths are being hardened for access to the lake and one or more campsites.

There is also a winter trailhead on the L at a curve in the road 1.7 mi from Eagle Bay. A 100-yd woods road leads from that trailhead to a jct. with the trail. ◀

FROM THE TRAIL REGISTER at the main parking lot (0.0 mi), turn L (SE) on a dirt road to start the circuit of the lake. (Turning R, one would hike the Circuit Trail in the opposite or counterclockwise direction.) For a view of the lake, walk straight ahead (SW) from the entrance for 135 yd to the shore of the lake at a beach. An island in the lake, a bluff on its W side, and white pines and beaches along the lakefront add to the attraction of the scene.

Hiking SE on the dirt road at the start of the circuit, you will note at some campsites openings to the R leading to sites of former camp buildings and to the lake shore. After crossing the edge of a bare clearing (where raspberries can be found in season), the route becomes a pleasant woods road, dropping through a gully at 0.3 mi. At 0.4 mi another woods road leads L (ENE) 100 yd to a parking area at a curve in Big Moose Rd. This can be used as a winter trailhead for skiing on the Circuit Trail.

At 0.5 mi there is a bridge over Moss Lake's main inlet (Cascade Lake's outlet). At 0.7 mi, with the lake visible through the trees, the Bubb Lake Trail (trail 29) comes in from the L (S) with yellow markers. It is 0.7 mi along that trail to the NE end of Bubb Lake, a route that may also be skied in winter. That route continues on past the Vista Trail (trail 30) to NY 28.

The Circuit Trail continues W along the woods road on the S side of Moss Lake, and at 1.2 mi crosses a bridge over the beginning of the lake's outlet. Here there is a view of the lake's S bay, one of the clearest views of the lake to be had from this trail. Tall white pines grace the shoreline here.

The trail passes through tall red spruce, hemlock, and yellow birch, and at 1.5 mi it descends almost to the edge of the SW end of the lake. From here NE along the W shore, one has views through the trees of the lake and of a 500-ft hill beyond it on the SE.

At 1.7 mi, a tree nearly three feet in diameter grows on top of a rock, its roots running several feet down the sides. An open area with ferns is traversed, followed at 2.0 mi by the first of several openings on the R leading to sites of former buildings, the lake shore, and another one of the campsites.

At 2.2 mi a cleared area off to the R, a campground framed with white pines, has abandoned stone steps going down to a beach at a N corner of the lake. The trail turns R at 2.4 mi (the route ahead goes to a parking lot for the disabled on nearby Big Moose Rd.). The starting point of the Circuit Trail is at 2.5 mi.

❊ Trail in winter: Easy skiing. Access can be from a winter parking place 0.4 mi E of the summer trailhead if the latter is not cleared.

👭 Distances: From trailhead clockwise to winter trailhead access, 0.4 mi; to Bubb Lake Trail (trail 29), 0.7 mi; to outlet, 1.2 mi; to beach, 2.2 mi; return to trailhead, 2.5 mi (4.0 km).

(29) **Bubb Lake Trail**

Map: C2

From NY 28, the route goes over the shoulder of Onondaga Mt., skirts Sis Lake and Bubb Lake on nearly level ground, and joins the Moss Lake Circuit Trail (trail 28). This is a scenic forest route. A round trip of the Bubb Lake Trail plus the circuit around Moss Lake would make a hike of 7.1 mi. A through hike to the Moss Lake trailhead on Big Moose Rd. would be 4.1 mi, taking the longer segment of the circuit trail around the lake's W side, or 3.0 mi taking the shorter part on the lake's E side.

Early settlers at Big Moose Lake used this route to reach Big Moose from Fourth Lake. After reaching Bubb Lake, they paddled to the inlet, portaged to Moss Lake, paddled to the N shore, portaged to Dart Lake, paddled across, and portaged to Big Moose Lake.

▶ Trailhead: From the jct. of NY 28 and Big Moose Rd. in Eagle Bay, drive 1.4 mi W on NY 28 and park on the L (S) side of the road opposite the trailhead, which may not have a sign. The N trailhead is on the Moss Lake Circuit Trail (28). ◀

FROM NY 28 (0.0 mi), the yellow-marked trail ascends 150 ft NW on an eroded section. At 0.2 mi, the Vista Trail (trail 30) ascends L, while the Bubb Lake Trail continues ahead, the broad trail leveling out but becoming muddier in places. At 0.4 mi a side trail forks R and goes 55 yd to Bubb Lake's S end. From here one can see most of this pleasant body of water.

The Bubb Lake Trail continues W, and at 0.7 mi it forks R. After 40 yd, a side trail forks L and goes 65 yd through conifers to the SE corner of Sis Lake. This pond-size lake has rocks along much of its shoreline.

The main trail continues R, going N along the E side of Sis Lake, on a smooth footway through a splendid stand of hemlocks. The trail then crosses a bridge over the stream between Bubb and Sis lakes at 0.9 mi. Both lakes are visible from here, but a full view of Sis Lake can be had by going a short way L to its rock-lined shore.

The trail continues parallel to the NW side of Bubb Lake past some stately hardwoods. Beyond them, the trail nears the lake in an attractive area of hemlocks. At 1.6 mi, it reaches the shore at the lake's narrowed NE end where there is a good view up the lake, with Onondaga Mt. rising from the far side. Soon the trail leaves Bubb Lake, bending L and heading NE. At 1.8 mi it crosses a bridge over the Bubb Lake outlet. On the downstream side is a dam with a spillway, built as a fish barrier.

The trail becomes broader and ends at 2.3 mi at the Moss Lake Circuit Trail (trail 28). The shortest route to Big Moose Rd. is to the R, but both directions end finally at the same trailhead (see trail 28).

❋ Trail in winter: Easy skiing, mostly level.

⚇ Distances: Trailhead to Vista Trail, 0.2 mi; to Bubb Lake, 0.5 mi; to Bubb and Sis Lake stream, 0.9 mi; to Moss Lake Circuit Trail, 2.3 mi (3.7 km); to Big Moose Rd., 3.0 mi (4.8 km).

(30) Vista Trail

Map: C2

This is a through trail with three trailheads. It has some nice views from several selected points along the way. One may enter the trail from either end, or use the Mountain Pond trailhead listed below to reach Cork Mt.

The Vista Trail is a more strenuous hike than most in the region, with a good deal of climbing (some of it steep), and many ups and downs, especially along Onondaga Mt. The trail passes through some handsome forest with notable hemlock stands in the SW section. The NE section of Onondaga Mt. offers some good views over Fourth Lake and elsewhere.

Onondaga Mt., a ridge extending 2.3 mi along Fourth Lake from just SE of Mountain Pond to SE of Bubb Lake, does not have an official or generally known name, but it is apparent from David H. Beetle's book, *Up Old Forge Way*, that this is what it has been called in the past.

The trail is described from W to E. Shorter trips can be had by traveling from Rondaxe Rd. to the Mountain Pond trailhead, or from the Mountain Pond trailhead to the Bubb Lake trailhead.

▶ Trailheads: To reach the W trailhead, from the Tourist Information Center in Old Forge, drive 4.4 mi NE on NY 28, turn L (NW) on Rondaxe Rd., and after 0.2 mi, park in the DEC parking area on the L, which also serves the Bald/Rondaxe Mt. trail and is likely to be overflowing on autumn weekends. The trailhead is on the other side of the road (NE).

To reach the center trailhead, go 5.5 mi from the Old Forge Tourist Information Center (3.4 mi from Big Moose Rd. in Eagle Bay). Turn L (NW) across from Daiker's Brookside Motel, and L again onto a dirt road. The trailhead is on the R, 0.2 mi from NY 28.

To reach the Bubb Lake trailhead on NY 28, go 1.4 mi W of Big Moose Rd. in Eagle Bay. Park on the L (S) side of the road, opposite the trailhead, which may not have a sign. ◀

STARTING AT THE W TRAILHEAD on Rondaxe Rd. (0.0 mi), the blue-marked trail drops through a tall forest mixed of conifers and broadleaf trees. At 0.2 mi, a red-marked spur trail goes L for 85 yd to Fly Pond, which is flanked by Rondaxe Rd. and a muddy wetland. The route reaches the SW end of the larger and more attractive Cary Lake at 0.4 mi, then goes N along the pond's W side on the lower slope of Bottle Mt., through a nice section of tall hemlocks.

Skirting the wetland at the N end of the pond, the trail reaches a dirt road at 0.75 mi and turns R on the road (no signs or markers). This road, used as a snowmobile and bicycle trail, goes L to Lake Rondaxe and R to NY 28, following the route of the old Raquette Lake Railroad, which operated from 1900 to 1933, as indicated on a sign next to the turnoff; the sign also cites the RR as the first to use oil-burning steam locomotives. The Mountain Pond trailhead is farther down this road.

After 160 yd along the road, crossing a wetland of Cary Lake, the trail turns L, again without a sign. After a muddy stretch along the wetland, the trail makes a 300-ft ascent N and E to the crest of Cork Mt. The climb, which uses switchbacks, has both moderate and steep grades on a picturesque slope of open forest with impressive hemlocks.

At 1.3 mi, a little below the crest, a red-marked spur trail goes L and climbs to the top of Cork Mt., where there is a partial view. (This spur trail climbs steeply N to Cork Mt.'s closed-in summit at 2280 ft elevation, a 0.3-mi round trip off the main route. The red-marked L fork at 0.1 mi goes to the summit. The R fork descends a short distance to a partial view of hills to the NE. Cork Mt. is so named because, from the Lake Rondaxe area on the NW, it supposedly looks like the cork of the bottle, a reference to Bottle Mt., to the SW.)

Continuing on the blue trail from 1.3 mi, the route crosses over a saddle and descends E to Mountain Pond (elevation 2005 ft). The trail skirts the S end of the pond, and at 1.6 mi a short side path leads L to the shore of the pond. To the R of this path is an attractive area for camping under hemlock trees on the E side of the pond.

The blue trail climbs SE a short distance through mud to the gap between Cork and Onondaga mts., where it passes an informal campsite and at 1.9 mi reaches a jct. Straight ahead is the red-marked Mountain Pond Trail, which descends very steeply to a dirt road connecting with NY 28, dropping about 250 ft in a quarter mile.

The blue route turns L at this jct. This is the beginning of a more rugged section going ENE along the entire crest of Onondaga Mt., with many ascents and descents, some steep. There are some attractive views along the way, narrow sections of crestline, tall hardwoods, stands of spruce, and areas of ferns and bedrock.

Immediately after the jct., the route is somewhat obscure. A climb of 300 ft up the W flank of Onondaga Mt. brings one to the mountain's highest point (2340 ft). At 2.3 mi there is a pretty view from the edge of a steep slope over a major section of Fourth Lake with hills and mountains beyond. At 2.6 mi there is another view of the larger E section of Fourth Lake.

At 2.8 mi the trail descends to a notch that separates the W and E segments of Onondaga Mt., and then makes a gradual ascent. After reaching another notch at 3.1 mi, the trail climbs to follow the first of several sections of narrow crest. At 3.5 mi there are limited views SE and E over parts of Fourth Lake.

The descent of the E end of the ridge starts at 3.7 mi. A red-marked spur trail climbs steeply L a short way to a fine open view N over both Bubb and Moss lakes. The trail becomes steeper; reaches Becker's Outlook, with a limited view over hills to the NE, including Blue Mt.; and makes a final steep descent to end at 4.2 mi (6.8 km) on the blue-marked Bubb Lake Trail (trail 29). To the L, the path reaches the S end of Bubb Lake in 0.3 mi, and continues on to Moss Lake. Going R, one descends SE for 0.2 mi to the Bubb Lake trailhead on NY 28.

❊ Trail in winter: Steep sections. Suitable for hardy snowshoers.

❧ Distances: Rondaxe Rd. to Fly Pond, 0.2 mi; to Cary Lake, 0.4 mi; to old Raquette Lake Railroad bed, 0.75 mi; to Cork Mt. spur, 1.3 mi; to Mountain Pond, 1.6 mi; to Mountain Pond trail jct., 1.9 mi (to Mountain Pond trailhead, 2.2 mi); to Bubb Lake Trail (29), 4.2 mi; to Bubb Lake trailhead, 4.4 mi (7.1 km). Highest elevation, 2340 ft (713 m).

(31) **Bald (Rondaxe) Mt. Trail**

Map: C3

This short trail climbs through woods and then through progressively more open rock to the fire tower at the open summit of Bald Mt., with great views. A restoration project is underway on the tower (see www.masterpieces.com/bald.htm).

▶ Trailhead: From the Tourist Information Center in Old Forge, drive 4.4 mi NE on NY 28, turn L (NW) on Rondaxe Rd., and after 0.2 mi, park in the large area on the L. Or, from the village of Eagle Bay at the jct. of NY 28 and Big Moose Rd., drive 4.5 mi W and SW on NY 28 and then turn R on Rondaxe Rd. There are trail signs and a register at the trailhead. ◀

FROM THE REGISTER (0.0 mi), the well-trodden red-marked trail ascends SW mostly along moderate grades, although there are some steep pitches. (Some say it's hard on the knees coming down.) As one climbs, the deciduous forest soon gives way to an attractive spruce-fir forest. A large part of the ascent is on bedrock. Starting at 0.4 mi, fine views are to be had of Second, Third, and Fourth lakes from the edge of cliffs on the L (SE). The final 600 ft to the fire tower on the summit at 0.9 mi is mostly along the rock spine with many viewing places.

The open views from the summit embrace First through Fourth lakes of the Fulton Chain on the S and E, part of Little Moose Lake on the S beyond First and Second lakes, Blue Mt. (3759 ft) in the distance to the ENE, and other mountains to the E. Climbing the fire tower to the cabin makes the view more extensive, and on very clear days one may see several of the High Peaks on the NE horizon L of Blue Mt., including Mt. Marcy, the highest of the Adirondack peaks (5344 ft), 55 mi away. SW of the fire tower, 375 ft along the rock crest, is another fine vantage point or two and a balanced rock of sorts: a boulder standing on a sloping ledge near the dropoff. Here the trail ends at 1.0 mi.

❋ Trail in winter: Snowshoe climb. Skis only for the expert. Crampons may be needed on the icy summit. Extra care needed on the open rock slopes.

🏔 Distances: Trailhead to tower, 0.9 mi; to end of trail, 1.0 mi (1.6 km). Ascent, 390 ft (119 m). Summit elevation, 2350 ft (716 m).

(32) **Eagle Cliff Trail**

Map: D2

This is an ascent nearly 200 ft from the village of Eagle Bay to the top of Eagle Cliff with its open view of Fourth Lake. The round-trip hike is only 0.5 mi. Access to the trail is on private land and the trail is privately maintained. There is no water.

▶ Trailhead: In Eagle Bay go to the intersection of NY 28 and Big Moose Rd. Park on the roadside near the intersection without blocking driveways. The trail starts on the R off Big Moose Rd. going up Ledge Rd. (gravel). ◀

FROM BIG MOOSE RD. (0.0 mi), the route goes E for 35 yd on Ledge Rd., passing one residence that faces Big Moose Rd. Look for an Eagle Cliff sign L on a dirt footpath. There are no markers, but the footpath is well worn.

After the L turn before the next dooryard, the trail goes between the cottages, bends a little R, climbs steeply N for a short distance, then climbs E along the edge of a steep slope to a rock outcropping at 0.2 mi with a view S of the nearby bay of Fourth Lake. A metal survey marker is embedded in the rock, signaling the boundary between Herkimer and Hamilton counties.

The route continues NE along the outcropping to reach the top of Eagle Cliff at 0.25 mi, an elevation of 2000 ft. From the edge of the cliffs one views Fourth Lake lying 300 ft below with Eagle Bay nearest at hand.

✸ Trail in winter: Suitable for snowshoes only. The trail reaches open, sloping rock above the cliff, which could be treacherous if icy, even with crampons.

🐾 Distance: 0.25 mi (0.4 km). Ascent, 200 ft (61 m).

(33) **Rocky Mt. Trail**

Map: D2

This short, popular trail—visited by busloads of people—ascends 445 ft from NY 28 to the ledges atop Rocky Mt. near the head of Fourth Lake, where a splendid view of the lake is to be had. It is a round trip hike of 1.2 mi, and there is no water on the trail.

▶ Trailhead: From the jct. of NY 28 and Big Moose Rd. in Eagle Bay, drive 1.2 mi E on NY 28 and turn L onto the old road, now a parking area off the highway. From the opposite direction drive 0.9 mi toward Eagle Bay on NY 28 from the public parking area in the center of Inlet, and turn R into the trailhead parking area. ◀

NEAR THE CENTER OF THE PARKING AREA, the yellow-marked trail (markers are sparse) starts (0.0 mi) in a NNE direction, then soon turns L. It is wide and eroded from much use and steep in several places.

Ascending through a hardwood forest, the trail turns NW and finally W along bedrock to the summit (elevation 2225 ft) at 0.6 mi. In another 60 yd along the open clifftop with a SW dropoff, there is a wide, open view over most of Fourth Lake lying 500 ft below. To the L on the wide E end of this large lake, one can see the village of Inlet and the highway going into town. The outlet of Fifth Lake, which is the inlet of Fourth Lake, can be detected in the middle of—what else?—Inlet.

To the R on the near shore, Eagle Bay seems to be almost hidden among the trees on a prominent peninsula. Cedar Island with its private facilities stands in the lake nearby. The road from Eagle Bay splits in the foreground just in front of Eagle Bay, the L and nearer branch being the road to Inlet. The less prominent R branch is Uncas Rd., which leads to trails 41, 42, and 43, and continues on to Raquette Lake.

In the distance, on the R shore of the lake, one can see the long ridge traversed by the Vista Trail (trail 30). Beyond that are the open rocky sides of Bald (Rondaxe) Mt. With binoculars, the old fire tower can be seen on its summit. Most of the highway from Old Forge is hidden along the R edge of the lake. It follows the route of the narrow gauge RR that once came from Carter Station W of Old Forge, crossed trail 30 at Cary Lake, followed along the lake through Eagle Bay, and chugged on to Raquette Lake, paralleling the route of Uncas Rd. mentioned above.

❋ Trail in winter: Suitable only for snowshoes. The route is steep. Care must be taken at the cliffs, where the rock can be windswept and icy.

⚹⚹ Distances: To summit, 0.6 mi (1.0 km). Ascent, 445 ft (136 m). Summit elevation, 222 ft (678 m).

(34) **Fourth Lake–Black Bear Mt. Trail**

Map: D2

Scenic Black Bear Mt., 2448 ft in elevation, stands 1.7 mi E of Fourth Lake and over 1.0 mi N of the W part of Seventh Lake. One has excellent views from this mountain, especially from the long expanse of open rock at the SE side of the crest. The mountain may be ascended from Fourth Lake on the W (trail 34) or from Uncas Rd. on the N (trail 35). The more traditional and popular route is from Fourth Lake, although the top part is steeper than the Uncas Rd. approach. The trails lend themselves to round-trip, circuit, and through hikes. Parts of the mountain hold beautiful stands of larger trees, with open woods beneath.

The Fourth Lake–Black Bear Mt. trail route has yellow ski trail markers and occasional yellow hiking trail markers. At the base of Black Bear Mt., the trail divides into two routes: the skiable yellow route L and the steep but shorter blue route R. As a ski trail in winter the last part of the yellow trail to the summit (part of the Uncas Rd.–Black Bear Mt. Trail) should be undertaken by advanced skiers only. In springtime and in wet weather, the blue route can be difficult, and hikers' boots will cause a lot of erosion damage. Both routes are described below.

▶ Trailhead: From the jct. of NY 28 and Big Moose Rd. in Eagle Bay, drive 1.2 mi E on NY 28 and turn L into an extensive parking area (part of the old highway) off the highway. From the opposite direction, drive 0.9 mi toward Eagle Bay on NY 28 from the public parking area in the center of Inlet and turn R into the trailhead parking area. From the end of the pavement at the SE end of the parking area (toward Inlet), walk 50 yd to the trail sign. The trail is marked with DEC yellow markers, with blue markers on an alternate route. ◀

FROM THE END OF THE PAVEMENT at the SE end of the parking area (toward Inlet) (0.0 mi), walk 50 yd to the trail sign, turn L onto the beginning of a woods road, and pass a barrier across it in another 30 yd. The yellow-marked route proceeds E on the woods road in a pleasant hardwood forest with a stream on the L. It ascends a rather wet grassy section.

At 0.7 mi, in a clearing, the route forks. Uphill R, first with yellow markers and later with blue, is the Old Black Bear Mt. Trail (trail 37). Continuing on the level straight across the clearing, the yellow trail follows a grassy old woods road through a partly wet area for 0.3 mi. In wet season, a pleasant 10-ft cascade can be heard on the L, just below the trail.

Beyond 1.2 mi, the trail becomes a narrow footpath with tall hardwoods and spruce trees along the way. The route passes on the N side of Black Bear Mt., and at 2.3 mi it ends at the Uncas Rd.–Black Bear Mt. Trail (trail 35), from Uncas Rd. past the end of the Uncas Trail (trail 39) on the NE to the summit of Black Bear Mt. The jct. does not have a sign and could be missed easily. Users should take a good look at the trail if they plan to return this way. The jct. is just downhill from a 2-ft-diameter blowdown with writing on it. Follow trail 35 R the rest of the way to the top for a total distance of 3.1 mi.

The most direct route from the summit back to the starting point is to follow the mostly blue-blazed trail W over the summit, and back to the jct. at the clearing on the yellow trail, making a 5.2-mi round trip. Backtracking on the two yellow-marked trails (35 and 34) will avoid the steep and slippery part, for a round trip of 6.2 mi.

The cross-country skier, whether ascending Black Bear Mt. or not, may return to NY 28 either over the same route, or by the Black Bear Mt. Ski Trail (trail 36). To reach this latter trail, not open in hiking season, go L down the Uncas Rd.–Black Bear Mt. trail (trail 35) for 0.3 mi NE from the end of trail 34. The yellow-marked ski trail (trail 36) goes R (S) then W for about 3.0 mi to reach NY 28 on the N edge of Inlet, just N of the telephone building (about 0.6 mi from the Fourth Lake–Black Bear Mt. trailhead).

❋ Trail in Winter: Suitable for snowshoes. Also skiable, but those who continue on trail 35 to the top would probably need to be expert skiers due to steeper slopes.

𝕸 Distances: NY 28 to jct. with Old Black Bear Mt. Trail (trail 37), 0.7 mi; to jct. with Uncas Rd.–Black Bear Mt. Trail (trail 35), 2.25 mi (3.6 km). To summit via trail 35, 3.1 mi (5.0 km). Ascent, 728 ft (222 m). Summit elevation, 2448 ft (746 m).

(35) Uncas Rd.–Black Bear Mt. Trail

Map: D2

The original Uncas Rd. began at Eagle Bay, went past Uncas Station on the Raquette Lake Railroad, then turned R and went SE and E to luxurious Uncas Camp on Mohegan Lake. At the R turn onto what is now trail 35, the Brown Tract Rd. (not to be confused with the original Brown's Tract Rd. from Moose River Settlement to Old Forge) continued on N to Raquette Lake. It was built as a public road in 1914.

Starting from the corner of Uncas Rd., its route as far as the Brown Tract Ponds ran next to the Raquette Lake Railroad (built in 1899), and more or less followed a previous road privately built in 1897-98 to Sucker Brook Bay of Raquette Lake. After years of confusion with people leaving the Eagle Bay end on Uncas and mysteriously coming out the other end on Brown Tract Road (as there were no signs where the road switched names next to the trailhead), the entire public highway is now called Uncas. Trail 35 follows the course of the old Uncas Rd. over the shoulder of Black Bear Mt.

This is the most gradual approach to Black Bear Mt., which is a good alternative to the crowded and often overflowing parking lot at Bald (Rondaxe) Mt. on a weekend during fall foliage season. This trail is also used for bicycling.

▶ Trailhead: In Eagle Bay at the jct. of Big Moose Rd., drive E on NY 28 for about 0.3 mi, then turn L onto Uncas Rd., paved for the first 1.7 mi. At 2.7 mi trailhead parking is on a slight uphill route to the R. This is 5.8 mi from the E end of the road off Antlers Rd. in Raquette Lake, 4.0 mi W of Browns Tract Campground, and 0.5 mi W of Ferds Bog, which could be hiked the same day. ◀

FROM THE ROAD (0.0 mi), the yellow-marked route crosses a stream and heads up a gentle hill on the old road. Soon the stately forest environment is interrupted by two grassy areas fringed by small conifers. At 0.8 mi the route turns R at a jct. onto a footpath. (Straight ahead leads down to NY 28 at Eighth Lake campground between Seventh and Eighth lakes. See trail 39.)

After the R turn, the trail heads down (S) to the base of the hill, then climbs again, turning gradually more W. At 1.2 mi, the Black Bear Mt. Ski Trail (trail 36) goes L. This trail is not open in hiking season.

At 1.5 mi, the yellow Fourth Lake–Black Bear Mt. Trail (trail 34) comes in from the R. Continuing ahead, yellow markers lead uphill toward Black Bear Mt. Along moderate grades on an attractive route, the forest changes from hardwood to spruce-fir. On the L are open areas along cliffs to which one may divert to observe the view.

At about 1.7 mi, open rock becomes more prevalent and paint blazes are used. The route arrives near the edge of the cliffs and then ascends SW along the open ledges near the drop-off. This is a highly scenic route with fine views of Seventh Lake and its forested surroundings on the L (SE). Behind to the NE one sees the extensive open wetland of No Luck Brook with Raquette Lake and Blue Mt. in the distance. The route up is easy enough to follow, but can be difficult to find going down. If you plan to return by this route, take careful note of landmarks along the way.

At 2.3 mi, the open summit has mostly the same views. On very clear days, some of the High Peaks can be seen on the far horizon above Raquette Lake, with Mt. Marcy appearing to the L of prominent Blue Mt. Other mountains are seen on the E and SE.

❄ Trail in winter: Snowmobile trail at the start. Suitable for backcountry skiing and snowshoeing, but the last part at the top is for expert skiers only. The exposed summit can be windblown and have arctic conditions.

🐾 Distances: Uncas Rd. trailhead to Uncas Trail, 0.8 mi; to Black Bear Mt. Ski Trail to Inlet, 1.2 mi; to Fourth Lake–Black Bear Mt. yellow trail, 1.5 mi; to summit of Black Bear Mt., 2.3 mi (3.7 km). Ascent, 592 ft (180 m). Summit elevation, 2448 ft (746 m).

(36) **Black Bear Mt. Ski Trail**

Map: D2

This route is open only in winter, owing to wet trail conditions.

▶ Trailhead: The trailhead is on NY 28 on the N side of Inlet, just N of a telephone building near Black Bear Trading Post, a quilt shop, and across the street from Stiefvaters Motel. Look carefully in the trees about 20 ft up the road from the building for the trailhead. Parking depends on snow conditions. For a loop trip, one may return to NY 28 via the Fourth Lake–Black Bear Mt. Trail (trail 34) without having to go over the summit of Black Bear Mt. ◀

PASSING THROUGH THE TREES at the road's edge (0.0 mi), this yellow-marked trail has a nondescript start. It follows nearly level terrain through an area that is very wet in summer.

At 0.2 mi, the route meets a woods road and turns L on the road. In another 500 ft, the route curves R and continues on easy ground until crossing Cedar Creek at 1.0 mi. The climbing leads to a jct. with the abandoned and impassable Seventh Lake–Black Bear Mt. Trail at 2.3 mi, and another jct., this one with the Uncas Rd.–Black Bear Mt. Trail (trail 35), at 3.0 mi.

To continue to the summit of Black Bear Mt., turn L and go up more steeply. This route to the summit, totaling 3.7 mi, is suitable for expert skiers only.

To continue on a loop of Black Bear Mt., turn L and follow the Uncas Rd.–Black Bear Mt. Trail (trail 35) up (SW) for 0.3 mi and turn R onto the Fourth Lake–Black Bear Mt. Trail (trail 34). This jct. is not well marked. Keep a careful watch for the yellow ski trail markers, just below a 2-ft diameter blowdown covered with writing (2004). It is an additional 2.3 mi of easy skiing down to the highway.

✳ Trail in winter: For cross-country skiers only. It is a generally easy trail, except for the summit of Black Bear Mt; that part is for experts only.

🐾 Distances: Telephone building to Cedar Creek, 1.0 mi; to Uncas Rd.–Black Bear Mt. Trail, 3.0 mi (4.8 km). To summit, 3.7 mi (6.0 km). Loop to NY 28 via Fourth Lake–Black Bear Mt. Trail, 5.3 mi (8.4 km). Ascent to highest point on ski loop, 335 ft (102 m).

(37) Old Black Bear Mt. Trail

Map: D2

This older, steeper section of trail, combined with the first part of the Fourth Lake–Black Bear Mt. Trail (trail 34), is the shortest route up Black Bear Mt.

▶ Locator: Interior trail starting at 0.7 mi from the NY 28 trailhead on trail 34. ◀

FROM THE CLEARING (0.0 mi) at 0.7 mi on the Fourth Lake–Black Bear Mt. Trail (trail 34), where that goes straight ahead on yellow markers but there is no sign, the Old Black Bear Mt. Trail heads R, uphill, following yellow and then blue markers. The trail climbs E on an old logging road to a nearly level clearing at 0.2 mi. Beyond the clearing, the old road curves L and continues on level ground as an open, grassy, but often wet route to about 0.4 mi.

After a gradual ascent on an eroding, rocky, and rooty trail to the base of the final slope—where a careful watch must be kept for markers—a steep ascent starts at 1.0 mi with the forest partly changing from hardwoods to conifers. The rest of the ascent is mostly on rock, with several pitches requiring some scrambling. Ledges provide fine S outlooks over Sixth and Seventh lakes, and at 1.3 mi one has a beautiful view W and SW of Fourth Lake, the only view of that lake to be had from the trails on this mountain. The summit is reached at 1.4 mi, or 2.1 mi from NY 28, including the section of trail 34.

✳ Trail in winter: Too steep to ski; also not suitable for snowshoers due to some steep sections.

⚜ Distances: Trail 34 to clearing, 0.2 mi; to steep ascent, 1.0 mi; to summit, 1.4 mi (2.3 km). Summit distance from trailhead, 2.1 mi (3.4 km). Ascent, 728 ft (222 m). Summit elevation, 2448 ft (746 m).

(38) Seventh Lake Trail

Map: D3

This is a nice trail, although difficult to get to. The W end has no parking and the E end is an unmarked path.

▶ Trailheads: At 1.5 mi SE of the public parking lot at Inlet, a paved town road—Seventh Lake Rd. or Drive—turns L (NE) to go to the back side of Seventh Lake. It turns to dirt and from there on is a private road with no parking available. Payne's Boat Livery has parking only for its boat/canoe rental customers. The trail is at the end of the road but there is no parking there, so users would have to park before the end of the town road if a spot could be found on public property. The E end of the trail is an unmarked path off trail 39. ◀

AFTER PARKING (0.0 mi), hikers can walk down the private road to the end, a private camp at a turn-around 1.4 mi. The trail continues past the garage for that camp and enters state land. The route becomes especially attractive here, going through a grove of paper birch and then, for most of the rest of the way, through stands of stately white pine that provide a footpath of needles. Informal campsites by the lake's clean-cut shoreline lie along the route.

The main attraction of the trail is at 2.8 mi from the start of the road: a point of land with a large rock (Arnold's Rock) rising from the lake, a lean-to, and a cleared area under the pines ideal for camping. The trail goes in front of the lean-to and continues along the lake shore past more informal campsites. At 3.2 mi it enters a 225-yd stretch of cleared forest floor looking like a long, continuous campground, at the end of which is a second, unusually large, lean-to.

The trail ends at 3.6 mi at a small beach opposite the W side of an island in Seventh Lake, with some stumps standing in the near part of the lake. The edge of the lake here has a shallow, sandy bottom. It is less than a half mile on unmarked path from here to the Uncas Trail (trail 39).

❄ Trail in winter: Parking may be difficult from either end. Suitable for skiing or snowshoeing.

Distances: Payne's Boat Livery to beginning of trail, 1.1 mi; to Arnold's Rock, 1.4 mi; to clearing before second lean-to, 1.8 mi; to end, 2.2 mi (3.5 km).

(39) **Uncas Trail**

Map: D2

The Uncas Trail, a broad, smooth trail with easy or moderate grades, goes through a majestic forest. It extends from the Eighth Lake Public Campground W and NW to the Uncas Rd., passing the W side of Bug Lake, which is popular for fishing. It has a side loop trail to Eagles Nest Lake and the SE end of Bug Lake, and provides access to the top of Black Bear Mt. It is designated as a hiking, mountain biking, and snowmobile trail.

The Uncas Trail is part of the original Uncas Rd., built by W.W. Durant in 1896 from Eagle Bay to Mohegan Lake as an access to Uncas Camp on that lake and to other luxurious camps he had built on Sagamore Lake and Lake Kora. (The camps up to then had been reached only by roads from the head of navigation of Raquette Lake's South Inlet.) After the Raquette Lake Railroad started operating in 1900, visitors to these camps could get off the train at Uncas Station and continue on the Uncas Rd. The present-day hiker on the Uncas Trail can imagine the New York financial tycoon J.P. Morgan riding along this route with his elegant carriage and team of horses to Uncas Camp, which he purchased from Durant in 1896.

▶ Trailheads: To reach the S trailhead, start from the public parking area in the center of Inlet. Drive 6.1 mi E and NE on NY 28 to the entrance of the Eighth Lake Public Campground on the L. Tell the registration booth attendant that you are going to hike the Uncas Trail (you will not have to pay the day-use fee). Sign in and out at the trail register near the booth. Go straight ahead (W) into the campground on the paved road, continuing into the woods on an unimproved vehicle track for 0.2 mi, and park on either side.

The N trailhead is at 0.8 mi on trail 35. ◀

FROM THE S TRAILHEAD (0.0 mi), the old road, marked with yellow DEC trail markers, goes W for 100 yd and crosses a bridge over the inlet of Seventh Lake, the northernmost arm of that lake lying on the L. (This is a takeout point for the canoe carry from Seventh to Eighth lake.) The route starts uphill.

At 0.6 mi, just before crossing the outlet of Bug and Eagles Nest lakes, the trail forks L, the R fork being the side trail to Eagles Nest Lake, also with yellow trail markers. There is no trail sign here. The loop trip recommended below starts at this point.

Continuing L, the trail crosses the stream and goes SW, then NW. The end of the side loop comes in on the R at 0.9 mi. The route goes along the W side of Bug Lake, passing a fishermen's launch site.

After climbing above the lake, the trail turns NW and crosses the divide between the Moose–Black River and Raquette River watersheds.

At 2.3 mi a snowmobile trail goes L (SW) toward NY 28 near Inlet, and at 2.4 mi the trail crosses No Luck Brook, the inlet to the Brown's Tract Ponds, on a long bridge. At 2.7 mi, the trail ends at the yellow-marked Uncas Rd.–Black Bear Mt. Trail (trail 35). L is the Black Bear Mt. summit, R is the Uncas Rd. trailhead.

The side trail mentioned above (0.6 and 0.9 mi) can be accessed from either end, although the one going from Bug Lake at 0.9 mi takes you down a steep bank to Eagles Nest, while coming the other way you climb the steep bank.

From 0.6 mi the trail goes N through splendid hemlocks, though not without a couple of muddy places. At 0.1 mi on the side trail, keep R at the fork, arriving in 30 yd at the edge of Eagles Nest Lake with its impressive stand of hemlocks on the R. This is, in reality, a modest pond, with dead wood lining the shore and an 80-ft cliff on the opposite side.

A narrow trail L along the pond's outlet leads in 40 yd to a point where an alternate stretch of the yellow side trail comes in on the L. Cross the wood-clogged outlet on the R and climb steeply NW for a short distance to a beautiful area at the SE end of Bug Lake at 0.3 on the side trail. Here on a forest floor carpeted with needles are tall hemlocks and a few great white pines. Tall pines grace part of the lake's shoreline.

To retrace your steps from here would make a round-trip hike of 1.8 mi. To return to the Uncas Trail so as to go farther N on it by Bug Lake, or return by it, go L (S) a short distance, cross the lake's outlet on the R, and follow a footpath that initially winds its way through a thick stand of spruce and then goes SW and S past majestic trees to reach the Uncas Trail at 1.1 mi. (There is no trail sign at this jct.) This completes a 0.4-mi side loop off the Uncas Trail. From here, it is 0.9 mi back to the trailhead.

❀ Trail in winter: Easy skiing or snowshoeing, but trail must be shared with snowmobiles. The steep bank between Bug and Eagles Nest would best be avoided. The campground is not open.

🐾 Distances: S trailhead to Eagles Nest Lake, 0.7 mi; to Bug Lake, 1.1 mi; to Uncas Rd.–Black Bear Mt. Trail (35), 2.7 mi (4.4 km). To N trailhead via trail 35, 3.5 mi (5.6 km).

(40) Cathedral Pines

Map: E2

This is one of the shortest circuit trails in the Adirondacks and one of the most rewarding for its length. Only 210 yd long, it visits a stand of great white pines lying between NY 28 and the upper, narrow section of Seventh Lake.

▶ Trailhead: The trail starts on the W side of the highway at a point 0.9 mi SW of the entrance to the Eighth Lake Public Campground and 1.0 mi NE of the Fishing Access Site on Seventh Lake. Park along the highway, cross a ditch by a DEC signpost (sometimes without a sign), and take the path marked with blue painted blazes. ◀

MOST OF THESE GREAT PINES are along the first, upper part of the trail, including a spur a few yards long. On the lower part, a stone pillar holds a plaque commemorating a young U.S. Air Force officer, the son of a local district ranger, killed in action in World War II. The plaque, dedicated by Governor Thomas Dewey in September 1946, was secured to a great white pine that snapped about 20 ft above the ground in 1989. The pillar in front of that tree was erected in 1992. The circuit ends at the highway a few yards from where it started.

❀ Trail in Winter: Suitable for snowshoes. One steep bank would make it difficult for skiers, unless they descend by sidestepping.

🐾 Distance: 0.1 mi loop (0.16 km). ◆

Swamp near Raquette Lake. MARK BOWIE

Raquette Lake Section

The trails are sparse in the Raquette Lake section, with widely separated trailheads E, W, and S of the lake. They are grouped in this section for ease in identifying and locating them on the map. The trails S of the lake were developed from old roads built in 1895–96 for the "Great Camps": Sagamore, Uncas, and Kamp Kill Kare. For a good introduction to these camps, see Craig Gilborn's book, *Durant*. Sagamore Lodge and Conference Center gives public tours daily during the summer, has a varied summer program of one-week educational programs, and is open for recreational skiing weekends during the winter. Uncas and Kill Kare are private and not open to the public.

Overlooking the lake is West Mt., 2902 ft, with trails going two ways from the top. This is the second highest point (behind the much more remote Sly Pond Trail, trail 90) in the west-central region.

EASY HIKE:
◆ Ferds Bog—0.7 mi (1.1 km) round trip. A wonderland for bird-watching and seeing bog plants between Eagle Bay and Raquette Lake. See trail 44.

MODERATE HIKE:
◆ Shallow Lake—3.2 mi (5.2 km) round trip. Near the village of Raquette Lake. A beautiful lake, with the appearance of great remoteness. See trail 41.

HARDER HIKES:
◆ Tioga Point—10.4 mi (16.8 km). On the E side of Raquette Lake. Access from Long Lake area. Leads to beautiful and popular Tioga Point. See trail 49.
◆ West Mt.—10.0 mi (16.1 km) round trip. A steep climb to a view over much of Raquette Lake. See trail 43.

TRAIL DESCRIBED	TOTAL MILES (one way)	PAGE
Shallow Lake Trail	1.6 (2.6 km)	106
Sucker Brook Bay Trail	3.1 (5.0 km)	106
Raquette Lake–West Mt. Trail	5.0 (8.1 km)	108
Ferds Bog	0.35 (0.5 km)	110
Uncas Rd. (Mohegan and Sagamore lakes) Trail	5.3 (8.5 km)	111
Sagamore Cascades Trail	3.3 (5.3 km)	113
Sagamore Lake Trail	3.9 (6.3 km)	115
Sargent Ponds North Trail	3.3 (5.2 km)	117
Tioga Point Trail	6.1 (9.8 km)	118
Death Falls	0.3 (0.5 km)	120

(41) **Shallow Lake Trail**

Map: E2

Shallow Lake is notable for its wilderness quality and its relative ease of access. It's an easily followed yellow-marked trail.

▶ Trailhead: The trail starts within Brown Tract Pond State Campground. To reach the state campground, take Uncas Rd. 6.7 mi from Eagle Bay, turning L at the campground. Or, from Raquette Lake, go N through the community of Raquette Lake for 0.7 mi from NY 28. Take Uncas Rd. L (W) for 1.8 mi and turn R (N) into the campground. A day-use fee is charged when the campground is open. Drive 0.6 mi through the campground to the parking for campsites 68–70 just down the hill from the end of the loop road. There is some parking for the trailhead. Park with care to avoid blocking a campsite.

An alternate trailhead is 0.9 mi farther W on the Uncas Rd., at the Sucker Brook Bay Trail (trail 42). The route is 0.7 mi longer, but there is no parking fee. ◀

STARTING E (UPHILL) OF CAMPSITE 68 (0.0 mi), the yellow-marked footpath goes W within view of Lower Brown Tract Pond. The pond is very attractive, with a rocky island opposite the trail. At 0.2 mi the route meets an old road which is now the Sucker Brook Bay Trail (trail 42).

Turning L for 10 yd, the Shallow Lake route then turns R uphill and leaves the old road. Again, there are yellow markers and the footpath is quite obvious. This upland route follows the contour. Then at 0.5 mi it plunges into a level, marshy area with pitcher and similar bog-loving plants and crosses the wide and deep Beaver Brook at 0.6 mi on a bridge of 6- to 8-inch logs. The trail continues NW in marshy terrain, passing tamaracks and gradually larger evergreens.

At 0.7 mi the route climbs slightly to provide a comfortable foot-path on the gentle hillside. This continues with small ups and downs until a turn at 1.3 mi takes the route NW over a slight rise, then down to the shore of Shallow Lake at a boat landing site at 1.6 mi. The lake does not seem particularly shallow. The view is one of untouched Adirondack beauty, with a sense of extreme remoteness. There are boulders along the shore R, from which one can get a better view.

✳ Trail in winter: Suitable for backcountry skiing or snowshoeing. The campground is closed in winter, so going through the campground would add 0.6 mi to the trip; one could also use the Sucker Brook trail-head.

🦌 Distances: Campsite 68 to Sucker Brook Bay Trail (trail 42), 0.2 mi; to Beaver Brook, 0.6 mi; to Shallow Lake, 1.6 mi (2.6 km).

(42) Sucker Brook Bay Trail

Map: E2

The Sucker Brook Bay Rd., also called West Mt. Rd., is a mostly broad, smooth woods road going from the gravel of Uncas Rd. N and NE to private camps on the NW shore of Raquette Lake's Sucker Brook Bay. According to Harold Hochschild's book *Township 34*, most of this route is the final section of a wagon road privately built in 1897–98 from Eagle Bay to Sucker Brook Bay.

▶ Trailhead: Go 5.8 mi E from Eagle Bay on Uncas Rd. To reach this point from NY 28 near Raquette Lake village, drive 0.7 mi N on a paved road through the hamlet and beyond (Antlers Rd). Turn L on unpaved Uncas Rd. and drive 2.7 mi. Park on the R (N) near the bar-ricade across the old road. Upper Brown Tract Pond is just to the W of the trail. ◀

THE BLUE-MARKED TRAIL starts beside Upper Brown Tract Pond (0.0 mi), with good views along the pond, bends R away from the pond past a trail register, and crosses the upper pond's outlet on a bridge. The route turns N and passes W of the lower pond. At 0.5 mi, an unmarked truck trail to the L should be avoided. An unofficial spur trail R at 0.6 mi leads to a large swimming rock with a good view at the edge of the pond.

The wide, easy old road continues N past a jct. at 0.9 mi. On the L (W) is the Shallow Lake Trail (trail 41) going W around the base of a hill. A sign says "trail" and there are yellow markers. The two trails share the path for another 10 yd before trail 41 heads R toward its trailhead at the Brown Tract Pond State Campground, also with a jct. marked "trail."

Beyond this jct., Sucker Brook Bay Rd. climbs a minor hillside and continues N on easy grades. The Raquette Lake–West Mt. Trail (trail 43) joins on the R (SE) at 2.3 mi, just before the road crosses Beaver Brook. The combined trails turn NW to cross the brook, then curve back NE over a broad hilltop to a road jct. at 3.1 mi. To continue L to West Mt., see trail 43. Trail 42 continues straight ahead (NE) 130 yd to the shore of Raquette Lake at the head of Sucker Brook Bay. This was the end of the original Sucker Brook Bay Rd. There is a narrow beach with a shallow sandy lake bottom and a view of the N part of this very large and handsome lake.

✤ Trail in winter: Easy on skis or snowshoes. If continuing on to West Mt., skiing the steep slopes is for experts only.

🐾 Distances: Uncas Rd. to Shallow Lake Trail (trail 41), 0.9 mi; to Raquette Lake–West Mt. Trail (trail 43), 2.3 mi; to Sucker Brook Bay, 3.1 mi (5.0 km).

(43) Raquette Lake–West Mt. Trail

Map: E1

This route extends along the W side of Raquette Lake from Uncas Rd., going roughly N and finally W to the summit of West Mt., 2902 ft in elevation. The round trip hike is 10.0 mi and the ascent is nearly 1100 ft from the road, of which 950 ft is a steady, moderately steep climb. With the fire tower gone, the view from West Mt. is limited to Raquette Lake. A handsome forest clothes most of the trail route, the northern part of which is in the Pigeon Lake Wilderness Area.

The first section of the route is a 1.4-mi path through the woods. The second section, 0.8 mi long, follows the Sucker Brook Bay Trail (trail 42) to a point 130 yd from Raquette Lake, where trail 42 diverges to the lake. Here a boat could be beached, shortening the hike to West

Mt. (see below). The third section, 2.8 mi long, is a trail going N from the Sucker Brook Bay Trail, then turning W 2.0 mi up the mountain. There are blue markers in this section because the route is a continuation of the blue-marked Constable Pond–West Mt. Trail (trail 21).

▶ Trailhead: From NY 28 by the community of Raquette Lake, drive 0.7 mi N on a paved road through the village and beyond (Antlers Rd.). Turn L on unpaved Uncas Rd. and drive W. The trailhead is at 0.6 mi, but a small area suitable for parking is 100 yd before it on the L. There is a sign.

An alternative is to start the trip on the Sucker Brook Bay Trail (trail 42). A shorter route on that trail can be had by using the Shallow Lake Trail (trail 41) and paying a day-use fee at the Brown Tract Pond State Campground when it is open. This variation crosses the Sucker Brook Bay Trail. ◀

AFTER DROPPING TO A REGISTER (0.0 mi), the blue-marked trail crosses an open grassy area, goes over the edge of Wadsworth Mt. and down and up over the shoulder of a smaller hill, then bends L (nearly W) along Beaver Brook. At 1.4 mi, the trail joins the old road that is the Sucker Brook Bay Trail (trail 42). The route follows the road R across Beaver Brook. At 2.2 mi there is a jct. where the trail goes L and the old road/trail 42 goes straight ahead 130 yd to the shore of Raquette Lake at the head (SW end) of large Sucker Brook Bay. There is a narrow beach with a shallow sandy lake bottom and a view of the N part of this very large and handsome lake.

(Arriving at this point by boat would reduce the hike up West Mt. from 5.0 to 3.6 mi one way. Canoes and motor boats may be rented in the community of Raquette Lake or nearby on NY 28 on the S shore of the lake. The distance by water is long but may be shortened, if canoeing or kayaking, by carrying 0.2 mi across the base of 1.5 mi-long Indian Point. The two-pronged end of Indian Pt. is private. When heading for the landing place at the end of Sucker Brook Bay, aim to the R of the wetland and its brook flowing into the lake.)

Continuing from the jct., the route passes a stand of tall white pines, and at 2.4 mi a side woods road leads R to a private camp. After a section of stately hardwoods and conifers, the route crosses Sucker Brook at 3.0 mi.

After an unmarked trail R, at 3.1 mi there is a roadway L and then at 3.2 mi an arrow indicates that the trail leaves the roadway, turning

L onto a footpath. The trail heads NE over a slight hill and crosses Stillman Brook at 3.6 mi.

At 4.0 mi, the ascent of West Mt. begins. The steady, moderately steep ascent is largely along straight stretches of broad trail. With the footpath increasingly on bedrock, the trail reaches a clearing near the summit at 4.9 mi, with the foundation of the former observer's cabin. There follows a short steep pitch through spruce to the summit. Partway up, the blue- or red-marked Constable Pond–West Mt. Trail (trail 21) joins on the R. (This 8.0-mi trail from Higby Rd. near Big Moose Lake travels through a remote section of the Pigeon Lake Wilderness Area. A more extensive trip can include this trail, but the trailheads are widely separated and there are no other trails looping back to Uncas Rd.)

The trail ends at the summit clearing at 5.0 mi, where there is a good, if narrow view SE of most of Raquette Lake. A few yards farther W along the crest is the site of the former fire tower. There are two U.S. Geological Survey bench marks here. The divide between the Raquette River watershed on the E and that of the Moose–Black River on the W passes over the summit.

❋ Trail in winter: Suitable for backwoods skiing or snowshoeing. Owing to the steep slope, West Mt. requires good skiing ability. Only groups with winter experience should attempt the full distance on an unbroken trail to West Mt.

❦ Distances: Uncas Rd. to Sucker Brook Bay Trail (trail 42), 1.4 mi; to Sucker Brook Bay, 2.1 mi; to split from roadway, 3.2 mi; to summit of West Mt., 5.0 mi (8.1 km). To trailhead on Higby Rd. (via trail 21), 13.0 mi (21 km). Using the Shallow Lake trailhead in the Browns Tract Pond Campground, the distances are 0.2 mi more. Using the Sucker Brook Trail adds 0.9 mi more each way. Ascent, 1100 ft (335 m). Summit elevation, 2902 ft (884 m).

(44) Ferds Bog

Map: D2

Tamaracks, pitcher plants, and other bog plants abound, along with many boreal (northern) birds, all visible from a plastic boardwalk floating on the bog at the end of a short walk on a state nature trail in the Pigeon Lake Wilderness Area. (This kind of boardwalk requires less maintenance and won't leak toxins as treated lumber might.) The bog is named for Ferdinand LaFrance, "who owned a cabin nearby and who discovered the good variety of resident boreal birds," according to the *New York State Conservationist* magazine (February 2004).

▶ Trailhead: From NY 28 at Eagle Bay, take Uncas Rd., which starts out paved, 3.2 mi E to a small parking area sufficient for three or four vehicles (be careful not to block the adjacent driveway). This parking area, on the L (N) side of the dirt road, bears a state marker. This point is also 5.3 mi from the E end of Uncas Rd. starting from NY 28 and driving 0.7 mi N through Raquette Lake. For those staying at Brown Tract Pond State Campground, it's 3.5 mi W of the campground. ◀

STARTING FROM A REGISTER (0.0 mi), the trail angles R from the corner of the parking lot, passing some side trails R that lead to private property and should be avoided on the way back. There may be state nature trail or blue markers.

After about 100 yd, the trail turns L and starts downhill, then turns R, passing along the base of a small ridge. It bends L onto a boardwalk at 0.3 mi. The boardwalk keeps visitors above the open bog mat but allows a view straight down into pitcher plants and a close-up look at tamaracks and numerous other bog flora growing next to, and sometimes trying to grow up through, the walkway. The trail ends at a viewing platform at just over 0.3 mi.

❋ Trail in winter: Suitable for backwoods skiing or snowshoeing.

🐾 Distance: 0.3 mi (0.5 km) round trip.

(45) Uncas Rd. (Mohegan and Sagamore Lakes) Trail

Map: E2, 3

Originally, Uncas Rd., built in 1896, began at Eagle Bay, went past Uncas Station on the Raquette Lake Railroad, then turned R (E) and went SE and E to luxurious Uncas Camp on Mohegan Lake. It then continued E to another great camp at Sagamore Lake. These were the summer homes of J. P. Morgan and Alfred G. Vanderbilt.

Today, the road, which is now named Uncas Rd. all the way through rather than changing to Browns Tract Rd. at the Raquette Lake end, is used for trails 35, 39, and 45. Trail 45 is the section running E from NY 28, from a point very near DEC's Eighth Lake Campground. Snowmobilers may loop back S and W to come out by the Seventh Lake Boat Launch, but that section, possibly an old logging road, eroded and considerably wetter, is not considered a hiking trail by DEC.

This section of Uncas Rd. is used by hikers to reach the road at Mohegan Lake. There is a private Camp Uncas on the NE peninsula. Coming from the Sagamore Lake (E) end, access is shorter, but not as woodsy.

▶ Trailheads: To reach the W trailhead, go 4.6 mi S from the turn-off to the community of Raquette Lake (or 5.0 mi N from Inlet, about 0.8 mi N of the Seventh Lake Boat Launch) on NY 28. The trailhead is on the E side about 300 ft S of the entrance to the Eighth Lake Campground. Park in the open area near the road. Two trails leave the open spot. The Uncas Road Trail is on level ground to the R (SE).

The E trailhead is the same as for the Sagamore Lake Trail (47). ◀

FROM THE W TRAILHEAD on NY 28 (0.0 mi), the old road, with only an occasional snowmobile marker, rises gently and crosses Seventh Lake Inlet at 0.15 mi, then bends L and starts to ascend. The next 1.5 mi is a gentle climb, with occasional flat spots on the grassy roadway. At 1.8 mi, an unnamed pond can be seen through the trees to the L for several yards. The trail tops out at 2.0 mi, turns S, and starts gently down.

There is a jct. at 2.6 mi with the old snowmobile trail heading uphill to the R. Uncas Rd. continues ahead, now with blue markers, passing another grassy road going uphill R and reaching an old cable barrier across the road at 2.8. Shortly beyond the barrier, the rotten stringers of a collapsed bridge dangle across a steep-banked stream. About 30 yd before the chasm, however, the trail leaves Uncas Rd., becoming a blue-marked footpath R going upstream to avoid the steep banks. It soon reaches another road which takes a southerly route that comes close to the W side of Mohegan Lake.

(A side trip R of up to 0.9 mi one way provides views of the W side of the lake with the road coming within 60 ft of the lake before bending away. That side road goes about 3.0 mi to a private camp of the Bear Pond Sportsmen's Club. The club's land extends for about 1000 ft around the clubhouse. The remainder is state land, including old unmarked routes to Bear Pond, which is on state land. The overgrown, mostly unmarked trail 84 can be used to reach Bear Pond from the S.)

From the point where the footpath along the outlet stream reaches the extension road, the blue-marked trail turns L, goes downhill, and uses the extension road's bridge to cross the outlet. Uphill, there is a bend to the R and a small clearing, then before 3.2 mi another bend R and a larger clearing. At this point the trail is back on Uncas Rd. At 3.5 mi, just yards E of small clearings on both sides of the road, there is an unmarked but well-used trail R (S).

(This path, with a slight bend R, leads through a pine grove to water's edge in a little over 0.1 mi. There are some benches, a fire ring, and sandy beach at the foot of the nice white pine grove, with views of the Great Camp from the point above.)

From the pine grove side trail, Uncas Rd. continues past the N side of the lake to a jct. at 3.8 mi. The road R leads to Camp Uncas on Mohegan Lake and the road ahead leads to Camp Sagamore and Sagamore Lake in another 1.5 mi. That route, along maintained road with no markers, heads NE, follows the contours of a hill, goes NE along a hilltop, goes N down a hill, and turns NE for 0.2 mi, reaching the gate at 5.1 mi. (The R fork at the gate goes to private land at Kamp Kill Kare.) It's another 0.2 mi to the DEC parking lot next to Sagamore on the L (N) side of the road.

Except for the footpath cutover from Uncas Rd. to the extension road and the pine grove path to the lake, both less than 0.2 mi, mountain biking would be an option. A sign at the Sagamore Lake end notes that hiking and biking are permitted.

❊ Trail in winter: Snowmobile trail, except for the last section near Mohegan Lake. If snowmobile traffic is light, this could be a nice trip for better skiers. The return trip is a long glide down.

❧ Distances: NY 28 trailhead to view of pond, 1.8 mi; to jct. with old snowmobile trail, 2.6 mi; to footpath off Uncas Rd., 2.8 mi; to jct. with extension road to Bear Pond Club, 3.0 mi; to pine grove campsite, 3.5 mi; to E trailhead at DEC parking lot by Sagamore Lake, 5.3 mi (8.5 km).

(46) Sagamore Cascades Trail

Map: E2

This route leads to the Cascades, formerly known as South Inlet Falls, a minor waterfall on Raquette Lake's South Inlet. Below the falls, the quiet water seems suitable for swimming, but the water appears nutrient-laden and the bottom is slick. A loop trip can be made by wading the inlet stream and returning on the trail along the E bank, although that section is wet in many places. Canoeists paddle to the falls from NY 28 at the edge of Raquette Lake's South Bay.

▶ Trailhead: From NY 28 across from the turnoff to Raquette Lake village, head S on Sagamore Rd. Go 2.9 mi to an old dirt road L, blocked by large boulders. There is space for several cars in front of the boulders. There is a DEC foot trail notice on a tree. The trail is an old road, marked occasionally by red ribbons. The second trailhead is 280 yd down the road at another old road L, just after the road crosses the South Inlet stream. ◀

FROM THE PARKING AREA (0.0 mi), the old road is nearly level, wide and smooth for 0.2 mi. The remaining trail heads very gently down, with a level section at a clearing at 0.5 mi. The trail approaches the creek, then curves to the W, following the contour above the water.

After a curve N again, another clearing has two roads leaving its N end. The trail follows the R one, proceeding along the high bank of the stream. At 1.3 mi, there is an S curve leading down to the stream and the first of several landings with views. A short section N along the stream leads to the Cascades at 1.4 mi and the trail ends at a canoe launch at 1.5 mi.

There was once a bridge across the Cascades, but hikers must now wade the stream above if they wish to cross. There is a shallow but slippery spot near an island above the cascades. A Sagamore trail guide leaflet notes that skiers, accompanied by a guide, could cross the inlet about 100 yd below the falls, but extreme caution is advised. The water is deep and the ice may be thin.

After crossing the stream, the trail follows a very wet old road (built by Durant in 1895) generally S along the stream bank to the second trailhead at 3.1 mi. The footpath is adequate and marked well enough with red ribbons, but in at least one spot leaves the soggy road for higher ground. There is a trail jct. on the L at 2.5 mi (1.0 mi from the Cascades). That unmarked trail is the Powerhouse Loop, on public land but mostly used by skiers from Sagamore. Farther along the creek, at 2.7 mi (1.2 mi from the Cascades), there is an old dam and brick powerhouse, once used for power at Sagamore.

The remaining route is a pleasant old road along quiet water, passing through a parking clearing and ending at the gravel Sagamore Rd. at 3.1 mi. Another 280 yd of road walking to the R will close the loop back to the first trailhead.

❋ Trail in winter: Easy skiing or snowshoeing, except the crossing of South Inlet, which can be dangerous if the ice is not thick enough.

Forest along South Inlet. RICHARD NOWICKI

🚶 Distances: First trailhead to end of trail below Cascades, 1.5 mi; to second trailhead, 3.1 mi. A complete loop is 3.3 mi (5.3 km).

(47) **Sagamore Lake Trail**

Map: E2

This trail is mostly used by guests at the Sagamore Lodge and Conference Center. Except for a minor section at the end, it is all on public land. Hikers and skiers not staying at Sagamore should follow the route described here and not enter private land. For those wishing to see the camp, public tours are given daily during the summer. For the tour, follow the signs at the entrance just across the road from the DEC parking lot. (See www.sagamore.org.) There are no state markers, but there is orange flagging at intersections and other spots. The description of this pleasant, mostly shaded trail is clockwise around the lake, forking R at trail jcts., except to avoid Sagamore property at the start and near the end, where L turns are necessary.

▶ Trailhead: From NY 28 across from the turnoff to Raquette Lake village, head S on Sagamore Rd. Go 3.3 mi to a jct., then turn R and cross a creek. At 3.4 mi, with some buildings of Sagamore on the L, turn

R into a DEC parking lot by a sign that says, "Tour parking, 300 ft." ◀

FROM THE PARKING LOT (0.0 mi), return to the road and turn L. Go downhill and across the outlet bridge you just drove over and to the road jct. 0.2 mi from the parking lot. Turn R and go toward the lake, reaching another jct. at 0.3 mi. A gated bridge R allows registered guests into Sagamore. Turn L onto an old road blocked at about 50 yd by boulders with a side path leading 20 yd to the lake.

Continue ahead on the old road as it follows along the W shore of Sagamore Lake. At 0.4 mi, there is a small trail R to the shore of the lake with a nice view. At 0.6 mi, there is another trail R, just steps to an overlook from near the NW corner of the lake. The view is very nice, but use caution looking out from the top of the cliff.

At 0.8 mi, the trail turns R (straight ahead N leads to South Inlet). Almost immediately (in 30–40 yd), there is another jct. The trail follows the R fork, marked with orange ribbon, whereas the other trail has yellow and blue flagging. The old carriage road passes near an open hilltop L and continues in pleasant woods.

At 1.3 mi, there is an iron cross planted 10 ft off the trail L. This is a monument to John Hoy. If you take the Sagamore tour, ask about this tale of tragedy.

Soon there are again glimpses of the lake R. There is another jct. with a yellow- and blue-flagged trail (L) in a clearing at 1.4 mi. The old carriage road continues straight through the clearing with orange flagging and soon starts gently downhill.

After leveling out, the trail crosses the inlet on a wide plank bridge at 2.0 mi. The trail turns R and follows the contour, keeping R at two old road jcts.

After 2.4 mi, there are again glimpses of the lake as the trail goes through mixed woods. At 2.7 mi, the trail heads toward the water. At the turn L, there is a path about 50 yd to a rocky edge of the lake. The trail then generally parallels the shore, close and then farther away, with another easy access (about 10 yd) to the lake at 3.0 mi.

Just before 3.5 mi, cars and buildings can be seen through the trees R as the trail makes a slight climb and reaches a clearing with a two-track road R, which goes onto the Sagamore Institute property and should be used only by guests staying there. "Lake Trail" signs point the way out, L, on a footpath S, which reaches the gravel road jct. a few yards away from the Mohegan Rd. gate before 3.7 mi. Turn R on the road and proceed another 0.2 mi to the parking lot entrance L, reaching the parking lot at 3.9 mi (6.3 km).

✳ Trail in winter: Suitable for cross-country skiing, although lot may not be plowed.

🐾 Distance: Parking lot to start of old road next to lake, 0.3 mi; to clearing and R turn at South Inlet trail, 0.8 mi; to bridge over inlet, 2.0; to edge of lake, 3.0 mi; to clearing next to Sagamore, nearly 3.5; to road, 3.7; back to parking lot, 3.9 mi (6.3 km).

(48) Sobel Ponds North Trail

Map: p. 119

This trail is also described as part of the Sargent Ponds Loop in ADK's *Adirondack Trails: Northern Region.*

This trail gives access to Upper and Lower Sargent Ponds. Both are very scenic. Side trails to both ponds lead to beautifully located campsites. In addition, the Lower Pond campsite has a lean-to.

▶ Trailhead: From NY 30 at Deerland, on the S end of Long Lake, take North Point Rd. W to the DEC trailhead at 6.3 mi. ◀

FROM NORTH POINT RD. (0.0 mi), the trail (with DEC red and snowmobile markers) heads S on easy ground above a creek. After passing over a slight hill at 1.0 mi, the path descends somewhat steeply to a jct. at 1.2 mi. To the L, the red trail goes to a campsite amid evergreens on the shore of Upper Sargent Pond at 1.4 mi. Nearby, an island in the lake adds great beauty to the scenery.

From the jct., the snowmobile trail turns R and continues along the edge of a hill N of the outlet creek. After some weaving along the contour, the trail reaches a jct. at 2.7 mi with the Tioga Point Trail (trail 49).

(Continuing ahead, the Tioga Point Trail soon crosses the outlet stream from Upper and Middle ponds. In another 0.1 mi, there is another jct. as the trail approaches a fish barrier dam on the outlet of Lower Sargent Pond. To the L, a DEC yellow-marked side trail leads 0.4 mi to Sargent Pond lean-to. This lean-to is very well located on a point of land with some tenting space nearby. The scenery is fine, and the fishing is apparently still good. Near the start of this side trail, a trail branch to the R leads quickly to the shore of the pond.)

✳ Trail in winter: Easy skiing most of the way, suitable for intermediate skiers familiar with wilderness travel. The trail down to Upper

Sargent Pond is somewhat steep. Shared with snowmobiles.

🐾 Distances: North Point Rd. to Upper Sargent Pond, 1.4 mi; to Tioga Point Trail (49), 2.7 mi. To Sargent Pond Lean-to via Tioga Point Trail (trail 49), 3.3 mi (5.2 km).

(49) **Tioga Point Trail**

Map: E1, p. 119

The portion of this trail past the jct. with the Sargent Ponds North Trail is described in ADK's *Adirondack Trails: Northern Region*.

Tioga Point is located at about the center region of Raquette Lake, and contains many lean-tos intended for canoe camping. This trail gives access to the point through a region of mature forests. The site receives heavy use during the summer from boat campers from the community of Raquette Lake and the surrounding area. In general, lean-tos must be reserved ahead of time. (Cost about $11. Call 800-456-2267 days for credit card reservations.) There are 15 lean-tos and 10 campsites administered by a caretaker at Tioga Point.

▶ Trailhead: From NY 30 at Deerland, on the S end of Long Lake, take North Point Rd. W to the second DEC trailhead at 7.8 mi (the first DEC trailhead at 6.3 mi is for trail 48). ◀

FROM NORTH POINT RD. (0.0 mi), the trail (with DEC red and snowmobile markers) heads S along the hillside W of Grass Pond outlet, with mild ups and downs in an older hardwood forest. Grass Pond, more or less living up to its name, is visible to the L at 1.0 mi. Beaver activity here has made the trail wet in several places.

The trail continues on easy ground to a jct. L with the Sargent Ponds North Trail (trail 48) at 2.0 mi. Continuing R (SW), the Tioga Point Trail soon crosses the outlet stream from Upper and Middle ponds. At 2.2 mi, there is another jct. as the trail approaches a fish barrier dam on the outlet of Lower Sargent Pond. To the L, a DEC yellow-marked spur trail leads four-tenths of a mi to Sargent Pond lean-to (see trail 48). Near the start of this spur trail, a branch to the R leads quickly to the shore of the pond.

At the trail jct. by the fish barrier dam, the trail goes R, crossing the outlet stream on a snowmobile bridge. There is a freshwater spring on the R just after this bridge. The trail climbs a ridge above the pond's W side and stays on the ridge until reaching a jct. at 2.4 mi. The unmarked

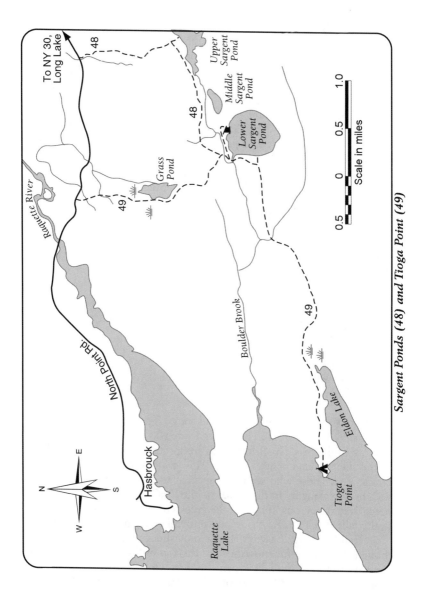

Sargent Ponds (48) and Tioga Point (49)

route L leads down 300 ft to the shore of Lower Sargent Pond at an unofficial camping area and boat landing.

From the jct., the trail turns R and heads W. There is a boggy stream crossing at 3.2 mi and another wet spot at 4.6 mi. The trail curves W and parallels the inlet bog of Eldon Lake as it approaches Raquette Lake. From there on, the route is on the pleasant high ground of Tioga Point peninsula. The water can be seen on the R for some distance before the trail reaches the Tioga Point lean-tos at 6.1 mi. The abundant lean-tos and manicured grassy areas here are in sharp contrast to the silent majestic forest passed through in reaching the point.

✳ Trail in winter: Easy skiing most of the way, suitable for intermediate skiers familiar with wilderness travel. Shared with snowmobiles.

⚹ Distances: North Point Rd. to Grass Pond, 1.0 mi; to Lower Sargent Pond, 2.2 mi; to Sargent Pond lean-to, 2.6 mi; to Tioga Point, 6.1 mi (9.8 km).

(49A) Death Falls

Map: E2

The falls are close to but not visible from NY 28 near Raquette Lake. They are situated on a broad headwall about 100 ft high, on a tributary creek of Death Brook.

▶ Trailhead: From the jct. with Raquette Lake village road, go E on NY 28. Pass the bridge over South Inlet at 2.5 mi. The trailhead is on the R at 3.3 mi near the top of a hill. There is a yellow barrier gate, but no sign. There are no trail markers. ◀

FROM THE GATE (0.0 mi), a dirt road goes 0.2 mi across level ground to a jct. at the base of a hill. The L fork leads 100 ft to an open view near the foot of the falls. The R fork leads around the hill with a gentle climb to the shelf of land above the falls. This "wide route" to the top is recommended. Those who scramble up next to the falls are creating erosion, or "wrecking it," in the words of one DEC official; this route is also potentially dangerous. Turn L at the creek crossing and follow the water to the falls at 0.3 mi. Take care, and remember the name of the falls.

✳ Trail in winter: Easy for skis or snowshoes to the foot of the falls, though short. Easy for snowshoes to the top of the falls. Access to the view at the top of the falls is dangerous in winter.

⚹ Distances: NY 28 to base of falls, 0.2 mi; to top, 0.3 mi (0.5 km).◆

Blue Mt. Lake Section

Blue Mt. Lake is considered one of the most beautiful lakes in the Adirondacks, with its variety of islands and Blue Mt. rising as a majestic sentinel from its E shore. It stands at the head of the Raquette River waterway in the St. Lawrence basin. There were three major resort hotels along its shores at the turn of the century. The village of Blue Mt. Lake lies along the SE corner of the lake. Lake Durant, the next largest lake in the area, lies nearby in the Hudson River watershed.

An outstanding cultural attraction in this area is the Adirondack Museum on NY 28N/30 a short distance N of the village center. It has many interesting exhibits pertaining to Adirondack culture and history, and is well worth a visit. Its Adirondack guideboat displays are outstanding. The lumbering exhibits are extensive and give a strong impression of the industry that dominated this region for a century. It is open from mid-June to mid-October.

The hiking trails described in this chapter lead mostly to ponds, the principal exception being the Blue Mt. Trail (trail 53). All are also described in ADK's *Adirondack Trails: Central Region*. Three trails S of NY 28 lie in the Blue Ridge Wilderness Area. The Northville–Placid Trail (N–P Trail) goes N–S on the E edge of the area. This 132-mi hiking route follows lower-lying terrain through the heart of the Adirondacks from Northville near the Sacandaga Reservoir N to Lake Placid. For a description of the entire trail, see *Adirondack Trails: The Northville–Placid Trail*, published by ADK.

Several trails in the area follow nineteenth-century roads. Most notable and oldest is the Cascade Pond Rd., cut through the forest in 1849–50 as a winter lumber road to Eagle Lake and later extended to the S shore of Blue Mt. Lake. From the Cedar River on the S it went N to Stephens Pond (the route followed by the N–P Trail), then W and NW to Cascade Pond and beyond (followed by the Cascade Pond Trail), and finally to Eagle Lake (the last part of it followed by the Wilson Pond Trail). This became part of the first stagecoach route from North Creek to Blue Mt. Lake, established in 1871 when the RR from Saratoga to North Creek was built (see Introduction). Starting in 1878, a different stagecoach route was used, and the Cascade Pond Rd. was thereafter seldom traveled.

Blue Mt. was an important survey point for Verplanck Colvin, who climbed the mountain on a horse in 1876. Today's hikers must do without the horse, but the sweeping view in all directions is no less rewarding. Castle Rock, a much lower peak, has an equally fine view, dominated by Blue Mt. Lake.

SHORT HIKE:
◆ Castle Rock—3.0 mi (4.8 km) round trip or 3.4 mi (5.5 km) loop with part of Sargent Pond East Trail. Great views from an open cliff overlooking Blue Mt. Lake after a 400- to 500-ft climb. See trail 51.

MODERATE HIKES:
◆ Blue Mt.—4.6 mi (7.4 km) round trip, 1560-ft climb. Moderately strenuous climb, but easily done at a slow pace. Great 360-degree view from the fire tower. See trail 53.
◆ Cascade Pond—5.4 mi (8.7 km) round trip. Pleasant wilderness setting, suitable for ski touring. See trail 55.
◆ Stephens Pond—6.6 mi (10.6 km). Gentle grades on a wide segment of the Northville–Placid Trail to a scenic pond with a lean-to. See trail 56.

HARDER HIKE:
◆ Northville–Placid Trail—This 132-mi N-S trail passes through this section; see *Adirondack Trails: Northville–Placid Trail*, published by ADK. The area S of Stephens Pond is open only to through hikers (2005); questions about this area may be e-mailed to DEC Supervising Forester Richard Fenton at rtfenton@gw.dec.state.ny.us. See trail 56.

TRAIL DESCRIBED	TOTAL MILES	PAGE
	(one way)	
Sargent Pond East Trail	4.7 (7.6 km)	123
Castle Rock Trail	1.5 (2.4 km)	124
Tirrell Pond Trail	3.0 (4.8 km)	126
Blue Mt. Trail	2.3 (3.7 km)	127
Wilson Pond Trail	3.4 (5.5 km)	130
Cascade Pond Trail	3.6 (5.8 km)	131
N–P Trail to Stephens Pond	3.3 (5.3 km)	132

(50) **Sargent Pond East Trail**

Map: p. 125

▶ Trailhead: From the jct. of NY 28 and NY 28N/30 in Blue Mt. Lake, drive N on NY 28N/30 for 0.6 mi and turn L on Maple Lodge Rd. Follow the paved and then gravel road for 1.3 mi to a DEC trailhead sign beside the Minnowbrook Conference Center control station. Minnowbrook has provided a long pullout for trailhead parking on the L just before the control station. If this is full, the closest parking is 1.3 mi back on NY 28N/30. ◀

FROM THE TRAILHEAD PARKING (0.0 mi), head W on a private road. Bear R uphill at a fork at 0.2 mi. At another DEC trail sign on the R at 0.3 mi, the trail leaves the road and enters the woods with red markers. The road straight ahead enters private land and should be avoided. At 0.4 mi, there is a jct. where the Castle Rock Trail (trail 51) goes L with yellow markers. Continue ahead on the red-marked foot trail, which leads N and then W on an old road around Chub Pond. The pond can be seen on the L shortly before the trail crosses the creek and turns W. At 1.5 mi, the Castle Rock Trail goes L with yellow blazes.

The Sargent Pond East Trail continues W, paralleling a wetland on the S for almost a mile. In this section a stand of spruce-fir offers a pleasing contrast to the predominantly deciduous forest of the trail route.

At 3.1 mi, the route descends to the level of an adjacent open wetland containing the inlet to Upper Sargent Pond (the outlet of Helms Pond). For the rest of its route, the trail parallels this stream on the S, descending very gradually as a narrow path through an open hardwood forest.

The trail ends at 4.7 mi at an informal campsite on a point of land on the E end of Upper Sargent Pond. A path continues 50 yd to the open, rocky end of the point. From this place, one may gaze W down the 1.3 mi-long pond with its conifer-lined shore and hills rising on the N side. The pond has a mucky bottom. Just to the R, the inlet enters the pond from a wetland.

❊ Trail in winter: Suitable for backcountry skiing and snowshoeing. Parking limited.

🐾 Distances: From parking near control station to turn off road, 0.3 mi; to first jct. with Castle Rock Trail, 0.4 mi; to second jct. with Castle Rock Trail (trail 51), 1.5 mi; to wetland, 3.1 mi; to Upper Sargent Pond, 4.7 mi (7.6 km).

(51) Castle Rock Trail

Map: p. 125

This small peak rises just 700 ft above Blue Mt. Lake, has an open summit, and provides a beautiful view over the lake. The trail has a mostly gentle slope, with one last steep but short section just below the top, with about 100 ft of elevation yet to climb.

▶ Locator: This interior trail starts at 0.4 mi from the trailhead on the Sargent Pond East Trail (50), passes spurs to Blue Mt. Lake and to the top, and ends at the 1.5-mi point on the Sargent Pond East Trail. ◀

FROM 0.4 MI (0.0 mi) on the Sargent Pond East Trail, the yellow-marked trail turns L (W) across a bridge. It bears R off the woods road at 0.1 mi, continuing on easy grades. Chub Pond can be seen R at 0.3 mi. Soon, the trail turns SW, following a stream down a gradual grade to a jct. at 0.4 mi.

(The blue-marked trail L heads down a stream to Blue Mt. Lake. It passes the ruins of a stone structure in the stream before reaching the lake, 0.3 mi from the jct., at a small clearing and sandy beach N of Long Island and other smaller islands W of Bluff Point. There is a DEC trail sign on a tree for those arriving by boat.)

From the jct., the yellow-marked trail continues W, first on the level but then increasingly steep. At 0.6 mi, the trail turns NW on easy to moderate grades, then goes through a hollow and ascends a short, steep pitch along the S face of Castle Rock to an overhang R at 0.9 mi. The herd path there rejoins the trail farther on.

The trail then heads nearly N on easy to moderate grades until a jct. at 1.0 mi where the R branch goes steeply up the W face of Castle Rock through a corridor with a high rock wall. The trail ends at 1.1 mi on the summit, an open cliff top 2480 ft in elevation. Blue Mt. Lake lies 700 ft below, and Blue Mt. (3759 ft) occupies the view to the L (E). Also seen are Lake Durant to the SE, Blue Ridge (3497 ft) to the S, Eagle Lake SSW, and Helms Pond WNW.

The trail ahead from the jct. at the W face continues 0.4 mi N to a jct. at 1.5 mi from the trailhead on the Sargent Pond East Trail; it can be used for the outbound trip (or to reach Castle Rock via a more gradual approach).

❊ Trail in winter: Suitable for snowshoeing, but extreme care is mandated on the upper part; it and the lookout ledge are quite dangerous in winter.

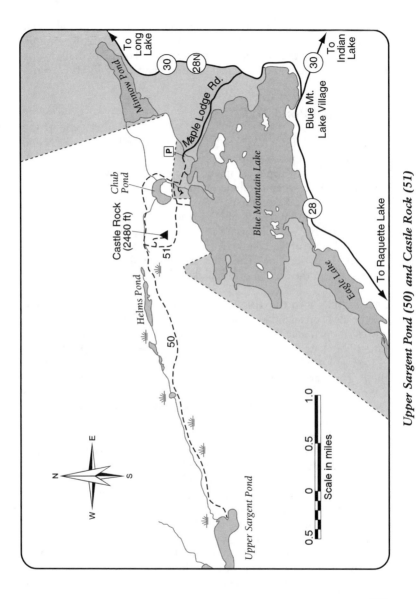

Upper Sargent Pond (50) and Castle Rock (51)

🜨 Distances: Sargent Pond East Trail (trail 50) to Blue Mt. Lake spur jct., 0.4 mi; to overhang, 0.9 mi; to turnoff to top, 1.0 mi; to summit, 1.1 mi (1.8 km); to N end at 1.5 mi on Sargent Pond East Trail, 1.5 mi (2.4 km). Ascent, 690 ft (210 m). Summit elevation, 2480 ft (756 m).

(52) **Tirrell Pond Trail**

Map: p. 128

This trail extends from NY 28N/30 NE to the N–P Trail near the N end of Tirrell Pond. It passes through private land that is leased to the Blue Mt. Lake Club by a paper company. It's a generally downhill route that makes a nice ski when combined with the portion of the N–P Trail S to NY 28/30 near Lake Durant.

▶ Trailhead: From the jct. of NY 28 and NY 30 in Blue Mt. Lake, go 1.4 mi N on NY 28N/30, past the Adirondack Museum, to a parking lot at the height of land on the R (E). The yellow-marked trail is at the N end of the parking lot. (The red-marked Blue Mt. Trail, trail 53, starts at a register in the middle of the parking lot.) ◀

FROM THE N END OF THE PARKING LOT (0.0 mi), the yellow-marked trail heads N on an old logging road but soon curves E and climbs a bit, passes an open area within earshot of traffic noise at 0.5 mi, and continues NE along the contour of steep-sided Blue Mt. The private gravel road at 1.4 mi goes to NY 28N/30 on the NW and up Blue Mt. to the R. There are also power lines here. In the level area from 1.8 mi to 1.9 mi (there is a glacial boulder on the L at the latter point), the trail crosses the St. Lawrence-Hudson River drainage divide at an elevation of 2360 ft. Blue Mt. can be seen to the S from here.

The trail gradually descends 400 ft to its end at the blue-marked N–P Trail at 3.0 mi. To the L, the N–P Trail continues N toward Long Lake. To the R, it leads 0.3 mi to Tirrell Pond Lean-to, which is a few hundred feet from the beach on the NE end of Tirrell Pond. Camping on the beach is prohibited. A yellow-marked trail leads to a campsite on the NE corner of the lake.

From in front of the lean-to, the blue-marked N–P Trail continues S along the W edge of the pond, muddy in spots due to Blue Mt. runoff, reaching O'Neil Flow Lean-to at 4.8 mi. Then it continues crossing several streams on walkways or rocks reaching NY 28/30 at 8.1 mi, where a car could be spotted for the trip back uphill to the trailhead above the museum.

✳ Trail in winter: Nice for backcountry skiing or snowshoeing, generally downhill from the parking lot near the museum to the roadside parking on NY 28/30 near Lake Durant. Listed by DEC as a skiable trail.

🐾 Distances: NY 28N/30 to gravel road, 1.4 mi; to N–P Trail, 3.0 mi; to Tirrell Pond Lean-to, 3.3 mi; to Tirrell Pond, 3.4 mi (5.6 km).

(53) Blue Mt. Trail

Map: p. 128

This popular trail ascends from NY 28N/30 E to the summit of Blue Mt. The fire tower on the summit provides a 360-degree view of Adirondack lakes, forest, hills, and mountains, including some of the High Peaks. The drainage divide between the St. Lawrence River watershed on the W and the Hudson River basin on the E goes in a N-

Fire tower on summit of Blue Mt. NORM LANDIS

S direction over the summit. The heavily-used, well-worn trail is steep and rough in places. Much of it goes over private land, so this is not a typical DEC trail. A hired trail crew worked on it for three weeks in the fall of 2004. To continue funding for work on this trail, an "iron ranger" has been installed next to the register kiosk. This is a square steel tubing with a slot for donations for trail work.

▶ Trailhead: From the jct. of NY 28 and NY 30 in Blue Mt. Lake, go 1.4 mi N on NY 28N/30, past the Adirondack Museum, to a parking lot at the height of land on the R (E). (The yellow-marked Tirrell Pond Trail, trail 52, starts at the N end of the same parking lot.) ◀

STARTING FROM A REGISTER in the middle of the E side of the park-

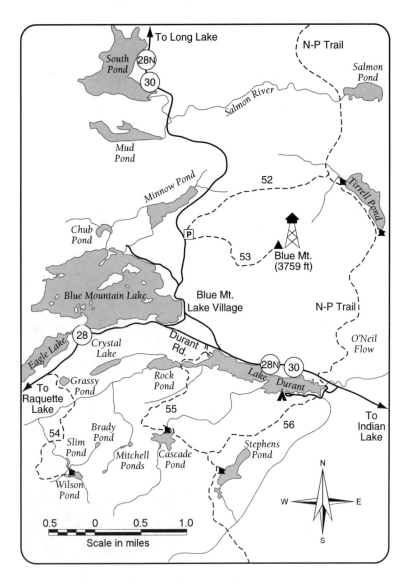

Blue Mt. Trails

ing lot (0.0 mi), the red-marked footpath goes over a little knoll and meets an old road at a box with nature trail brochures. It then begins a gentle climb. The old road ends in 0.3 mi, but the route ahead is still easy. A steeper climb doesn't last long. The trail turns SE, climbing gently across the slope, as it heads for the old trail route on the SW ridge.

Numerous walkways lead over wet spots, then there is a short, steep climb to meet the old trail at 1.1 mi. From there on the route is steadily uphill, sometimes on bare rock, sometimes on jumbled rock, and sometimes on the little bit of soil not yet torn loose by hikers' feet and spring runoff. Spruce and balsam fir become more prevalent, along with paper birch, mountain ash, and mountain maple. The fragrant balsam eventually predominates.

At 1.6 mi the bedrock footway becomes continuous, and between 1.8 mi and 2.0 mi some views back (W) are possible. Then for 0.3 mi the trail is nearly level with glimpses of the tower above short trees. The trail reaches the tower at 2.3 mi.

The cabin atop the DEC fire tower on the open rock summit is closed, but hikers can climb the tower to the landing just below the cabin. The summit view is partly blocked by trees in some directions, but improves dramatically at the last stair landing just below the cabin. This panorama includes Tirrell Pond, with its sandy N beach, just below on the NE; Third Lake of the Essex Chain on the E; O'Neil Flow and Rock Lake to the SE; the E end of Lake Durant on the S; Stephens Pond and, in the distance, the Cedar River Flow to the SSW; prominent Blue Mt. Lake as well as Minnow Pond, Eagle Lake, Utowana Lake, and Crystal Pond to the W and SW, with very large Raquette Lake beyond; Forked Lake, Mud Pond, and South Pond on the NW; and, in the distance, more to the N, Lake Eaton. The Adirondack High Peaks panorama lying from 25–70 degrees on the NE includes Algonquin Peak, Mt. Colden, and Mt. Marcy, highest of the Adirondack peaks (5344 ft), 28 mi away. Closer by, the rock face of Tirrell Mt. is seen on the NE. The highest Adirondack mountain outside the High Peaks region, Snowy Mt. (3899 ft), peeks up from the S just L of Buell Mt., and Wakely Mt. (3760 ft) is to the SW. Both Snowy and Wakely mts. have fire towers still standing; Snowy's has been refurbished, but Wakely's is currently (2005) unmaintained.

From the ground on the summit there are some views over the trees, but one should walk a short way E of the summit to a rocky area near the site of the observer's cabin for a fine open view from N to SE. This includes the High Peaks panorama and, closer at hand on the NE, the prominent Fishing Brook–Dun Brook Mt. range. The foundations of old radar installations can be seen on the summit area which, together with the fire tower, was served by a road climbing the mountain on the NW from NY 28N/30. This route has been closed.

✸ Trail in winter: Snowshoe trip for properly equipped and experienced winter mountaineers. The summit weather can be overpowering, with whiteouts and vicious sub-zero winds.

❧ Distances: Trailhead to summit of Blue Mt., 2.3 mi (3.7 km). Ascent, 1550 ft (473 m). Summit elevation, 3759 ft (1146 m).

(54) **Wilson Pond Trail**

Map: p. 130

Starting opposite Eagle Lake on NY 28, this trail goes in a mostly S direction past Grassy Pond to attractive Wilson Pond and its lean-to. The trail goes past impressively large yellow birches, through extensive stands of conifers and past wetlands, with wet and muddy portions. The first part of the trail, to a little beyond Grassy Pond, is wide and smooth, being the route of the old Cascade Pond Road mentioned in the introduction to this section. Thereafter, the trail tends to be narrower. Like the trails S of NY 28/30, this trail is in the Blue Ridge Wilderness Area.

▶ Trailhead: From the jct. of NY 28 and NY 30 in Blue Mt. Lake Village, go SW for 2.8 mi on NY 28. Park at a small inset on the SE side of the road. ◀

LEAVING THE PARKING AREA (0.0 mi), the red-marked trail goes NE parallel to the road for about 125 yd, then turns abruptly away from the road, heading SE through conifers, mostly balsam fir, and crosses a wetland. At 0.3 mi another trail on private land crosses the Wilson Pond Trail at a Forest Preserve sign.

At 0.5 mi, the trail crosses the boggy outlet of Grassy Pond. The pond is small and lined by tamaracks, and can be seen on the L (E) across a short section of wetland.

At 0.8 mi, the route crosses the outlet stream from Long Pond, which flows through a wetland with open water lying on the R (W). After traversing fields of ferns, the trail starts, at 0.9 mi, a 420-ft crossing of a wetland containing the outlet stream of Wilson Pond (also the outlet stream of Slim Pond). Corduroy footing and a bridge provide some help in the crossing. At the far edge of the wetland, a short side trail leads L to a spring. As you proceed up the trail from here, turn and notice the view of Blue Mt. and its tower.

For the next 0.3 mi, the trail gradually ascends (with a downslope on the R) SW through an airy hardwood forest. At 2.1 mi, it crosses the Wilson Pond stream which, upstream on the L (E), goes through a wetland with open water.

The route continues in a forest of spruce and fir followed by hardwoods, and has several short ups and downs. Again it crosses the Wilson Pond stream at 3.2 mi.

Climbing uphill through a stand of tall spruce, the trail ends at 3.4 mi at the lean-to, near the N shore of Wilson Pond. The lean-to faces a dense clump of spruce-fir on the side of the pond. The pond is lined with boggy growth and conifers but has a nice rock ledge on the shore near the lean-to with an island nearby. Beyond the pond on the S is the Blue Ridge range, which rises to an elevation of 3497 ft.

❄ Trail in winter: Beautiful snowshoe trip. Can be skied by intermediate backcountry skiers, but breaking trail uphill all the way can be a big chore.

🐾 Distance: Trailhead to corduroy, 0.9 mi; to middle crossing of Wilson Pond stream, 2.1 mi; to Wilson Pond, 3.4 mi (5.5 km).

(55) **Cascade Pond Trail**

Map: p. 128
The trail passes Rock Pond near the start, and Cascade Pond and its lean-to at 2.7 mi, near the other end. The N–P Trail at the far end at 3.6 mi (5.8 km) leads S past Stephens Pond Lean-to, 4.1 mi from the Cascade Pond trailhead.

▶ Trailhead: From the highway jct. in Blue Mountain Lake Village, drive 0.8 mi E on NY 28/30. Turn R on Durant Rd. and go W for 0.2 mi. Turn L (S) on a dirt road next to a cemetery. Drive 0.1 mi on the dirt road and park in the area on the L. (The road continues another 0.1 mi to the W end of Lake Durant, where there is a boat-launching site and an informal campsite and privy in an open area by the lake.) There is a privy and informal campsite E of the trailhead parking area. The trail starts on the W side of the road. ◀

THE RED-MARKED TRAIL crosses a brook a few yards from the start (0.0 mi) and forks R just beyond. At 0.6 mi there is a long board bridge over the beginning of the waterway connecting Rock Pond with Lake Durant. The trail then crosses the end of a ridge SE of Rock Pond and turns R to climb a notch between it and the next ridge.

After ascending a steeper slope at the end of the notch and leveling out, the trail turns L (E) at an arrow at 2.2 mi onto the broader, smoother route of an old woods road coming in from the R. The woods road, which is followed all the way to the N–P Trail, was once the Cascade Pond Rd. mentioned in the Blue Mt. Lake section introduction. The old road passes through increasing quantities of spruce and balsam fir.

The Cascade Pond Lean-to is at 2.7 mi, on a cove at the pond's NE end just W of the outlet. Rocks by the shore provide good viewpoints on this attractive pond.

The trail continues, crossing the pond's outlet and going SE as a broad, smooth path, to end at the blue-marked N–P Trail at 3.6 mi at a Y jct. From the L fork, it is 2.7 mi on the N–P Trail to the highway and the Lake Durant Public Campground. To the R, Stephens Pond and its lean-to are 0.5 mi S on the N–P Trail (on a short side trail L).

❋ Trail in winter: Suitable for backcountry skiing and snowshoeing. Listed as a skiable trail by DEC.

𖠰 Distances: Trailhead to Rock Lake crossing, 0.6 mi; to Cascade Pond lean-to, 2.7 mi; to N–P trail, 3.6 mi (5.8 km). To Stephens Pond, 4.1 mi (6.6 km).

(56) N–P Trail to Stephens Pond

Map: p. 128

This section of the N–P Trail extends from a prominent trailhead on NY 28/30 SW to the lean-to at the S end of Stephens Pond. The route follows a woods road with easy grades. The woods road as far as the jct. with the Cascade Pond Trail (55) is an old logging road cut through the forest in the early 1850s from the Cascade Pond Rd. to a dam at the foot of present Lake Durant.

▶ Trailhead: From the jct. of NY 28 and NY 30 in Blue Mt. Lake, go E on NY 28/30 for 2.7 mi to a well-marked trailhead. To save 0.2 mi of hiking, you can also go 3.0 mi from the jct. and turn in at the Lake Durant Public Campground. Park near the bathhouse, after paying a day-use fee. ◀

STARTING ON THE S SIDE of NY 28/30 (0.0 mi), the blue-marked trail goes L (SE) along the former highway, past the forest ranger's headquarters area and across the bridge over the beginning of the Rock River (Lake Durant's outlet). It turns R (SW) along the paved road of the Lake Durant Public Campground.

At 0.5 mi, by Campsite No. 3, the route goes L onto a DEC truck trail, shortly passing a sizeable hemlock growing on a rock. The trail leaves the truck trail at 0.8 mi, and 135 yd beyond that at a register a side trail goes acutely R to the public campground area. Stands of spruce-fir and scrub hardwood are traversed, and there follows just over 2.0 mi of pleasant walking on a broad footway to the jct. with the red-marked Cascade Pond Trail (trail 55) at 2.7 mi. The Cascade Pond lean-to is 0.9 mi to the R (NW). This jct. is a sharp L turn going S. Returning on the blue-marked trail, hikers must be careful to avoid going straight ahead (W) on the red-marked Cascade Pond Trail (trail 55) and turn back over their R shoulder to continue N on the N–P Trail.

The N–P Trail continues SE and S another 0.5 mi, descending steeply in places to the SW end of Stephens Pond, where a lean-to is located on a short spur going L at 3.3 mi. Tall white pines are among the conifers adorning the perimeter of the pond. A narrow trail from the lean-to goes N along the shore to a small point, with good water access.

The N–P Trail continues S for another 66 mi; however, it remains closed where it passes over private land at the former McCane's Resort on the Cedar River Rd. Parking is not permitted at this location. Through hikers are allowed to continue along the N–P Trail. Questions about this area may be e-mailed to DEC Supervising Forester Richard Fenton at rtfenton@gw.dec.state.ny.us. For more details, refer to the *Adirondack Trails: Northville–Placid Trail*, the fourth volume in ADK's Forest Preserve Series.

❊ Trail in winter: Suitable for snowshoeing or backcountry skiing. Listed by the DEC as a skiable foot trail.

❧ Distances: To end of DEC Lake Durant Truck Trail, 0.8 mi; to Cascade Pond Trail (trail 55), 2.7 mi; to Cascade Pond lean-to, 3.6 mi; to Stephens Pond lean-to, 3.3 mi (5.3 km). ◆

Fallen aspen leaves. RICHARD NOWICKI

Brantingham Section

Brantingham is unique among the trailhead sections of the West-Central Region; it is the only section not on a through road. The road may be a dead end, but the community is not. Brantingham Lake is a center for summer activity with resorts, a marina, a golf course, many stately summer homes, fine dining, two tiny general stores, and a motel. As with the Independence River Section, access roads to the area are local and complicated. A Lewis County highway map shows town roads that may not appear on state maps, as well as state and county highways. They are $3 each (verify cost at 315-376-5350) with a check to the Lewis County Highway Dept. at 7660 State St., Lowville, NY 13367.

The hiking trails of this section are intimately linked to the two major roads passing through it. Brantingham Rd. enters from the highway network to the W and continues E to merge into Steam Mill Rd., a principal trailhead route going 5.7 mi E. The old steam-driven lumber mill is long gone, although timbers cut at this mill and used in the roadway were found preserved under the road and still in good condition when it was reconstructed in the mid-1970s. Partridgeville Rd. crosses Brantingham Rd. going N, then curves E around the lake. After passing the site of the former village of Partridgeville NE of the lake, it continues E to trailheads at the former Dolgeville, and goes beyond that all the way to Big Otter Lake (as a snowmobile and hiking trail). Dolgeville was also known as Botchfordville. It once had a live-in community with sawmills and tanneries.

In winter, the more distant trails are not decently accessible on foot for day trips, but they are used by snowmobilers. Many of the closer trails, such as Catspaw Lake Rd. and the Centennial Ski Trail, then become more attractive.

The area also includes the Otter Creek Horse Trail system (DEC has a map); those trails are also open to hikers, mountain bikers, and cross-country skiers—the mix not being the problem DEC had anticipated. Bicyclists especially should use caution, particularly at bends or corners, to avoid spooking horses.

Short Hike:

◆ Catspaw Lake—2.0 mi (3.2 km) round trip. A 4WD road goes around the N side of the lake, with access at the NE and NW corners. The lake is very nice, and the walk pleasant. See trail 58.

Moderate Hikes:

◆ Pine Lake—5.8 mi (9.4 km) round trip. This very remote wilderness lake and lean-to is accessible via a good trail on an old road, now the Pine Lake Trail. See page 67.

◆ Big Otter Lake—9.4 mi (15.2 km) round trip. An old jeep road leads to a fine camping spot on the NW side of the lake. See trail 64.

Harder Hike:

◆ Independence River—15.6 mi (25.2 km). The Silvermine Trail leads to the river near Balsam Flats, and then to the East Bridge (to be removed) over the Independence River (and a small campsite).

Trail Described	Total Miles (one way)	Page
Confusion Flats	Various	137
Branaugh Trail	0.3 (0.5 km)	137
Fletcher Horse Trail	1.3 (2.1 km)	140
Little Otter Lake Rd.	1.0 (1.6 km)	140
Florence Pond Rd. and Horse Trail	1.5 (2.4 km)	140
Pitcher Pond Horse Trail	1.0 (1.6 km)	141
Erie Canal Horse Trail	1.0 (1.6 km)	141
Streamside Horse Trail	1.7 (2.7 km)	141
Blueberry Snowmobile Trail	1.5 (2.4 km)	142
Glenfield Railroad Snowmobile Trail	2.4 (3.9 km)	142
Shingle Mill Falls Trail	0.5 (0.8 km)	143
Crooked Creek Horse Trail	0.7 (1.1 km)	143
Centennial Ski Trail	3.8 (6.1 km)	144
Silvermine Trail	7.4 (11.9 km)	145
Big Otter Lake West Trail	5.4 (8.7 km)	147
Otter Creek–Pine Lake Trail	2.6 (4.2 km)	148
Pico Mt. Trail	2.4 (3.9 km)	149
Pine Lake Trail	6.0 (8.5 km)	150
Mudhole Trail	1.2 (1.9 km)	152

(57) **Confusion Flats**

Map: pp. 138–139

Confusion Flats is a vast region of big sand dunes and scrub vegetation, mixed with scrubby pines. It is covered with old two-track roads. Some are passable by car (passenger car on the main routes, but 4WD is better). These roads are principally horse and snowmobile trails, while a few (shown on the map as roads) are marked for motor vehicle use. Motorists, including ATV drivers, may not use those paths not specifically marked for vehicular use. Hikers are welcome to use all trails.

Among the many attractions of this region, Pitcher Pond and Little Otter Lake are especially pretty evergreen-ringed lakes. Some trails cross Otter Creek and connect to trails in the Brantingham area. Other trails on the N go as far as Beach Mill Rd., near the trailhead at Beach Mill Pond.

Trails in this region are linked for continuous horse and snowmobile travel. All of them provide opportunity for a pleasant walk in the woods. The trails listed below have particular appeal for the hiker because of ponds, streams, or longer distances.

There are nice campsites in the Otter Creek State Forest at the southern trailhead. Camping is by advance permit only; call the Lowville office of the DEC at 315-376-3521.

▶ Trailheads: To reach the N trailhead from Chases Lake Rd. S of Chase Lake (E of Lowville), go E on Sand Pond Rd. There is a large parking lot at the jct. with Confusion Flats Rd. Take Confusion Flats Rd. S.

To reach the S trailhead, from Pine Grove Rd. N of Grieg, go E on Eatonville Rd. Van Arnum Rd. connects on the R at 1.2 mi. Eatonville Rd. then goes downhill to Otter Creek at 1.4 mi. The bridge over the creek marks the start of the Otter Creek Truck Trail, a DEC road. This 1.5-mi road ending at private land gives access to some of the southernmost trails of Confusion Flats. ◀

(57A) **Branaugh Trail**

Map: pp. 138–139

SAND POND, E of Chase Lake, is not entirely private. There is a slice of state land on the E side, with a nice sand beach. Starting from the N trailhead, go E on Sand Pond Rd. for 0.5 mi to a parking area on the R, next to a gate. Walk around the vehicle barrier and go 0.3 mi on the

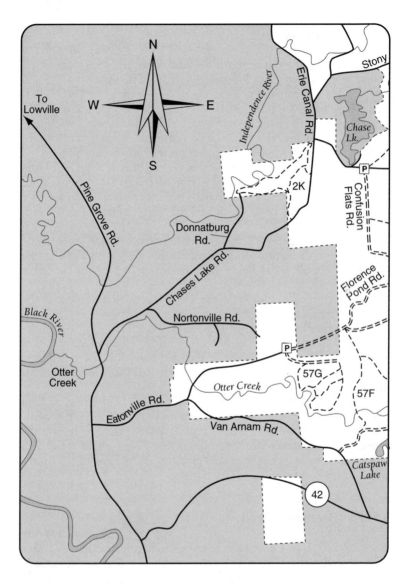

Confusion Flats and Brantingham (57)

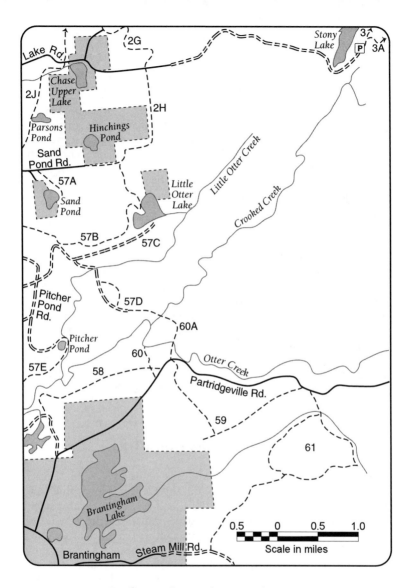

Lake Rd.

2G

Stony Lake

3

P 3A

Chase Upper Lake

2J

2H

Parsons Pond

Hinchings Pond

Sand Pond Rd.

Little Otter Creek

57A

Sand Pond

Little Otter Lake

Crooked Creek

57B

57C

Pitcher Pond Rd.

57D

60A

Pitcher Pond

60

Otter Creek

57E

58

Partridgeville Rd.

59

61

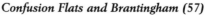

0.5   0   0.5   1.0

Scale in miles

Brantingham Lake

Brantingham   Steam Mill Rd.

Confusion Flats and Brantingham (57)

old road, which turns R into a field at the head of the beach. The area to the N and E of the lake is state land.

(57B) Fletcher Horse Trail

Map: pp. 138–139

STARTING FROM THE N TRAILHEAD, use Confusion Flats Rd. to reach Florence Pond Rd. Turn L. Go 0.7 mi and park nearby. Starting from the jct., the Fletcher Trail goes N, then E through the scrub pines. The trail turns N at 1.0 mi and skirts Little Otter Lake, then turns E onto a peninsula with a beautiful view of the lake. The route leaves the peninsula headed W for 0.3 mi, then turns N around Airport Pond and continues to Bull Rd. at 1.3 mi.

(57C) Little Otter Lake Rd.

Map: pp. 138–139

STARTING FROM THE N TRAILHEAD, use Confusion Flats Rd. to reach Florence Pond Rd. Turn L. At 0.7 mi, the Fletcher Horse Trail (57B) enters from an old road on the L and leaves on a path straight ahead. Turn R and go another 0.2 mi to an unmarked Y jct. Take the L fork if you have a 4WD or park and walk the route otherwise. The rutted old road winds through scrub pine for 1.0 mi, first passing a footpath which connects to the Fletcher Horse Trail, then a short path down to the lake, and finally ends at a sort of campsite just above the middle of the lake's S shore.

(57D) Florence Pond Rd. and Horse Trail

Map: pp. 138–139

STARTING FROM THE N TRAILHEAD, use Confusion Flats Rd. to reach Florence Pond Rd. Turn L. At 0.7 mi, the Fletcher Horse Trail (trail 57B) enters from an old road on the L and leaves on a path straight ahead. Turn R and go another 0.2 mi to an unmarked Y jct. (the L fork is trail 57C). Turn R again and continue another 0.5 mi to Little Otter Creek. One may wish to park here, as the road becomes ever less drivable (but still pleasantly walkable) as the distance increases, and becomes hopeless at 1.3 mi from Little Otter Creek. The old road then goes down somewhat steeply to reach Crooked Creek, 1.5 mi from

Little Otter Creek. The Crooked Creek Horse Trail (trail 60A) joins on the other side (Crooked Creek must be waded).

There is an alternate route on the L at 0.2 mi from Little Otter Creek. It heads E for 0.5 mi to cross an open ridge between two lower wet areas, then turns S to meet the main route at 0.9 mi from Little Otter Creek.

(57E) Pitcher Pond Horse Trail

Map: pp. 138–139

STARTING FROM THE N TRAILHEAD, use Confusion Flats Rd. for 2.5 mi. Park at the jct. with Shortcut Rd. and Erie Canal Horse Trail (trail 57F) L. Take Erie Canal Horse Trail for 0.2 mi to the jct. with Pitcher Pond Horse Trail (L). The trail drifts through sand flats for 1.0 mi, then descends gently to the S bank of Pitcher Pond. It continues around the pond to meet Pitcher Pond Rd. on the N side.

(57F) Erie Canal Horse Trail

Map: pp. 138–139

STARTING FROM THE N TRAILHEAD, use Confusion Flats Rd. for 2.5 mi. Park at the jct. with Shortcut Rd. and Erie Canal Horse Trail (L). Starting from the S trailhead, take Van Arnum Rd. E 2.2 mi to the jct. with Catspaw Lake Rd., a dirt road on the L. That road splits in a Y jct. Take the R fork. Go 0.3 mi to the Erie Canal Trail on the L. The trail is a pleasant, easygoing 1.0-mi trip across Otter Creek.

(57G) Streamside Horse Trail

Map: pp. 138–139

FROM THE S TRAILHEAD, go 1.4 mi from Otter Creek to Mike's Rd. on the R. Turn onto Mike's Rd. and go 0.9 mi to the jct. with Ridgeview (or Ridge Top) Trail on the R. This is the end of the officially drivable road. Continue ahead on foot. The old road ends 0.4 mi from the parking point, but the trail turns R and continues along the high, steep bank of Otter Creek. At 0.7 mi, the route turns N and descends to meet the Valley Trail and the bot-

tom end of the Ridge Top Trail (two short trails that go E to join the Streamside Trail). By the Ridge Top Trail, it is 0.4 mi back to the starting point. Streamside Trail continues along low ground near the creek, then climbs back up to meet Mike's Rd. From there, the start of the trail is 0.4 mi to the R on Mike's Rd. It's 1.7 mi around the full loop.

(58) **Blueberry Snowmobile Trail**

Map: pp. 138–139

▶ Trailhead: See trail 60. ◀

THE SNOWMOBILE TRAIL meets Partridgeville Rd. just E of the Shingle Mill Falls Trail (0.0 mi), but hikers have little need to use that short section. Go down the Shingle Mill Falls Trail and turn L (W) onto the Blueberry Trail. It goes to Otter Creek, around a very high esker, and meets Catspaw Lake Rd. at 1.5 mi. It is another 1.0 mi from there to Partridgeville Rd. The best part of the trail is the section near Catspaw Lake.

The start of the Catspaw Lake Rd. is 0.9 mi N on Partridgeville Rd. from its jct. with Brantingham Rd. It is a simple two-track road, almost unnoticeable on the L. At 1.0 mi on this old road, trail 58 joins on the R. Catspaw Lake is on the L at the bottom, and is interesting in its own right.

　❋ Trail in winter: Snowmobile trail and good ski trail.
　🐾 Distance: Trailhead to Catspaw Lake Rd., 1.5 mi (2.4 km).

(59) **Glenfield Railroad Snowmobile Trail**

Map: pp. 138–139

▶ Trailhead: See trail 60. ◀

THE ROUTE STARTS SLIGHTLY E of the Shingle Mill Falls Trail (trail 60), on the opposite side of the road. It goes S to meet the bed of an old lumber RR, then heads NE to rejoin Partridgeville Rd. at the edge of a private land block, 2.4 mi from the first trailhead. It is not worth coming a long way for, but is a pleasant level hike for those staying in Brantingham.

　❋ Trail in winter: Snowmobile trail.
　🐾 Distance: Trailhead to trailhead, 2.4 mi (3.9 km).

(60) Shingle Mill Falls Trail

Map: pp. 138–139

Shingle Mill Falls is a broad, wide, 10 ft high drop in Otter Creek, with some auxiliary falls above and below. Access is easy, and the falls are pretty. A large pool at the bend below the falls looks inviting for swimming.

▶ Trailhead: From the crossroads on Brantingham Rd. in Brantingham, go N on Partridgeville Rd., curving to the NE. At 1.6 mi there is a jct. Partridgeville Rd. turns L. At 2.7 mi on the L is a slight grassy region suitable for parking next to Shingle Mill Falls Rd. (no markings). Check the distance carefully; there are many turnoffs in the area. This two-track dirt road goes nearly to Shingle Mill Falls. It may be improved in the future, allowing easy access right to the falls. Otherwise, the ruts make it advisable to park passenger cars at the grassy spot next to the paved road. ◀

FROM PARTRIDGEVILLE RD. (0.0 mi), follow the two-track road N. At 0.2 mi is a jct. where the Blueberry Snowmobile Trail (trail 58) crosses. That trail is marked for both snowmobile and horse trail use. At 0.5 mi there is a sort of parking lot. Shortly beyond, the route reaches the water on open rock slabs just above the falls. Don't bother with the good footpath going L just before the falls; it leads nowhere. Walk along the rocks just back from the water to reach the area below the falls.

❋ Trail in Winter: Easy showshoe or ski, but a bit short.

🐎 Distance: Partridgeville Rd. to end of road and falls, 0.5 mi (0.8 km).

(60A) Crooked Creek Horse Trail

Map: pp. 138–139

This horse trail connects Partridgeville Rd. with Confusion Flats. It is an easy and pleasant trail, but does involve wading Otter Creek at the start and Crooked Creek at the other end (if continuing on into Confusion Flats).

▶ Trailhead: From the crossroads on Brantingham Rd. in Brantingham, go N on Partridgeville Rd., curving to the NE. At 1.6 mi there is a jct. Partridgeville Rd. turns L. At 2.7 mi on the L is a slightly overgrown grassy parking spot next to the two-track Shingle Mill Falls Trail (trail 60). The next trail, at 2.8 mi on the L, is the Blueberry

Snowmobile Trail (trail 58). Beyond that, the two-track road on the L at 3.0 mi is the Crooked Creek Trail. Park along the road as best you can. ◀

FROM PARTRIDGEVILLE RD. (0.0 mi), the old road descends a short distance to Otter Creek, where the stream must be waded. It then goes through pleasant open woods N, then curves W and goes down to cross Crooked Creek (wading, no bridge) to meet Florence Pond Rd. and Horse Trail (trail 57D) at 0.7 mi.

❊ Trail in winter: Snowmobile trail, suitable for skiing and snowshoeing if the two creeks are crossable.

⚹ Distance: Trailhead to Crooked Creek, 0.7 mi (1.1 km).

(61) Centennial Ski Trail

Map: pp. 138–139

This trail is a through route from Partridgeville Rd. to Steam Mill Rd. An extra trail section in the middle allows one to ski or hike a loop trip through interesting country. The through route is called the Centennial Scoot and the loop trip uses a section known as the Bear Ridge Run.

▶ Trailheads: To reach the N trailhead, from the crossroads in Brantingham, go N on Partridgeville Rd. At 1.5 mi, there is a jct. Partridgeville Rd. turns L. This part of the road was formerly known as Dolgeville Rd., but is now the continuation of Partridgeville Rd. At 4.6 mi, a gravel road goes L. Trailhead parking is on the R, almost opposite this gravel road.

To reach the S trailhead, continue ahead (E) on Brantingham Rd. at the intersection with Patridgeville Rd., passing the golf course. At 0.9 mi from the intersection, where the pavement turns L, continue straight ahead on gravel Steam Mill Rd. At 2.3 mi from the Partridgeville Rd. intersection, the trailhead is on the L (N). ◀

FROM PARTRIDGEVILLE RD. (0.0 mi), the yellow-marked trail goes SE past a trail register and curves S as it passes over some ups and downs. A mild climb leads to a jct. at 0.5 mi on a hilltop overlooking a pond to the L (E). The trail L is Bear Ridge Run (see below).

Continuing ahead, the Centennial Scoot goes W following easy terrain above Brantingham Inlet Creek, then turns S across a smooth hilltop. After a gentle descent, at 1.7 mi it reaches a jct. at the other end of Bear Ridge Run. Ahead, the trail leads over gentle terrain to the Steam Mill Rd. trailhead at 3.1 mi. That trailhead is 0.4 mi from the end of the plowed road in winter.

Back at the jct. at 0.5 mi from Partridgeville Rd., the trail to the L (S) is the Bear Ridge Run, which curves around the pond on a long ridge. This route is very interesting, but definitely not for beginning skiers. It even has "Caution, steep hill" signs. It has significant ups and downs. Next to an open area R, the trail drops to a T jct. at 1.2 mi. The trail L is abandoned and should be avoided. Turning R, the route is gentler than the first part. It continues across an open area, then through evergreens with red hiking trail markers.

At 2.2 mi, after crossing a bridge, the trail reaches the other jct. with the Centennial Scoot. To the L (W), it is 1.5 mi to Steam Mill Rd. The route R (N) leads gently up and over a broad hill to a jct. at 3.4 mi marking the completion of a loop, before it heads back to the starting point L (N) downhill to reach Partridgeville Rd. at 3.7 mi.

❄ Trail in winter: Cross-country ski trail.

ᛟᛟ Distances: To jct. of Bear Ridge Run and Centennial Scoot, 0.5 mi; to second jct. of two routes via Centennial Scoot, 1.7 mi; to Steam Mill Rd., 3.2 mi (5.2 km). Road-to-road distance using Bear Ridge Run, 3.8 mi (6.1 km). Round trip using both trails, 7.0 mi (11.3 km).

(63) **Silvermine Trail**

Map: A2, 3

This trail from the Brantingham area allows access to the Independence River. It is mostly a gentle trail, wide and dry, with a few notable mudholes. Most of the bad spots are easily bypassed in the open hardwood forest. Trail connections near the Independence River allow through trips across the backcountry, but this requires cars at two trailheads. Access is possible by trail from Stony Lake and from Beach Mill Rd. Of these, Beach Mill Rd. has a good smooth access for automobiles. Stony Lake Rd. is decidedly rough. (See Independence River section.)

▶ Trailhead: From the crossroads in Brantingham, turn L (N) onto Partridgeville Rd. At 1.5 mi, there is a jct. Partridgeville Rd. turns L. This part of the road was formerly known as Dolgeville Rd., but is now the continuation of Partridgeville Rd. At 7.5 mi, park in the trailhead parking lot on the R, just before a bridge over Otter Creek. This is upstream of the former Dolgeville (Botchfordville), which had sawmills and tannery operations. ◀

FROM THE PARKING LOT (0.0 mi), cross the bridge on Partridgeville Rd. over Otter Creek, then turn L onto the snowmobile trail. At first the wide old road goes N, then E to bypass a section of private lands. It then turns NE through open hardwoods, until a set of beaver ponds sends the trail to higher and drier country (mostly). These uplands have more undergrowth, and some unexpected boggy spots.

The gentle higher route drops down to cross Crooked Creek at the site of the old Silvermine Dam at 3.6 mi. Crossing on a bridge, the path turns R and follows around a hill, then touches once more on a lowland beaver meadow to the R. After this, the old road heads uphill, continuing the NE trend.

At 5.2 mi, a slight footpath leads R a few paces to the foundation of an old cabin, the first sign of Balsam Flats ahead. At 5.8 mi, a dirt road leads R to private land in 100 ft. The trail turns L on this road and soon continues N, reaching a good but restricted access gravel road, which also leads R to private land. The trail crosses this road and heads diagonally L downhill.

There is an access point to the Independence River at 7.2 mi. The trail then leaves the river briefly to end at the Mt. Tom Trail (trail 3A) at 7.4 mi. Ahead, the Mt. Tom Trail crosses private land to reach a trailhead at Stony Lake. The trail is open to the public for foot, horse, and snowmobile use (no bicycles), but hikers must stay on the trail.

Turning R, the route reaches the river at 7.8 mi. There is an informal campsite on the R, about 60 ft from the East Bridge over the Independence River. The bridge is closed to snowmobilers but could be used by cautious hikers, while it's still there. It is to be removed under the Unit Management Plan for this area.

❅ Trail in winter: Snowmobile trail, lightly used. Gentle, easy going.

⚶ Distances: Partridgeville Rd. trailhead to Silvermine bridge, 3.6 mi; to gravel Balsam Flats restricted access road, 5.8 mi; to Mt. Tom Trail, 7.4 mi (11.9 km); to Independence River, 7.8 mi.

(64) **Big Otter Lake West Trail**

This trail is actually an old road, still technically open, with numerous large mudholes. It is marked and used as a snowmobile trail, but is also hiked. It is the shortest route from a trailhead to Big Otter Lake.

DEC has proposed reopening this road to automobile traffic as far as Big Otter Lake, with a parking lot at the end. Budget constraints, among other things, make this unlikely for some years to come. Reopening would allow transport of canoes, kayaks, and car-top boats to the lake. The parking lot exists, but access would be difficult even for a rugged 4WD, as there are spots where even the ATVs leave the road to go around.

Note that near the end of the lake, where trails 67 and 69 meet, there are some erroneous signs. Some overstate the distance to Steam Mill Rd., measuring to a former trailhead before the Drunkard Creek trailhead was made, and others make reference to the parking lot at the end of the lake, which is virtually impossible to reach, apparently anticipating the road improvement.

▶ Trailhead: See trail 63. ◀

BEGINNING AT THE BRIDGE by the parking lot (0.0 mi), the route goes through a small block of private land, past summer homes, and then enters state land on a rocky but easy old road. At 0.5 mi, there is a wet creek crossing, the first of several. Farther on, a 50-ft washout has left the route under water.

At 3.0 mi on the R there is a trail to a footbridge referred to as the Otter Creek Trail. It is not maintained by the state but serves as a cutover to the Pine Lake Trail (trail 67).

Continuing E, at 3.6 mi the Big Otter Lake West Trail goes straight ahead. To the R, through the "parking lot," a trail soon crosses Otter Creek on a two-section bridge no longer usable by snowmobiles and joins the blue-marked Big Otter Lake East foot trail from Thendara (trail 69). The red and snowmobile trails continue SW on the S side of Otter Creek toward Pine Lake.

From the jct. at 3.6 mi, the Big Otter Lake West Trail continues E, crossing the Lewis-Herkimer County line at a post at 3.7 mi. The route is unmarked for a ways, but older snowmobile trail markers show up eventually. The road has numerous wet spots, with wet bypasses, but the woods are open and detours are easy.

At 4.5 mi, a shallow and swampy part of Big Otter Lake comes into view. Two clearings on the trail at 4.6 and 4.7 mi are apparently the sites of an old resort hotel in use around 1900. An informal campsite in the second clearing is well located near shore with a beautiful view of the lake from a sand beach.

Continuing along the lake, the route passes a tiny sand beach, then climbs, providing nice views out over the lake. At the end of Big Otter Lake at 5.3 mi, a muddy, boggy crossing must be accomplished as best one can. On the other side, now aiming SW, the route leads past a large hemlock and a gigantic white pine to another stream crossing, probably requiring wading. A steep bank on the other side inhibits crossing upstream.

Beyond, the route enters the Ha-De-Ron-Dah Wilderness Area and ends at an elaborate unofficial campsite on a point of land at 5.4 mi (8.7 km). The setting is very nice, and the lake views are excellent. A road once continued N from here, but it is long gone, and the private land a short distance up the creek is posted.

❊ Trail in winter: Snowmobile trail to jct. with trail 67; otherwise suitable for backcountry skiing and snowshoeing. Loop trips for parties of strong skiers are possible using the Otter Creek–Pine Lake Trail (trail 65) for a return.

❧ Distances: Trailhead parking to last houses, 0.4 mi; to jct. with Otter Creek cut-off trail, 3.0 mi; to jct. with Big Otter Lake East Trail (trail 69), 3.7 mi (to Herreshoff Rd. trailhead at Thendara, 11.6 mi); to old hotel site, 4.7 mi; to E end of Big Otter Lake, 5.4 mi (8.7 km).

(65) Otter Creek–Pine Lake Trail

Map: A3

▶ Trailhead: See trail 63. The trail is marked with snowmobile trail markers. ◀

STARTING AT THE BACK of the parking lot on Partridgeville Rd. (0.0 mi), the snowmobile trail goes S up a hillside, bends R at the top, and goes W to join the old Pine Lake Rd. at 0.5 mi, where that old road leaves private land gated nearby to the R. Continuing L on the old road, the mostly dry trail heads SE along the hilltop to Hubbards Jct. at 0.9 mi. The trail R (S) is the Pico Mt. Trail, leading in 2.4 mi to the trail jct. at Spring Hill (see trail 66).

The route ahead (SE) continues over the hill and down the side of a slight ridge, with numerous mudholes and ATV tracks, and continues on to a jct. with the red-marked Pine Lake Trail (trail 67) at 2.8 mi. To the R, it is 2.4 mi to the Spring Hill jct. and 4.0 mi to the Drunkard Creek trailhead on Steam Mill Rd. To the L, it is 0.1 mi to the Pine Lake lean-to spur (the lean-to being about 200 ft N) and 2.0 mi to Big Otter Lake.

❋ Trail in winter: Snowmobile trail. Otherwise suitable for skiing and snowshoeing.

🐾 Distances: Otter Creek trailhead to Hubbards Jct. and Pico Mt. Trail (trail 66), 0.9 mi; to Pine Lake Trail (trail 67), 2.4 mi; to Pine Lake, 2.6 mi (4.2 km).

(66) Pico Mt. Trail

Map: A3

▶ Locator: This is an interior trail. The N end can be accessed from the Otter Creek–Pine Lake Trail (trail 65) 0.9 mi from Partridgeville Rd. The S end can be accessed from the Pine Lake Trail (trail 67) 1.6 mi from the Drunkard Creek trailhead at the E end of Steam Mill Rd. ◀

STARTING AT THE OTTER CREEK–PINE LAKE TRAIL JCT. at Hubbards Jct. (trail 65) (0.0 mi), the route, marked with snowmobile trail markers, follows an old road S, going gently downhill. The old road is generally wide and pleasant.

After crossing Fish Creek on a bridge at 1.0 mi, the route continues S to 1.1 mi, then turns nearly E and begins to climb a gentle slope. After reaching a broad ridge, the route turns S again and finishes the climb. Near the top at 2.1 mi, the trail crosses to the SE side of the hill (unofficially named Pico Mt.) and starts angling down. The bottom is only a short distance down, with a small, easy creek crossing, and the trail starts up again on a wet slope.

In a short distance, the trail ends at a jct. on Spring Hill at 2.4 mi. Ahead, up the hillside on trail 68, it is 1.2 mi to Pine Creek near The Mudhole. To the L on the Pine Lake Trail (trail 67) it is 2.5 mi to the Pine Lake Lean-to. To the R on the Pine Lake Trail it is 1.6 mi to the Drunkard Creek trailhead.

❋ Trail in winter: Snowmobile trail. Otherwise suitable for skiing and snowshoeing.

❧ Distances: Hubbards Jct. on Otter Creek–Pine Lake Trail to Fish Creek bridge, 1.0 mi; to jct. at Spring Hill, 2.4 mi (3.9 km).

(67) **Pine Lake Trail**

Map: A3, 4

This trail, part of which is a snowmobile trail, extends from Steam Mill Rd. at Drunkard Creek trailhead to Big Otter Lake, passing Pine Lake on the way. Several connecting trails along the path allow for many varied routes. Pine Lake camping is at a lean-to constructed in 2004, slightly W of the site of the lean-to destroyed in early 2000.

▶ Trailhead: From the jct. with Partridgeville Rd. in Brantingham, go E on Brantingham Rd., continuing straight ahead past the golf course. In 0.9 mi, where the pavement turns L, continue ahead on a gravel road (Steam Mill Rd.). The road crosses Poison Creek at 3.1 mi, the approximate site of the old steam-driven lumber mill. At 5.4 mi, by Drunkard Creek, the road ends at a barricade and parking lot. The trail is marked with DEC red and snowmobile markers. ◀

STARTING AT THE DRUNKARD CREEK PARKING LOT (0.0 mi), the old road crosses the creek, bends R, and climbs gently to a trail register at 0.1 mi. Bending L, the old road curves to the NE under open canopy and climbs gently, crossing several bridges, reaching the four-way jct. on Spring Hill at 1.6 mi. To the L (N), the Pico Mt. Trail (trail 66) goes over a shoulder of Pico Mt. toward Hubbards Jct. and Otter Creek. To the R (S), Mudhole Trail (trail 68) goes toward The Mudhole. The snowmobile trail turns L onto the Pico Mt. Trail.

Continuing ahead (NE) on a foot trail, the route curves over a slight hill and descends to the outlet creek of Eight-Foot Swamp at 2.6 mi. The bank is steep. On the E side, the trail goes steeply up to the top of an S-shaped esker and passes along nearly its entire length, about 0.2 mi. The steep-sided esker seems just like a man-made earth dam. At its E end, the trail turns down the side and continues through heavy undergrowth on a ridge above Pine Creek.

At 2.8 mi, the trail overlooks a beaver dam, R, apparently the end of Pine Lake, which extends NE for nearly 1.25 mi. At 3.8 mi, a couple of walkways assist in crossing a wet area, although hikers may have to wade to get to them as the water covers the steps up to the walkways. At 3.9 mi, there is a side trail R to an overlook, and an opening through brush that drops to a picnic spot next to the lake.

At 4.0 mi, the route joins the old Pine Lake Rd. To the L (NW), the road forms the route of the yellow-marked Otter Creek–Pine Lake Trail (trail 65). Turning R (E), the red Pine Lake Trail continues on the old road and at 4.1 mi passes a spur trail which leads N about 200 ft to a relatively new lean-to, slightly W of the location of the former lean-to. At a jct. at 4.3 mi, the blue-marked trail R (S) is the Lost Lake Trail (trail 70). At about 4.5 mi, there is a fine view of East Pine Pond to the S.

The trail continues NE, then curves around a hill, heading N. Where the trail turns R (E) at 5.7 mi, an unmarked connecting trail continues N on an old road. This is the Otter Creek Trail, leading in a short distance to Otter Creek and then to a jct. with the Big Otter Lake West Trail (trail 64). This is a shortcut route for continuing W toward the trailhead on Partridgeville Rd. The footbridge is not maintained by the state.

The Pine Lake Trail continues E on the old road to a jct with the blue-marked Big Otter Lake East Trail (trail 69) at 6.0 mi. That trail goes E through the Ha-De-Ron-Dah Wilderness Area to the Herreshoff Rd. trailhead at Thendara. To the L (N), the Pine Lake Trail continues over a two-section bridge, blocked to snowmobilers, over Otter Creek just W of Big Otter Lake. It joins the Big Otter Lake West Trail (trail 64) at 6.1 mi. To the L, that trail leads W to a trailhead on Partridgeville Rd. To the R, the trail leads to campsites on Big Otter Lake.

✽ Trail in winter: Suitable for backcountry skiing or snowshoeing, but Steam Mill Rd. is not plowed in winter, adding about 4.5 mi to the distance. The unplowed road and the trail as far as Spring Hill are also used by snowmobiles. The section from Spring Hill to Pine Lake is rougher, with a few short, steep banks at Eight-Foot Swamp outlet.

🐾 Distances: Drunkard Creek trailhead to Spring Hill jct., 1.6 mi; to Pine Lake, 3.3 mi; to Otter Creek–Pine Lake Trail (trail 65), 4.1 mi; to Lost Lake Trail (trail 70), 4.3 mi; to Otter Creek Cutover Trail, 5.7 mi; to Big Otter Lake East Trail (trail 69), 6.0 mi; to Big Otter Lake West Trail (trail 64), 6.1 mi (8.5 km); to campsite on N side of Big Otter Lake, 7.1 mi (10.9 km).

(68) Mudhole Trail

Map: A4

▶ Locator: This is an interior trail which heads S from the jct. of trails 66 and 67. ◀

FROM THE JCT. AT SPRING HILL (0.0 mi), the trail goes S gently over a hill, rising about 60 ft and then descending about 100 ft to reach Pine Creek. The short spur trail to The Mudhole leads through grass and bushes to a swampy crossing of a small creek 1 ft wide. Just beyond is a boat launching site on Pine Creek, which is deep, slow, and wide in this area. There is a large boulder at the water's edge just beyond, from which a better view can be had.

An extensive open wetland, The Mudhole, can be seen on the N and NE. Mudhole Pond is out of sight beyond the trees to the NE, and would not be easy to reach without a boat.

❄ Trail in winter: Former snowmobile trail.

🐾 Distances: Spring Hill jct. to Pine Creek near The Mudhole, 1.2 mi (1.9 km). ◆

Wood sorrel in the West-Central Region. RICHARD NOWICKI

Old Forge–Thendara Section

The village of Old Forge, the largest in the West-Central Region, fronts on Forge Pond at the foot of the Fulton Chain of Lakes. Although the iron mining in this area never got very far, a romantic image of the old iron forge persists. In the center of town, a triphammer wheel from the "old forge" is still on display. This would have been powered by a water wheel to lift and drop a large forging hammer that repeatedly smashed red-hot but brittle cast iron until it was mixed well enough to be a low-grade workable steel.

The smaller hamlet of Thendara is adjacent to Old Forge on the SW, both communities being in the Town of Webb (honoring Dr. William Seward Webb, builder of the nearby RR and owner at one time of much land in the area). Thendara was actually the first community in the region, but Old Forge was at the head of lake navigation and soon became the center of activity.

The main hiking trail network in the area lies W and SW of the two communities in the Ha-De-Ron-Dah Wilderness Area on the NW side of NY 28. (Bicycles are not allowed in wilderness areas.) *Ha-De-Ron-Dah* is an attempt at a more accurate phonetic spelling of the native pronunciation of "Adirondack." On the S and SW there is a trail system around Nicks Lake extending to Remsen Falls and Nelson Lake in the Black River Wild Forest. These trails include long circuit routes that lend themselves to backpacking. Leading to remote ponds and lakes, they do not have long climbs or reach viewpoints over the surrounding terrain. Moderate grades prevail. This section is one of relatively low hills, and there are considerable open spaces, the result of forest fires around the turn of the twentieth century.

For a view of the lower lakes of the Fulton Chain (First through Fourth lakes), one may walk up the ski slopes of McCauley Mt. just SE of Old Forge, or take the chairlift, which operates in summer and early fall in addition to the ski season. It is a 500 ft ascent to the 2320 ft summit. The ascent of Bald (Rondaxe) Mt. (trail 31) just N of Old Forge gives a similarly good view of the lakes. See the Big Moose Section for this trail.

Short Hikes:

◆ Lock and Dam—2.0 mi (3.2 km) round trip (or 3.0 mi round trip from RR station at Thendara). Easy walking on an old woods road with only one brief hill, providing views of the Middle Branch of the Moose River along the start and at the end.

◆ Humphery Hill, Lock and Dam Loop—3.8 mi (6.1 km) round trip from Bisby Rd. including side trip to lock and dam, or 2.6 mi (4.2 km) loop from Green Bridge Rd. parking lot (total 3.6 mi from RR station at Thendara). Bicycles permitted. See trail 79A.

Moderate Hikes:

◆ Nicks Lake Circuit—4.7 mi (7.6 km) round trip. Beautiful evergreens, one-mile-long woods lake. A day-use fee is charged at the trailhead campground (free access with 2.0-mi round trip addition from trail 78). See trail 79.

◆ Middle Settlement Lake via Scusa Trail—6.4 mi (10.3 km) round trip. Generally easy going to a beautiful clean lake in a wilderness setting with lean-to. See trails 77, 76, 75, and 73.

◆ Middle Branch Lake from Thendara RR station—13.4 mi (21.6 km) loop. Nice two-day backpack with a stay at a scenic lake via Browns Tract, Cedar Pond, Middle Branch, Big Otter E. trails, and NY 28 and Herreshoff Rd. See trails 76, 74, 72, and 69.

Harder Hikes:

◆ Big Otter and Pine Lakes Loop—24.9 mi (40.1 km) round trip. Small pieces of several trails and two lean-tos make a good loop trip for two or three days. Start at Herreshoff Rd. trailhead, go to East Pond, Big Otter Lake, Pine Lake, Lost Lake, Middle Settlement Lake, Middle Branch Lake, and return by the Big Otter Lake East Trail. See trails 69, 71, 67, 70, 73, and 72.

◆ Remsen Falls, Nelson Lake, Jones Mt. Loops—18.1 mi round trip. Smooth trail (snowmobile trails in winter). Overnight at lean-to by Remsen Falls on the Moose River. See trails 78, 78A, 78B, and 79.

TRAIL DESCRIBED	TOTAL MILES *(one way)*	PAGE
Big Otter Lake East Trail	7.9 (12.7 km)	156
Lost Lake Trail	4.0 (6.5 km)	158
East Pond–Lost Creek Trail	6.7 (10.8 km)	159
Middle Branch Lake Trail	1.7 (2.7 km)	162
Middle Settlement Lake Trail	5.0 (8.1 km)	164
Cedar Pond Trail	2.2 (3.5 km)	166
Middle Settlement Lake Access Trail	1.2 (1.9 km)	167
Browns Tract Trail	7.5 (12.1 km)	168
JBT Gull Lake Trail	0.5 (0.8 km)	170
Scusa Access Trail	0.6 (1.0 km)	171
Remsen Falls, Nelson Lake, Jones Mt. Loops	Various	171
Remsen Falls	12.9 (20.8 km)	172
Nelson Lake Trail	6.9 (11.1 km)	173
Jones Mt. Trail	3.9 (6.3 km)	174
Nicks Lake Circuit	4.7 (7.6 km)	175
Humphery Hill, Lock and Dam Loop	4.0 (6.5 km)	177
Humphery Hill–Nicks Lake Connector	0.3 (0.5 km)	179

PRINCIPAL DESTINATIONS	MILES	TRAILS USED
Distances from trailhead using most convenient trails		
East Pond	4.4 (7.1 km)	69-71
Middle Settlement Lake	3.2 (5.2 km)	77-76-75
Remsen Falls	6.9 (11.2 km)	78

Take note that the distances given are not always from a trailhead, but indicate length of the trail named. Most of these trails connect points in the interior.

(69) **Big Otter Lake East Trail**

Map: A, B3

This is a truck trail built by the Civilian Conservation Corps in the 1930s. In addition to being a hiking trail, it is a DEC-designated ski touring trail. It extends from the trailhead N of the hamlet of Thendara W to the SW end of Big Otter Lake, the last 0.4 mi of the route being a footpath. The trail is broad, with a good number of moderate ascents and descents, and it goes through a second-growth hardwood forest. It is generally easy walking.

The East Pond–Lost Creek Trail (trail 71), the Middle Branch Lake Trail (trail 72), and the Pine Lake Trail (trail 67) all start or end at the Big Otter Lake East Trail; these four trails lend themselves especially to circuit hikes.

▶ Trailhead: Heading N on NY 28, upon rounding the bend at the RR station at Thendara, turn L (N) on the dirt Herreshoff Rd. (formerly Tower Rd.) before going under the RR underpass. If southbound, from the Old Forge Tourist Information Center, drive SW on NY 28 for 2.0 mi; just after the RR underpass in Thendara turn R onto Herreshoff Rd. Drive N 0.4 mi on the unpaved road and park by the gate at its end. This is also a designated horse trail on the woods road portion. ◀

FROM THE GATE (0.0 mi), the blue-marked trail starts N but in 70 yd leaves the snowmobile/bicycle trail and turns L(W) on a broad, smooth woods road in a second- or third-growth forest. At 0.4 mi a barrier marks the beginning of the Ha-De-Ron-Dah Wilderness Area, where bicycles are prohibited. A 300 yd traverse of an open wetland of Indian Brook begins at 1.0 mi, with part of an esker (stratified sediments deposited by the melting continental ice sheet) on the R looking like an elongated pile of fill.

The yellow-marked East Pond–Lost Creek Trail (trail 71) goes R at 1.5 mi. From a clearing at height of land at about 2.2 mi—apparently a former truck turnaround—the recently reopened red-marked Moose River Mt. Trail angles L. (This trail makes a gradual but steady climb of about 300 ft, bending R shortly before the end at 0.6 mi at the site of a fire tower removed in 1977. Views are limited. The trail allows a ski glide all the way to the East Pond–Lost Creek Trail, trail 71. The mountain is sometimes referred to as Petes Mt. in honor of long-time fire observer Pete Walters, even though he was there in the 20s and 30s.)

At 4.9 mi, the yellow-marked Middle Branch Lake Trail (trail 72) goes L (S). At 6.0 mi, the trail enters an extensive open area, including a wetland fringed by tamarack and spruce that flows N into the South Inlet to Big Otter Lake. The route is flooded for approximately 200 yd because of beaver damming. Wading on the firm road surface through shallow water may be a better option than searching for grass clumps along the edge, which is likely to prove unsuccessful at keeping dry anyway.

At 6.6 mi the red-marked East Pond–Lost Creek Trail (trail 71) comes in from the R (NE). Beyond this jct. the woods road narrows somewhat. In approx 175 yd it passes by the wetland of the Big Otter Lake inlet on the R with a large boulder beside the trail.

The woods road (truck trail) ends at 7.5 mi; a little before this a woods road goes R for a short distance to the edge of the narrow W section of Big Otter Lake. From here a distant view may be had of the broader part of the lake to the NE.

The Big Otter Lake East Trail continues ahead as a blue-marked footpath. At 7.9 mi, the footpath ends at a woods road on the boundary of the wilderness area. This is the Pine Lake Trail (trail 67), marked red for hikers and snowmobilers. To the L, it goes to Pine Lake and beyond. Going R for 50 yd, one reaches a two-section bridge over the beginning of Otter Creek, the outlet of Big Otter Lake, which flows W to the Black River. The bridge is closed to snowmobilers but can be used by hikers. Here are the remains of a dam once used for log drives down Otter Creek. The narrow, boggy W end of Big Otter Lake is on the R.

The red markers continue beyond the bridge a very short way, ending at 8.0 mi from the beginning of the Big Otter Lake East Trail. This point is a jct. with the Big Otter Lake West Trail (trail 64). The snowmobile markers continue to this jeep road and then go L on it toward Partridgeville Rd. To the R the Big Otter Lake West Trail goes NE along the W side of Big Otter Lake to some fine camping sites.

⁂ Trail in winter: Easy snowshoeing or backcountry skiing. Listed by the DEC as suitable for skiing. A switch-key ski or hike—where two groups start from opposite ends and exchange vehicle keys midway, driving to a pre-arranged meeting point afterwards to swap back vehicles—is possible from Herreshoff Rd. to Partridgeville Rd. (trail 64), although the trailheads are far apart.

Distances: Herreshoff Rd. trailhead to East Pond Trail jct., 1.5 mi; to Moose River Mt. Trail, 2.2 mi; to Middle Branch Lake Trail jct., 4.9

mi; to Middle Branch Lake lean-to, 5.9 mi; to Lost Creek Trail jct., 6.6 mi; to Pine Lake Trail and Otter Creek, 7.9 mi (12.7 km). Continuations: to Big Otter Lake West Trail (trail 64), 8.0 mi (12.9 km); to Big Otter Lake campsite on trail 64, 9.0 mi; to Pine Lake lean-to via Pine Lake Trail (trail 67), 9.8 mi (15.8 km).

(70) Lost Lake Trail

Map: A3, 4

This trail goes from Pine Lake and East Pine Pond SE to Lost Lake and then E to the SW end of Middle Settlement Lake. It connects the Pine Lake Trail (trail 67) with the Middle Settlement Lake Trail (trail 73). It is a narrow trail, with much encroachment. In some years, Lost Lake may not be much more than a boggy pond, but when the beavers are active, the pond is especially scenic. The trail also goes through wetlands of some interest. The route is described from the Pine Lake end, assuming a circuit hike is being made from that direction. The Pine Lake Trail is described in the Brantingham Section, and can also be reached from the Big Otter Lake East Trail (trail 69).

▶ Locator: This trail is deep in the interior. It runs from near Pine Lake on the Pine Lake Trail (trail 67), 3.1 mi (5.0 km) from Partridgeville Rd. via the Otter Creek–Pine Lake Trail (trail 65), and ends at a jct. with the Middle Settlement Lake Trail (trail 73) 0.6 mi W of the lean-to and 3.8 mi (6.1 km) from NY 28 via the Scusa Access Trail. ◀

STARTING AT THE RED-MARKED PINE LAKE TRAIL at the NE corner of Pine Lake (0.0 mi), the blue-marked Lost Lake Trail goes S between Pine Lake and East Pine Pond, with good views of East Pine and some views of Pine. At 0.4 mi it enters an open area in which there are expanses of wetland, open water, and stands of balsam fir and tamarack trees.

The outlet of East Pine Pond flows under a long boardwalk bridge, then the trail goes over a ridge and through a wet area. At 0.7 mi, the trail enters a young forest; fields of ferns stretch for as far as one can see, a sight to behold. They do try to cover the trail but it is well marked.

The trail enters a second open area at 1.2 mi, encompassing Middle Branch Creek and its wetland. After a small footbridge over a tributary, a long bridge crosses the creek at 1.4 mi. At the end of this bridge the trail climbs a short steep pitch and continues to a section where it disappears in marshy growth heading across a gully.

The trail reenters the forest and starts passing through some tall timber. There are a number of ups and downs as an outlet of Lost Lake is crossed, and the N end of that lake is reached at 2.5 mi, with a view of the boggy shoreline and dead standing timber. Beavers have dammed the adjacent outlet. The trail passes along part of the pond for approximately 0.3 mi, with a view of steep bedrock banks on its far side.

For the rest of the route the trail is rougher. The Lewis and Herkimer county boundary lines cross, marked by a sign. Near the trail's end, rugged rock outcroppings and boulders lend interest to the scene. At the jct. with the yellow-marked Middle Settlement Lake Trail (trail 73) at 4.0 mi, impressive cliffs stand on the L. Going L (NE) on the yellow trail, it is 0.6 mi to the lean-to on Middle Settlement Lake and 3.8 mi to NY 28 via trails 75, 76, and 77. Going R on the yellow-marked trail 73, it is 1.7 mi S to the Browns Tract Trail (trail 76), and another 2.2 mi to NY 28 via the W end of trail 76.

❈ Trail in Winter: Suitable for snowshoers and possibly expert skiers, but interior trail not recommended for day trips.

🐾 Distances: Pine Lake to Lost Lake, 2.5 mi; to Middle Settlement Lake Trail (trail 73), 4.0 mi (6.5 km).

(71) East Pond–Lost Creek Trail

Map: B3

This loop provides access to the N portion of the Ha-De-Ron-Dah Wilderness Area from the Big Otter Lake East Trail (trail 69). The area has had signs stating that it was on limited maintenance to provide a wilderness experience. The trail extends from mile 1.5 on the Big Otter Lake East Trail NNW past Little Simon Pond and East Pond. (A round-trip hike to East Pond from the Herreshoff Rd. trailhead of the Big Otter Lake East Trail would be 8.8 mi.) Near East Pond, a red side trail goes NE to Blackfoot Pond and the remnants of a mica mine. The trail continues W past East Pond to Lost Creek, then turns SW to rejoin the Big Otter Lake East Trail S of Big Otter Lake. The trail goes through wetlands, and parts of it, especially the last half mile before the Big Otter Lake inlet, are overgrown or muddy.

▶ Locator: The trail is a loop N of Big Otter Lake East Trail (trail 69), starting on the R (N) 1.5 mi from the Herreshoff Rd. trailhead, with the other end also on the Big Otter East Trail (69), 6.6 mi from Herreshoff Rd. trailhead. ◀

THE TRAIL TURNS **R** (N) at 1.5 mi on the Big Otter Lake East Trail (0.0 mi). At 0.3 mi, the East Pond Trail uses the remains of a half-log walkway to cross an open, brushy, and grassy area, which includes a branch of South Inlet Creek and its wetland. Here the trail is especially overgrown, sometimes nearly obscuring what's left of the walkway.

At 0.7 mi, the route crosses another branch of South Inlet Creek on a sturdy split-log bridge. At 1.1 mi, the trail turns L (NW) and passes fields of ferns and stands of spruce, which give some variety to the forest. At 1.6 mi the trail traverses another extensive open area of herbaceous and scrubby growth lined by tamarack and spruce, then crosses a stream several yards downstream from a beaver dam, turning L and down along the stream.

Just before 2.0 mi, the trail reaches some of the massive blowdown around Simon Ponds, then crosses the outlet of Little Simon Pond which curves out of sight to the NE.

The pond here is shallow, with water lilies and a wetland fringe.

After the trail crosses the outlet it continues by the W side of Little Simon Pond, with a further view of part of it. After crossing an inlet, the route provides a glimpse of Simon Pond L and climbs more than 150 ft through tall hardwoods, including some large yellow birches, only to descend through more stately growth to a trail jct. at 2.6 mi overlooking an inlet to East Pond. Here the trail goes L (W) toward Lost Creek.

EAST POND SPUR

To reach East Pond, a spur trail continues ahead 0.3 mi N and NW, ending at 2.9 mi, or 4.4 mi from the Thendara trailhead. Less than 0.1 mi before the end, a red-marked trail goes R (NE) to Blackfoot Pond (see description below). The East Pond side trail passes an informal campsite on the R before reaching the site of a former lean-to. This site has a blowdown and is partly grown in and thus no longer suitable as a campsite, even if it weren't so close to the water. A trail leads a few yards to the pond itself with a rock step into the water; the shoreline has a good deal of dead standing timber but is graced with occasional towering white pines and red spruce.

BLACKFOOT POND SPUR

From the jct. near East Pond, the red-marked Blackfoot Pond Trail heads NE to Blackfoot Pond and the remains of a mica mine W of the pond, a round-trip distance of 2.0 mi. The first part of the trail is in tall hardwoods. At 0.7 mi, the path reaches the SW end of the W segment of Blackfoot Pond, fringed by a wetland (easy to miss). The only view of the pond from the red-marked trail is from here. The pond appears on the map as two ponds, but is more like one C-shaped pond. The trail continues on the W side of the pond but at some distance from it, and is encumbered in places by mud and partly obscured by ferns. It ends at 1.0 mi, where a clearing (an old cabin site) has been filled with criss-crossed blowdowns, with the unimpressive remnants of a mica mine on the L about a hundred yards before the end.

The mine is more accurately described as a prospecting hole. Mica was used for windows in wood- and coal-burning stoves, but the sheets must be large to be useful. No doubt, this "mine," like many others, proved to have so few large sheets that it wasn't worth the trouble to get them out.

At the jct. with the East Pond and Blackfoot Pond spurs at 2.6 mi, the main trail turns W with blue markers. At 3.2 mi the wide outlet of East Pond and its wetland appear R. At 4.7 mi, the blue-marked section of trail ends at the red-marked section near Lost Creek. To the R is the Lost Creek spur trail (not to be confused with the Lost Lake Trail, trail 70).

LOST CREEK SPUR

From the jct., the red-marked Lost Creek spur trail heads NE. In 50 yd it crosses the East Pond outlet and climbs a steep bank. It goes N on an old road to Lost Creek. Blowdowns are encountered along the way. At 0.5 mi, the red markers end at Lost Creek on the L. This is an attractive, broad stream on bedrock with tea- or copper-colored water. This phenomenon occurs in certain other streams and ponds of the region and is caused principally by tannic acid leached from conifer needles.

RESUMPTION OF MAIN TRAIL

From the jct. at 4.7 mi, the East Pond–Lost Creek Trail goes L (SW) with red markers past majestic sugar maple and yellow birch with occasional tall spruce and hemlock. At 5.8 mi, Big Otter Lake comes into view through the trees to the R. This is the only view of the lake from this trail.

The last part of the trail is dense as it leads through a semi-wetland fern-spruce environment. At 6.6 mi the route reaches the broad South Inlet of Big Otter Lake with metal sticking up from a rock in the middle, apparently from a former bridge. The trail goes upstream L along the bank for 100 yd to cross the inlet on a bridge. At 6.7 mi, the trail ends at a jct. with the blue-marked Big Otter Lake East Trail (trail 69). To the R (NW) it is 1.3 mi to the W end of Big Otter Lake and 1.2 mi to the edge of the Ha-De-Ron-Dah Wilderness Area at Otter Creek. To the L (SE) it is 6.6 mi to the Herreshoff Rd. (Thendara) trailhead (14.8 mi round trip from parking lot).

❄ Trail in winter: Suitable for snowshoers and possibly expert skiers, but interior trail not recommended for day trips.

🚶 Distances: Big Otter Lake East Trail jct. to Little Simon Pond, 2.0 mi; to East Pond/Blackfoot Pond spur, 2.6 mi (to East Pond, 2.9 mi; to old mica mine and Blackfoot Pond, 3.8 mi); to Lost Creek spur, 4.7 mi; to second jct. with Big Otter Lake East Trail, 6.7 mi (10.8 km).

(72) Middle Branch Lake Trail

Map: A, B3

This trail goes from the end of the red-marked Cedar Pond Trail (trail 74), roughly N to the Big Otter Lake East Trail (trail 69). It passes E of Middle Branch Lake, with a red-marked side trail to the lake.

▶ Locator: S end at Cedar Pond clearing, 3.1 mi from NY 28, using the Scusa Access Trail (trail 77), Browns Tract Trail (trail 76), and Cedar Pond Trail (trail 74); N end at the Big Otter Lake East Trail (trail 69) 4.9 mi W of the Herreshoff Rd. trailhead. The trail is described from S to N. ◀

FROM THE TRAIL JCT. at a boulder beside a clearing at the end of the Cedar Pond Trail (trail 74), this is one of two yellow-marked trails. The other (L) is the Middle Settlement Lake Trail (trail 73). Taking the R (E) fork (0.0 mi), the Middle Branch Lake Trail heads N. There is an ascent of more than 100 ft over a ridge with a corresponding descent on the other side, followed by the more gradual crossing of a wider ridge, passing rock outcroppings before 0.6 mi.

Another brief rise precedes a drop to a jct. at 1.0 mi. Here, a red-marked spur trail goes L (W), down a gully and then up along a ridge

Middle Branch Lake in the Ha-De-Ron-Dah Wilderness. JAMES APPLEYARD

for 0.3 mi, passing a glacial boulder, and ending at a lean-to on a point of land on the E side of Middle Branch Lake. This is a nice location at the edge of an attractive lake with several rocky access points for swimming. The main trail continues on through moderate terrain to the Big Otter Lake East Trail (69) at 1.7 mi.

The most direct access to Middle Branch Lake is Scusa Access Trail (77) from NY 28, 0.6 mi; R on Browns Tract Trail (76), 0.2 mi; L on Cedar Pond Trail (74), 2.2 mi; R on Middle Branch Lake Trail (72), 1.0 mi; L on red spur trail, 0.3 mi. Total distance: 4.3 mi.

❅ Trail in winter: Suitable for snowshoers and expert skiers.

🐾 Distances: Cedar Pond clearing to lean-to spur trail, 1.0 mi (to lean-to on Middle Branch Lake, 1.3 mi); to Big Otter Lake East Trail (trail 69), 1.7 mi (2.7 km).

(73) Middle Settlement Lake Trail

Map: A4, B3

This trail meets the Middle Branch Lake Trail (trail 72) and the Cedar Pond Trail (trail 74) at a clearing and boulder. From that jct. it goes L (SW) to Middle Settlement Lake and then S to the Browns Tract Trail (trail 76). It passes a field of giant boulders, has a short side trail to a cliff top, and goes by the most prized campsite of the Ha-De-Ron-Dah Wilderness Area, a beautifully located lean-to on Middle Settlement Lake.

Two blue-marked trails connect in the middle of this yellow trail, the Middle Settlement Lake Access Trail on the SE and the Lost Lake Trail on the W (trails 75 and 70). The yellow and blue trails are best used as parts of circuit hikes. For easiest access to Middle Settlement Lake, see the Middle Settlement Lake Access Trail (trail 75).

▶ Locator: E end at Cedar Pond clearing, 3.1 mi from NY 28 using the Scusa Access Trail (77), Browns Tract Trail (76), and Cedar Pond Trail (74), or 6.6 mi from Herreshoff Rd. using the Big Otter Lake East Trail (69) and Middle Branch Lake Trail (72). W end on Browns Tract Trail (76) 2.2 mi from NY 28 at its W end. The trail is described from E to W. ◀

BEHIND A BOULDER at the N edge of the Cedar Pond clearing, the Middle Settlement Lake Trail is the L of two yellow-marked trails (0.0 mi). It goes WSW, paralleling a wetland and the outlet of Cedar Pond, which it crosses as a wide brook at 0.5 mi, either by wading or on downed trees. The trail crosses a small swamp before starting uphill on dry ground at 0.8 mi. At 1.0 mi, over the hill, a giant boulder sits on the L, broken off from the high cliff on the R.

The blue-blazed Middle Settlement Lake Access Trail (trail 75) comes in from the Browns Tract Trail (76) on the L (SE) at 1.1 mi. The trail then passes great boulders, some stacked to make a room-sized shelter. Some yards after the R turn, the trail crosses an inlet to the lake and skirts a wetland at the NE end of Middle Settlement Lake, then passes along the lake itself.

[Just after the trail rounds the corner where the inlet enters the lake, about 75 yd from the jct., a somewhat obscure red-marked side trail goes R (where most visitors are enjoying the view of the lake L). This side trail, called the Vista Trail, climbs NE about 150 ft to the top of a cliff with a view of the nearby hills, and a partially blocked view of the lake. The round trip from the yellow trail is 0.4 mi.]

The yellow trail follows the shore of Middle Settlement Lake and reaches the lean-to on the W side at 1.6 mi. This is a delightful location on a clean-cut rocky section of shoreline, an inviting spot to swim. (While there are few conifers lining the lake, there are loons that add to its pristine character.) The lean-to, behind which stands a large boulder, is in good condition. The only water supply is the lake, which is held in place by beaver dams.

Beyond the lean-to, the trail passes two marked informal campsites, then descends to cross the lake's outlet at 1.8 mi either on one of the beaver dams or following flagging a little downstream to cross on rocks. The trail continues past what could be termed the "back bay" L, the SW end of Middle Settlement Lake. After going along the top of a hill, the trail drops down along an inlet and is muddy for a short stretch.

At 2.2 mi, near impressive cliffs on the R, the route reaches a jct. with the blue-marked Lost Lake Trail (70). The Middle Settlement Lake Trail (signs may refer to this section as the Stony Creek Trail) continues L, curving around the S end of a beaver pond, and follows the shore NE, turns R, and ascends through stately hardwoods. After crossing the ridge summit, the route curves R (SW), descends gradually along the hillside, then starts downhill.

At 3.3 mi, the trail reaches a branch of Stony Creek and turns L to cross it. Continuing on the other side, the Middle Settlement Lake Trail joins the Browns Tract Trail (trail 76) at 5.0 mi. The route R (S) on the Browns Tract Trail continues to Copper Lake Rd., a private road on public land, which leads on both ends to private land. A state trail goes down the road, however, into John Hancock Timber Group woods to a trailhead near NY 28 in another 2.3 mi. To the L (NE), the Browns Tract Trail leads 3.5 mi to NY 28 via the Scusa Access Trail (trail 77).

❀ Trail in winter: Suitable for backcountry skiing or snowshoeing.

ﾊ Distances: Cedar Pond jct. to Middle Settlement Lake Access Trail, 1.1 mi; to Middle Settlement Lake lean-to via spur, 1.6 mi; to Lost Lake Trail (trail 70), 2.2 mi; to Stony Creek branch, 3.3 mi; to Browns Tract Trail (trail 76), 5.0 mi (8.1 km).

(74) Cedar Pond Trail

Map: B4

This trail goes from the Browns Tract Trail (trail 76) NW to the Cedar Pond clearing (a former lean-to site). It does not visit a pond, but it has a spur trail to Grass Pond and ends at a jct. with the trails to Middle Branch Lake and Middle Settlement Lake (trails 72 and 73). It is best hiked as part of a circuit route. The trail crosses many brooks, most of these easily.

▶ Locator: S end on Browns Tract Trail 0.2 mi E of the Scusa Access Trail (trail 77) and 1.3 mi W of the Okara Lakes trailhead. N end in a clearing at the jct. of two yellow-marked trails, Middle Settlement Lake (trail 73, L) and Middle Branch Lake (trail 72, R). ◀

THE RED-MARKED TRAIL HEADS NW from the Browns Tract Trail (0.0 mi), first up but then bending briefly L and then R. It skirts a small hill, continuing to a trail jct. at 0.4 mi. (The yellow-marked spur R, N, goes 0.5 mi to Grass Pond. It gradually descends to an informal campsite in the woods at a trail sign and then R through wetland to a point near the pond's outlet with a measuring stick in view beyond the beaver dam. Shallow water, mud flats, and water lilies can be found.)

From the Grass Pond spur jct., the main trail continues NW, and at 0.9 mi crosses Grass Pond outlet stream, follows a contour, and then descends. At about 1.5 mi the waters of bog-fringed Cedar Pond show through the trees on the L. The trail reaches a clearing at 2.2 mi, ending at a jct. with two yellow-marked trails. The Middle Branch Lake Trail (trail 72) goes R (roughly N) and reaches that lake and lean-to via a side trail in 1.25 mi. The similarly marked Middle Settlement Lake Trail (trail 73) behind the boulder goes L (SW) and reaches that lake's lean-to in 1.6 mi.

❋ Trail in winter: Suitable for backcountry skiing or snowshoeing.

⚶ Distances: Browns Tract Trail to spur to Grass Pond, 0.4 mi (to Grass Pond, 0.9 mi); to Grass Pond outlet, 0.9 mi; to Cedar Pond clearing, 2.2 mi (3.5 km).

(75) Middle Settlement Lake Access Trail

Map: B4

This connecting trail goes NW from the Browns Tract Trail (trail 76) to the Middle Settlement Lake Trail (trail 73) at a point just NE of that lake. The lake and lean-to are among the nicest places to stay in the Ha-De-Ron-Dah Wilderness.

▶ Locator: S end on the Browns Tract Trail (trail 76), 0.9 mi W of the jct. with the Scusa Access Trail (trail 77) from NY 28. N end at the W end of Middle Settlement Lake at a jct. with the Middle Settlement Lake Trail (trail 73). The trail is described from S to N. ◀

FROM BROWNS TRACT TRAIL (0.0 mi), the blue-marked trail heads N. At 0.2 mi it crosses a small stream and at 0.4 mi a larger creek on rocks. There is an open wetland on the R. This is a creek that flows E through the wetlands and then into Grass Pond Outlet. There follows a gradual ascent of 160 ft (steep for skiers) and a steeper descent of about the same vertical distance to the trail's end at the yellow-marked Middle Settlement Lake Trail (trail 73).

This connecting trail provides the shortest access to the Middle Settlement Lake lean-to. Starting from NY 28, one goes 0.6 mi on the Scusa Access Trail (trail 77), then L on the Browns Tract Trail (trail 76) for 0.9 mi, R on the Middle Settlement Lake Access Trail (blue) for 1.2 mi, and finally L on the Middle Settlement Lake Trail (trail 73) for 0.5 mi to the lean-to, for a total distance of 3.2 mi.

❋ Trail in winter: Suitable for backcountry skiing or snowshoeing. Listed by DEC as an intermediate-level ski trail.

⚶ Distances: Browns Tract Trail to Middle Settlement Lake Trail, 1.2 mi (1.9 km).

(76) **Browns Tract Trail**

Map: B4

This trail roughly parallels NY 28 from Thendara SW to Copper Lake Rd., mostly following the route of the old Browns Tract Rd. established in 1811 (see Introduction). Most of the way it's broad and easy hiking, although in some places where the trail is notched into hillsides with both sides higher it tends to be wet, and going around Okara Lakes it's a footpath where the old road is on private property. The trail visits no lakes or ponds, but connects with three trails that lead into the Ha-De-Ron-Dah Wilderness Area. The trail is used primarily in sections for loop trips and for access from Thendara to the other trails. There is no convenient parking at the Thendara trailhead, which is 0.7 mi from the RR station.

▶ Trailheads: There are three trailheads that give direct access to this trail, as well as the Scusa Access Trail (trail 77).

To reach the Thendara trailhead, permission to park at the Thendara RR station might be granted. If so, walk 0.4 mi SW on NY 28 from the station (the S shoulder is wider), then turn R on Quarry Ave. and just yards later L (W) on Browns Tract Rd. At 0.2 mi from NY 28 the road becomes unpaved, and in another 0.2 mi it simply becomes the trail at 0.8 mi from the RR station. There is no suitable place to park in the area.

To reach the Okara Lakes trailhead (in the middle section of the trail), drive 1.8 mi SW on NY 28 from the Thendara RR station and look for the "state land access" sign. This is 6.5 mi NE of the Moose River bridge on NY 28. Turn N onto the gravel road. At 0.2 mi along this old highway, turn R onto Okara Rd. E, go 0.2 mi and park on the L at a sharp L turn in the road. A sign here shows the yellow-marked Browns Tract Trail on the R with a register.

To reach the S trailhead, drive 5.5 mi S from the RR station in Thendara (3.1 mi N of the Moose River bridge) on NY 28. Turn W into a gravel parking area. It's 0.2 mi N of the Nelson Lake trailhead on the E side of the road. In the parking area turn R (N) in the first parking lot and follow the gravel road for another 0.5 mi to a designated parking area. ◀

FROM THE THENDARA TRAILHEAD (0.0 mi), the route rises more than 60 ft from NY 28. After the yellow-marked trail starts, the climb continues along a road-width path nearly 100 ft higher before generally following the contour line for a while with sounds and occasional views of NY 28 L while heading SW along the route of the old Browns Tract Rd. At 0.5 mi avoid an old road L; the trail continues straight.

At just under 1.0 mi a Wilderness Area sign on the right has "Cold Hill" scratched onto it. There are small ups and downs until at 1.2 mi a structure can be glimpsed and at 1.3 mi, with houses nearby, the trail bends R, fords a stream, and goes slightly uphill off the old road. Shortly, it drops back down the hill to the Okara Lakes trailhead at 1.4 mi.

From the register, the trail forks L back uphill into the woods, leaving the old Browns Tract Rd. route for the next 1.3 mi. Any trails L are access trails from private land and should be avoided. The trail is close to private property markers.

After some ups and downs, the trail crosses the end of a wetland at 1.7 mi and reaches a flooded area at 1.8 mi with crossing possible on a beaver dam R. At just over 2.0 mi the trail crests an esker in open woods. It then stays R of property line markers toward a hillside until a jct. at 2.7 mi. The red-marked Cedar Pond Trail (trail 74) heads uphill R and the Browns Tract Trail continues L across a walkway of more than 90 ft. At 2.8 mi, the trail turns R, rejoining the old Browns Tract Rd. Eastbound hikers should take care to turn at this well-signed point to avoid private land.

At 2.9 mi, the red-marked Scusa Access Trail (trail 77) comes in on the L from NY 28.

The trail W from here is easy walking, mostly a slight decline. At 3.3 mi there is a cut through a hillside. The route crosses a stream and rises through a notch in the opposite hillside. At 3.8 mi, the blue-marked Middle Settlement Lake Access Trail (75) goes R (NW) to that lake.

After a couple of streams (no bridges), at 4.0 mi a meadow marks the crossing of Middle Settlement Creek. Just beyond this crossing is a clearing where the Middle Settlement House once stood, accommodating nineteenth-century travelers going to and from the Old Forge area. Here, also, Abbey Rd. came in from the W to join the Browns Tract Rd.

The trail follows the open wetland of Middle Settlement Creek below on the L, sometimes going a little uphill from the roadway to stay dry, and passes some large black cherry trees in an otherwise second-growth hardwood forest.

At 5.5 mi the trail noticeably drops and at 5.8 mi the Middle Settlement Lake Trail (trail 73), referred to on state signs as the Stony

Creek Trail, also yellow-marked, is on the R. After crossing a wetland that included two brooks, the trail reaches the dirt Copper Lake Rd., 6.0 mi from the Thendara trailhead. Both ends of Copper Lake Rd. are on private posted land.

The trail turns L (SE) and continues on the road. To avoid private land, watch for the sharp R (S) turn away from the road where the trail goes gently uphill. It then drops the rest of the way. This section is criss-crossed by a number of old logging roads, so care must be taken to watch for markers while navigating around the ruts.

The trail gradually curves E and starts gently downhill. A trail register is located at 7.4 mi, where the trail turns R on an old road. A barricade and parking lot mark the trail's end at 7.5 mi (0.5 mi from NY 28 on a gravel road which may not be plowed in winter).

❄ Trail in winter: Suitable for snowshoeing or backcountry skiing.

🚶 Distances: Thendara trailhead to Okara Lakes trailhead, 1.4 mi; to Cedar Pond Trail (trail 74), 2.7 mi; to Scusa Access Trail (trail 77), 2.9 mi; to Middle Settlement Lake Access Trail (trail 75), 3.8 mi; to Middle Settlement Lake (Stony Creek) Trail (trail 73), 5.8 mi; to Copper Lake Rd., 6.0 mi; to S trailhead, 7.5 mi (12.1 km).

(76A) **JBT Gull Lake Trail**

Map: B4

Gull Lake is a very scenic aspect of the John Brown Tract. The odd name distinguishes it from the other Gull Lakes in the region.

▶ Trailhead: On NY 28 a state sign on the L (N) 2.9 mi NE of the Moose River is a driveway for this trailhead and the W trailhead for Browns Tract Trail (trail 76). If headed S, it's on the R (N) 5.3 mi SW of the RR station in Thendara. Turn W into a gravel parking area and turn L for Gull Lake parking. Access to the Browns Tract Trail is by a gravel road R. ◀

FROM THE L (S) END of the parking lot (0.0 mi), go S a few steps, turn R (W) into the woods, and in 100 ft stop at the trail register. Just beyond, the red-marked trail joins an old truck road L, going up a couple of steep slopes before leaving the truck trail onto a footpath R at 0.2 mi. The path seems to be wide enough for hauling a canoe.

The trail rises a little more for a total of about 90 ft from the trailhead, then drops several feet as the lake becomes visible on the L at 0.4

mi. At 0.5 mi, the trail ends at the rocky shore of the lake. The lake, with an island, is camera ready.

❋ Trail in winter: Suitable for snowshoeing and for experienced skiers. The trailhead will probably not be plowed.

❧ Distances: Trailhead to lake, 0.5 mi (0.8 km).

(77) Scusa Access Trail

Map: B4

This trail allows access to several lakes, notably Middle Settlement and Middle Branch, both with lean-tos, in conjunction with the Browns Tract Trail (trail 76) which links with other lakes.

▶ Trailhead: Park in a large parking loop on the S side of NY 28, 2.8 mi SW of the Thendara RR station and 5.8 mi NE of the Moose River bridge. A state land access sign is just NE of the parking loop on the N side of the road, with a bridge over the ditch. ◀

THE TRAIL LEAVES the parking loop (0.0 mi), passes a register and mapboard, and about 50 yd from the loop turns L and ascends SW steeply 120 ft. It turns R, drops L across a bridge and after climbing the other bank slopes down until a short rise just before the jct. with the yellow-marked Browns Tract Trail (trail 76) at 0.6 mi. Going L on the Browns Tract Trail, it is 0.9 mi to the jct. with the blue-marked Middle Settlement Lake Access Trail (trail 75). Going R on the Browns Tract Trail, it is 0.2 mi to the jct. with the red-marked Cedar Pond Trail (trail 74) after a sharp bend L to stay on state land.

❋ Trail in winter: Suitable for snowshoeing or backcountry skiing. Skiers may have to walk the hill at the start of the trail, just over 0.1 mi.

❧ Distances: Trailhead to Browns Tract Trail (trail 76), 0.6 mi (1.0 km).

(78) Remsen Falls–Nelson Lake, Jones Mt. Loop

Map: B4, B5

Three sections of trail make two adjacent loops in the Black River Wild Forest. Either loop can be taken separately, or a longer (21.7 mi) trip can be done by hiking the outer sections of both loops, which are between the Middle Branch of the Moose River on the N and W and the South Branch of the Moose River on the S. Because it's zoned Wild

Forest, bicycles are allowed.

The Nelson Lake Trail goes all the way from Bisby Rd. to the Middle Branch of the Moose River near the NY 28 trailhead described below (although some old signs include part of this with the Jones Mt. Trail). The loop N is the Jones Mt. Trail and the loop S is the Remsen Falls Trail. A popular section of trail is the more easterly one leading to Remsen Falls Lean-to, although a shorter trip is possible to Nelson Lake using the NY 28 trailhead. Combining the two loops together, the Nelson Lake section passes down the middle through hardwood regrowth forest. This network can be reached via a common section of trail accessed either by the Bisby Rd. trailhead, through Nicks Lake Campground (a fee is charged), or from NY 28 S of Thendara.

▶ Trailheads: To reach the E trailhead on Bisby Rd., follow the Nicks Lake Public Campground signs from the jct. with NY 28 in Old Forge, finally turning L on Bisby Rd. Almost immediately on the R is a trailhead for the Humphery Hill, Lock and Dam Loop (79A) with snowmobile markers, and 0.1 mi farther on the R is the hiking trailhead, parking space, and trail register (1.2 mi from NY 28).

The W trailhead is on NY 28 2.8 mi NE of the Moose River bridge and 5.4 mi SW of the RR station at Thendara. ◀

FROM THE BISBY RD. TRAILHEAD (0.0 mi), the blue-marked trail goes S on a broad woods road. At 0.3 mi, the old road straight ahead leads to Nicks Lake, but the trail route turns R. At 1.0 mi, the Nicks Lake Circuit trail (trail 79) joins on the L. Hikers on that route use this common section of trail, marked both in blue and in yellow, to either the Nelson Lake Trail (trail 78B) or Remsen Falls trail (trail 78A).

The next jct., at 1.7 mi, requires a major decision. To the L is the Remsen Falls trail. Straight ahead the Nelson Lake Trail continues 0.6 mi to the start of the Jones Mt. Trail.

(78A) **Remsen Falls**

AFTER A L TURN AT THE JCT., 1.7 mi from Bisby Rd., this trail heads S and E along the contours, just out of sight of Nicks Lake. It then turns S and climbs the hill just S of Nicks Lake. At the high point, 2.6 mi, a trail to the L, Nicks Lake Circuit (trail 79), leads downhill 0.8 mi to the beach at Nicks Lake Campground.

The Remsen Falls Trail continues S, descending nearer to Nicks Creek, then ascending again to twist through the forest on the rim of the hill above and out of sight of the creek. At 5.0 mi, a side trail R once led 0.3 mi to little, undistinguished Bloodsucker Pond.

The route continues along the hillside above Nicks Creek, crossing the outlet stream of Bloodsucker Pond, and reaching the Remsen Falls lean-to on the Moose River at 6.9 mi. Remsen Falls is nicely framed in the view straight up the river from the lean-to. The falls, only a few feet high, are created by a natural rock barrier across the river.

To reach the Remsen Falls Spur Trail, which connects to the Woodhull Mt. Trail (trail 98), wade across above the falls at the place where the old road crossed. Some hikers prefer to wade across at the lean-to. In either case, it can be dangerous when the water is high. This river gets very deep 24 hours after a rainstorm.

Continuing on past the lean-to, the trail is always in the woods, but seldom more than 200 ft from the river. At the confluence of the South Branch and Middle Branch of the Moose River, the trail turns N and follows the Middle Branch, often just out of sight of the river. The water is sometimes calm and sometimes swift.

At 11.0 mi, a level area makes an inviting place to stop. The river is quiet here, but still swift. It is hard to believe that this beautiful, remote location is just across the river from the RR tracks (on which excursion trains operate), not far from NY 28.

At 11.2 mi, after leaving the river, the route joins an old woods road, turning R (E). The old road follows up the valley of a creek, eventually leaves it, continues climbing NE past informal camping access to Nelson Lake on the L, and finally joins the Nelson Lake Trail (trail 78B) on level ground at 12.9 mi. The route R leads back to the trailhead (18.5 mi total). The route L leads to Nelson Lake, the South Branch of the Moose River, the NY 28 trailhead, and the W end of the Jones Mt. Trail.

(78B) Nelson Lake Trail

CONTINUING FROM THE TRAIL JCT. 1.7 mi from the trailhead, this route, marked with blue and snowmobile markers, leads SW, going uphill. After gentle climbing the trail levels off. At 2.3 mi, a snowmobile sign marks the start of the Jones Mt. Trail (trail 78C) R.

The Nelson Lake Trail continues straight ahead through hardwoods, deadwood, and beaver country. At 5.2 mi there is a trail jct. The Remsen Falls trail (trail 78A) is to the L and the Nelson Lake Trail continues ahead. Nelson Lake can be accessed from either. One may take the Remsen Falls trail L, continuing SW to the S side of Nelson Lake, where there are several informal campsites and access to the shore of this 0.7 mi long lake.

Continuing ahead on the Nelson Lake Trail from the jct., one may descend a hill and approach the N side of Nelson Lake. At 5.5 mi (0.3 mi from the jct.), there is an unmarked trail to picnic spots along the E shore of the lake. The trail continues around the N end of the lake, crossing an inlet that provides nice views. Then it bends SW around the lake, reaching an obvious truck road jct. at 6.2 mi. From here an unmarked side trail goes L about 85 yd to an informal campsite and turns L to go another 50 yd to a picnic spot among birches at a sandy edge of the lake. This turnoff is 0.7 mi from the South Branch of the Moose River and about 1.2 mi from the NY 28 trailhead across the river. From that jct., the Nelson Lake Trail continues W, ending at the river at 6.9 mi, about 0.5 mi across from the NY 28 trailhead.

Coming from the NY 28 trailhead, a yellow-marked trail goes down an old truck road, reaching tracks of the Adirondack Scenic Railroad at 0.3 mi (0.3 mi S of a RR bridge over the river). From there it is less than 0.1 mi to the river's edge, with rough water L and calmer water R below some islands, across from the Nelson Lake Trail and Jones Mt. Trail jct.

(78C) Jones Mt. Trail

STARTING FROM THE JCT. at 2.3 mi W of Bisby Rd. on the Nelson Lake Trail (trail 78B), this snowmobile route leads R (NW) on an old woods road. The trail crosses some minor wetlands, easily negotiated, turning gradually to the SW. It drops at 1.1 mi but rises again at 1.3 mi, although the total elevation change over the trail is less than 200 ft.

The Middle Branch of the Moose River comes into view on the R at 2.3 mi. After passing close to the river, the trail climbs away from the water, then approaches it again at 2.9 mi. Minnehaha is just across the river, but out of sight. The route climbs L, turning away from the river just before 3.0 mi to pass through a notch just W of Jones Mt. It then descends to the river, ending at 3.9 mi, at the water's edge in a level field. There was once a bridge across the river here, but now no trace remains. This is about 0.5 mi across from the NY 28 trailhead.

❄ Trail in winter: Suitable for snowshoeing or backcountry skiing. If you can get across the river, use of a portion of the Nelson Lake Trail with the Jones Mt. Trail would be less than 10 mi. Shared with snowmobiles.

🐾 Distances: Bisby Rd. trailhead to Nicks Lake Circuit Trail (trail 79), 1.0 mi; to jct., 1.7 mi; to Remsen Falls, 6.9 mi; Remsen Falls, Nelson Lake, Jones Mt. Loops, 18.5 mi (29.6 km); Middle Branch of Moose River via Nelson Lake Trail, 6.9 mi (with less than 0.5 mi more across the river to NY 28 trailhead); Nelson Lake Trail and back via Jones Mt. Trail, 13.1 mi (21.1 km).

(79) Nicks Lake Circuit

Map: B4

Nicks Lake, S of Thendara, has beautiful stands of conifers on its shores and is surprisingly wild for a lake that has a public campground reachable by a paved road. By combining trails and a campground road you may hike a 4.7 mi circuit of this mile-long lake, starting at the campground where a day-use fee is charged. This is the Nicks Lake Circuit.

A longer access to the circuit, where no fee is involved, is via a woods road going S from the Bisby Rd. trailhead of the Remsen Falls, Nelson Lake, Jones Mt. Loops (trail 78), adding 2.0 mi round trip to the route. That trail uses part of the Nicks Lake Circuit. There are ups and downs around the lake, especially some ridges on the NE end of the lake, but the elevation variation is only about 100 ft all the way around.

▶ Trailhead: From Old Forge, turn SE from NY 28 by the school at the Nicks Lake campground sign and drive 1.7 mi, following campground signs and finally going E on Bisby Rd. Then turn R (SW) onto the campsite entrance road, paying a day-use fee at the registration booth. For the circuit hike, two trailheads are in the campground. The one that is more convenient for the additional activities of swimming and picnicking is in the beach area near the lake's SE end, reached by driving SW through the campground to the parking area at the road's end. For the other trailhead, take the first R after the registration booth onto Loop A road, drive 0.2 mi and park on the R. The trailhead is another 50 yd down the road, where a side trail begins. ◀

FROM THE BEACHFRONT TRAILHEAD (0.0 mi), a clockwise route around the lake starts at the far end of the beach with a sign. The yellow-marked trail crosses a bridge over the lake's inlet, goes along a boardwalk over a wetland, and continues on a well-worn footpath along the S side of the lake through a handsome stand of spruce and hemlock.

At 0.7 mi there is a red-marked spur trail L to a fish barrier dam on Nicks Creek, the lake's outlet. (This spur is less than 0.3 mi, round trip.) In another 100 yd a bridge carries the trail over Nicks Creek. The trail leads uphill on a woods road to a jct. at 0.8 mi with another woods road, part of the blue-marked Remsen Falls trail (trail 78A). To the L it is 4.3 mi to the Remsen Falls Lean-to. R on this yellow trail, the Nicks Lake Circuit goes N and W on the W side of the lake, but out of sight of it. The woods road passes through a second-growth hardwood forest.

At 1.7 mi, the trail L goes to Nelson Lake, while the Nicks Lake Circuit goes R on the yellow- and blue-marked woods road. The trail heads N and then E, still out of sight of the lake. Much of the route here is grassy, and it goes through an open section as well as more second-growth forest.

At a jct. at 2.5 mi, the blue trail continues ahead to a trailhead on Bisby Rd., 1.0 mi away. This is the trail that can be used to avoid the fee at the campground or when the campground is closed for the winter. The Nicks Lake Circuit turns R (E) on a broad trail, with yellow markers, on the N side of the lake. At 2.7 mi a broad path goes R 100 yd to the edge of the lake where there is a picnic spot. From here one looks S down this handsome lake to the narrows at its midsection.

At 2.8 mi, the Nicks Lake Circuit forks R onto a footpath, initially wet in places. At 3.0 mi an unmarked woods road crosses the trail and goes to the edge of the lake. This marks the boundary of the public campground and is the most direct access to the Nicks Lake Circuit from the Bisby Rd. trailhead on the N. From here on, the trail is more attractive and interesting, passing through stands of spruce, hemlock, and white pine along the lake, with views of the latter.

At 3.1 mi, the trail crosses an inlet stream on a bridge and ascends to traverse an area of splendid white pines with nice views of the lake. At a map board at 3.2 mi, yellow markers go L on a side trail to a trailhead in the public campground (on Loop A road), while the Circuit trail continues on the yellow markers. It follows around a cove at the NE corner of the lake, an especially beautiful section with handsome conifers and narrow beaches going up and over a ridge on a peninsula.

The Nicks Lake Circuit continues down the E side of the lake, passing several campsites on the L. At 4.1 mi the trail leaves the lakeside to reach a paved road on loop E. There is no trailhead parking here. The Circuit goes R along the campground road, keeping R at junctions, and reaching the beach parking area. Crossing the beach takes one back to the trailhead and register, where the Nicks Lake Circuit started, at 4.7 mi.

❄ Trail in winter: Suitable for snowshoeing or backcountry skiing. The campground is not open in winter, so the Bisby Rd. trailhead would have to be used.

🐾 Distances: Trailhead near beach to Nicks Creek, 0.7 mi; to jct. with Remsen Falls trail (trail 78A), 0.8 mi; to jct. with Nelson Lake Trail (trail 78B), 1.7 mi; to map board, 3.2 mi; complete circuit, 4.7 mi (7.6 km).

(79A) Humphery Hill, Lock and Dam Loop

Map: B4

This snowmobile trail—shaped like a capital *P* on its side with its foot to the E—offers a combination of a woods walk and Moose River views, including a visit to a lock and dam, where hikers may see canoeists and kayakers portaging. (The name "Humphery Hill" is shown on a local DEC sign, and does not appear on maps of the area.) Some may prefer just the lock and dam visit from the Green Bridge Rd. parking lot (2.0 mi round trip), while others may want to start at Bisby Rd. to enjoy the entire 4.0 mi woods walk (including the side trip to the lock and dam).

▶ Trailheads: From NY 28 in Thendara just NE of the RR bridge (0.2 mi NE from the RR station), turn S on Beech St. This becomes Green Bridge Rd. before a turn L and then, staying on paved road, turns R to cross a bridge. Green Bridge Rd. trailhead parking is to the R just across the bridge. From there, continue L (E), taking two R turns onto Bisby Rd. with the trailhead almost immediately on the R.

From Old Forge, you can reach the Bisby Rd. trailhead from NY 28 by following the Nicks Lake Public Campground signs from the jct. with NY 28 next to the school. Conclude by turning L on Bisby Rd.; the trailhead is almost immediately on the R. ◀

FROM BISBY RD. (0.0 mi) snowmobile markers beyond a gate lead gently uphill on a woods road, gaining 100 ft over the 0.6 mi to a three-way jct. The trail R (N) comes out at Green Bridge Rd. and can be used

Butterfly and dew. Richard Nowicki

on the return trip. Turn L (S) for about 40 yd to another jct. Trail 79B ahead connects with the Remsen Falls, Nelson Lake, Jones Mt. Loops (trail 78). Turn R (W) on a footpath through road-width grass on a level section, which soon begins a mostly gentle decline.

At 1.3 mi, a sharp R turn starts a moderate drop. Heading N at 1.4 mi the trail drops to cross a snowmobile bridge over a stream flowing to the L, then levels off until reaching the jct. with the spur trail to the lock and dam at 1.5 mi. (The trail L leads 0.3 between fields of ferns and gently down to a clearing at the lock and dam.) Ahead, the trail is level, then drops about 40 ft, leveling out again to come alongside the river at 2.0 mi. It reaches the gate at Green Bridge Rd. at 2.3 mi.

Crossing the parking lot there, and passing a gate R (S), the trail heads sharply up the hill to the three-way jct. at 2.7 mi. A L turn returns you to Bisby Rd. on the section you started on, for a total trip of 4.0 mi, including the side trip to the lock and dam.

For the shorter lock and dam section only, start from the Green Bridge Rd. trailhead. After the gate and register, the woods road follows along the Moose River's Middle Branch with views across including buildings at the Thendara RR station. At 0.2 mi, the trail bends L, leaving the river. At 0.4 mi, avoid a road-width opening to the R with a footpath and continue ahead on a woods road heading up a sharp hill, the greatest elevation change on this section. There's a large clearing on the L at 0.7 mi. At 0.8 mi there is a jct., with the trail ahead looping back over Humphery Hill and the trail R leading slightly down to a clearing next to the river at the lock and dam at 1.0 mi.

✴ Trail in winter: State snowmobile trail, probably lightly used because there's only an indication of a state trail on local snowmobile maps. This is not maintained by local clubs or considered part of the Old Forge-Inlet system. The section from Green Bridge Rd. S to the jct. is quite steep, good for snowshoers but more difficult except for advanced skiers. The rest is suitable for snowshoers or skiers.

Ɱ Distances: Bisby Rd. trailhead to jct., 0.6 mi; to spur to lock and dam, 1.7 mi; to Green Bridge Rd. trailhead, 2.5 mi; return to three-way jct., 2.9 mi; return to Bisby Rd., 3.5 mi (5.6 km). With side trip to lock and dam, 4.0 mi (6.5 km). Green Bridge Rd. trailhead to lock and dam spur, 0.8 mi; to lock and dam, 1.0 mi (1.6 km).

(79B) Humphery Hill–Nicks Lake Connector

Map: B4

▶ Locator: This connector trail runs from a three-way jct. on trail 79A, 0.4 mi from Green Bridge Rd. and 0.6 mi from Bisby Rd., to trail 78, 1.0 mi from Bisby Rd. ◀

FROM THE THREE-WAY JCT. on the Humphery Hill, Lock and Dam Loop (trail 79A) (0.0 mi), this wide, woods trail with snowmobile markers raises slightly, passing the continuation R (W) of trail 79A in about 40 yd, continues ahead S gently uphill for 0.1 mi, then drops to the Remsen Falls, Nelson Lake, Jones Mt. Loops (trail 78) at 0.3 mi.

✴ Trail in winter: Suitable for snowshoeing or backcountry skiing.

Ɱ Distance: 0.3 mi (0.5 km). ◆

Birch in the Moose River Plains. RICHARD NOWICKI

Moose River Plains Wild Forest Section

This is a remote tract of land that includes a 50,000-acre piece purchased by the state from the Gould Paper Company in 1963. It lies SE and E of Limekiln Lake, its S portion bounded by the West Canada Lakes Wilderness Area and its NE portion bounded by the Blue Ridge Wilderness Area. Formerly called the Moose River Recreation Area, the MRPWF is mostly drained by the South Branch of the Moose River. At its heart are the Moose River Plains, the principal flood plain of the South Branch, including that of lower Sumner Stream flowing W and S into the South Branch. The Plains are flat and largely open, with grass, bushes, and expanses of wetland.

A study with field work done over six years, 1995–2000, by Brian and Eileen Keelan of Rochester, NY (http://www.frontiernet.net/~keelan/), found that a 200-square-kilometer area centered on the MRPWF contains 522 species of vascular plants of 254 genera and 86 families. Under a special DEC permit, the Keelans collected hundreds of specimens, later donated to the State Museum in Albany, that were found for the first time in Hamilton and Herkimer counties, as listed on the *Revised Checklist of New York State Plants* (Mitchell, R.S. & G. C. Tucker). Threatened species found included Farwell's water milfoil in two spots, alga pondweed in seven locations, and mountain goldenrod and balsam willow in three locations. Others species, "uncommon but not really rare," included 19 species of orchids. (See the N.Y. Natural Heritage Program Web site at http://www.dec.state.ny.us/website/dfwmr/heritage/.)

A state brochure calls this "the largest block of remote land in the Adirondacks readily accessible by motor vehicle," but that depends on the season, because the roads are closed except to snowmobilers from the end of hunting season in the fall until about Memorial Day. The area includes a deer yard where large numbers of deer spend the winter.

Although it was one of the last great wild areas to be cut down, the forest of the Moose River Plains Wild Forest is primarily second or third growth, most of it having been extensively logged before state acquisition. Some impressive stands of conifers, especially white pine and balsam fir, remain in tracts purchased by New York State before the rest of the region was logged.

The MRPWF has sizeable hills and a mountain range, with Little Moose Mt. reaching 3620 ft. Except for the Sly Pond Trail (trail 90), the hiking trails do not climb these hills. Some of the ponds and lakes are unusually high, topped by Sly Pond at 2872 ft, one of the highest bodies of water in the Adirondacks (compare to Lake Colden at 2764 ft, or even Avalanche Lake at 2863 ft, both in the High Peaks).

The trails of the MRPWF, maintained by the DEC, are largely on old logging roads leading to ponds and lakes. In winter the trails (except those in the adjacent Wilderness Area) are open to snowmobiling. Access to the trails is mildly affected by the seemingly long distances on winding, unpaved roads with a 15 MPH speed limit. The access problem can be alleviated by a stay at one of the primitive camping areas within the area; these have fireplaces, picnic tables, and privies, and are located along the roads. Car-top boats are permitted, without motors. There are informal campsites at the ends of some of the trails, a few reached by boat that one would have to carry in. Registration is required for all entering at either the Limekiln or Cedar River gates.

The MRPWF is open to cars, trucks (up to one ton), and trailers usually from Memorial Day through November. Trailers and RVs are permitted from Memorial Day through Labor Day. Chains or 4WD are required after Oct. 1. The main road as well as the Sly Pond Loop, Lost Ponds, Mitchell Ponds, Beaver Lake, Seventh Lake Loop, Old Uncas Rd., Bear Pond Rd., Benedict Creek, Fawn Lake, and Otter Brook truck trails are designated as snowmobile trails. Note that some of these trails are listed in the Big Moose section of this book.

No motorcycles, motorized bicycles, or all-terrain vehicles are allowed at any time.

Entry by foot or bicycle is permitted at any time.

After the gates close in the fall, access for hikers is nearly shut off. Limekiln Rd. is plowed only to the area of the W gate, and Cedar River Rd. on the E is not plowed past the last home.

The W entrance to the wild forest is reached by driving toward Raquette Lake from Inlet on NY 28. At 0.8 mi from the center of Inlet, turn R (S) down Limekiln Rd. and then keep L when you see Limekiln Lake downhill, turning onto the unpaved road. From the control station at this entrance, the MRPWF's through road, Moose River Rd., extends for 21.2 mi to the Cedar River (E) entrance. The latter is at the end of Cedar River Rd., which comes in 11.8 mi from NY 28/30, about 2.0 mi W of the village of Indian Lake.

As one drives along Moose River Rd. from the Limekiln entrance, Rock Dam Rd. goes SW at 4.6 mi (16.6 mi from the Cedar River entrance), and at 8.2 mi (12.9 mi from the Cedar River entrance). Otter Brook Rd. goes S, while Moose River Rd. goes L at each jct. Otter Brook Rd. goes 3.3 mi to a fork just across the bridge over Otter Brook, where it bears L (E) a short distance to its end. At the fork, Indian River Rd. goes R (W and SW). There are no road signs at these jcts. or along these unpaved roads, only trail signs.

At the entrances to the Moose River Plains Wild Forest, one may obtain a leaflet showing the roads, trails, and camping areas. The trails usually bear DEC yellow markers, and the trailheads have signs. Parking is on the road or, in some cases, one can drive off the road a short distance to park. All hikes are on relatively level terrain unless otherwise indicated.

Some trails on the E edge of the MRPWF are outside the area of the large map accompanying this guide, but are shown on individual page maps. Refer to the Cedar River section. The E part of the West Canada Lakes Wilderness Area is covered more extensively in *Adirondack Trails: Northville–Placid Trail*, a publication of the Adirondack Mountain Club.

Improvements to make much of the area handicapped accessible are planned, pending the approval of the unit management plan. The proposal includes road improvements and better access with some docks for Hell Diver, Ice House, Mitchell, and Lost ponds and Squaw and Beaver lakes along with ATV use, by permit, for the disabled.

Also included in this section are a few trails outside the W gate of the wild forest near Inlet.

SHORT HIKE:

◆ Rock Dam—2.8 mi (4.5 km) round trip. Gentle traveling to the "rock dam" on the Moose River. See trail 83.

MODERATE HIKE:

◆ Beaver Lake—4.2 mi (6.8 km) round trip. Walk a pleasant old road to Beaver Lake. One highlight are the magnificent old white pines along the way, but there is good water access as well. See trail 88.

HARDER HIKE:
◆ Sly Pond—15.4 mi (24.8 km) round trip. One of the highest lakes in the Adirondacks. Gives a good impression of a really remote wilderness lake and is generally a good choice for solitude. See trail 90.

TRAIL DESCRIBED	TOTAL MILES	PAGE
	(one way)	
Limekiln Creek–Third Lake Trail	5.6 (9.0 km)	184
Limekiln Ski Routes	Various	186
Whites Pond Trail	3.1 (5.0 km)	188
East Shore Path and Snowmobile Trail	2.7 (4.4 km)	188
Rock Dam Trail	1.4 (2.3 km)	190
Bear Pond Trail	2.5 (4.0 km)	191
Benedict Creek Trail	Your choice	191
Mitchell Ponds Trail	2.8 (4.5 km)	192
Helldiver Pond Trail	0.15 (0.24 km)	193
Ice House Pond Trail	0.4 (0.6 km)	194
Beaver Lake Trail	2.1 (3.4 km)	194
Lost Ponds Trail	1.3 (2.1 km)	195
Sly Pond Trail	7.7 (12.4 km)	196
Squaw Lake Trail	0.3 (0.5 km)	198
Muskrat Pond Trail	0.1 (0.2 km)	198
Indian Lake Trail	0.1 (0.2 km)	198
Indian River (Horn Lake) Trail	7.4 (11.9 km)	199

(80) Limekiln Creek–Third Lake Trail

Map: C, D3

This trail connects Limekiln Rd. and South Shore Rd. It is designated as both a ski touring and hiking trail. It is a generally level route extending from the SW end of the Limekiln Lake Public Campground along Limekiln Creek, then NW to Third Lake Creek and the trailhead at South Shore Rd. near Third Lake, a through hike of 5.6 mi. At the start the route follows the W segment of a DEC self-guided nature trail, which makes an interesting 1.5 mi trip in its own right. The longest section of the trail route, going NW toward Third Lake, passes through extensive wet areas heavy with mosquitoes through June.

▶ Trailheads: To reach the Limekiln Rd. trailhead from the parking area in the center of Inlet, drive 0.8 mi on NY 28 toward Blue Mt. Lake, turn R on Limekiln Rd., and go 1.7 mi S. Turn R on the entrance road to the public campground and pay a day-use fee at the booth. With attractive Limekiln Lake on the L, drive the whole length of the campground to its SW end and park by Campsite 87. Because the campground is closed after Labor Day and reopened in early May, it is necessary to park near the gate during that period and go an additional 1.5 mi on foot.

To reach the South Shore Rd. trailhead from the parking area in Inlet, go one short block toward Raquette Lake and turn R at the first corner. Drive 5.5 mi (passing the Inlet Ski Touring Center and the Fourth Lake Picnic Area) on South Shore Rd. Turn L at the large clearing 0.3 mi past the picnic area. To reach the South Shore Rd. trailhead from the Tourist Information Center in Old Forge, go S on NY 28 and turn L at the first corner. Keep L until you leave the lake headed SE. Go about 5 mi and turn R into the large parking area. ◀

FROM CAMPSITE 87 at the E trailhead (0.0 mi), the yellow-marked trail goes S on a barricaded driveway for 100 yd, turns L past a pump house at the end of the field, and reaches the beginning of the Old Dam Self-Guiding Nature Trail at 0.2 mi. At the register, there are descriptive leaflets for the nature trail. On the L is a fish barrier dam in Limekiln Creek, just out of Limekiln Lake. The nature trail returns over the dam to this spot.

To the R (SW), the trail goes through tall conifers with a boggy pond on the L, following yellow ski trail markers. At 0.6 mi, the trail crosses Limekiln Creek at the site of the "old dam," used in the first half of this century in connection with log drives down the creek to the South Branch of the Moose River. 40 yd beyond, the nature trail goes L (E) at a jct. The ski/hiking trail goes R and heads SW through tall conifers, paralleling Limekiln Creek and its wetland. At 1.3 mi, there is a good view R of a beaver meadow.

Beyond the wetland the trail follows above the creek in an attractive section at 1.5 mi, passing a small but pretty waterfall and pool, worth the bushwhack of a few yards down to them. At 1.6 mi, the trail crosses a bridge over the creek. Approximately 100 yd downstream on the R bank, a larger waterfall can be seen. This is a good turning-back point for a round-trip hike.

The rest of the trail toward Third Lake goes generally NW. Beyond the bridge one passes through stately hardwoods and fields of ferns, which are much in evidence from here on. At 2.0 mi, the trail goes R onto a weedy snowmobile trail, follows it for 40 yd, and turns L off of it. (Be alert to this turn.) Herbaceous growth continues under foot.

The trail enters a conifer forest at 2.3 mi and crosses a bridge over the outlet of Limekiln Swamp, which lies on the R. Shortly after the trail reenters the woods, one of the Limekiln Ski Routes (trail 81) comes in on the R at 2.8 mi. This trail can be used for a good loop ski trip.

For the next couple of miles, the route crosses mostly flat, swampy, or semiswampy terrain in a mixed conifer-hardwood forest. In this section the trail follows a vehicle track, turns R off it at 3.7 mi where the footpath temporarily disappears in the ferns, and goes along the edge of Third Lake Creek Swamp with nearly half a mile of continuous wet footing. The trail then regains the vehicle track, following it for a little over a quarter mile only to turn R off it again (be alert here), and then follow Third Lake Creek.

At 4.7 mi, the trail again regains the vehicle track on private land and follows it through dense conifers and along muddy places for 360 yd to a chain barrier. Just beyond, at 4.9 mi, the route turns R on a widened jeep road with ruts and mud puddles and follows it through deciduous woods to the trail's end at 5.6 mi at South Shore Rd., E of Third Lake. There is an open area for parking (formerly the site of the Third Lake Campgrounds) but there may be no trail sign.

❀ Trail in winter: DEC ski trail. The entire trail cannot be used easily for a loop trip, but the first 2.3 mi can be used in connection with the Limekiln Ski Routes (trail 81) for a good day's outing.

ᴍ Distances: Limekiln Lake parking area to creek with waterfall, 1.6 mi; to Limekiln Ski Trail, 2.8 mi; to W trailhead, 5.6 mi (9.0 km). Limekiln Rd., looping back via the longest Limekiln Ski Route, 8.6 mi. Nature Trail loop, 1.5 mi.

(81) **Limekiln Ski Routes**

Map: D3

▶ Trailhead: To reach the trailhead from the parking area in the center of Inlet, drive 0.8 mi on NY 28 toward Blue Mt. Lake. Turn R on Limekiln Rd. and go 1.7 mi S. Park at the entrance road to the Limekiln

Lake Campground if space has been plowed. The route is marked with DEC yellow markers. ◀

IN SKI TOURING SEASON, one may ski from Limekiln Rd. to the Limekiln Creek–Third Lake Trail (trail 80) on two different routes. To reach the start of that hiking-skiing trail, just W of Limekiln Lake, ski W from Limekiln Rd. along the public campground's entrance road. Then follow the route of the yellow ski markers, which leaves the main campground road to make shortcuts nearer the lake through the remainder of the campground. An alternative to part of this route is to ski on Limekiln Lake from the boat launching site, which the main campground road passes, to the shore of the bay at the NW corner of the lake.

The other route, also marked with DEC yellow cross-country ski markers, leaves the W side of Limekiln Rd. at a point 1.0 mi S of the road's jct. with NY 28 and 0.7 mi N of the public campground's entrance road. The trail goes mostly SW for over 3.0 mi to end at the Limekiln Creek–Third Lake Trail (trail 80) N of where the latter crosses the outlet of Limekiln Swamp. Near the start of the route, several trails go R as part of the Town of Inlet's network, and thereafter a snowmobile trail is crossed at an angle (actually followed a short ways).

At about 1.4 mi there is a jct. with signs, where a connecting ski trail goes L to the Limekiln Lake Public Campground. This connecting trail, also with yellow ski markers, goes mostly SE, making turns at three jcts. with snowmobile trails, and reaches the NW area of the campground by Campsite 184. From there one should follow the ski and snowmobile markers L to a broad jct. at Campsite 47, and then descend toward the campground's beach to pick up the ski route through the campground, as described above.

Omitting the final 3.0 mi of the Limekiln Creek–Third Lake Trail, one has the choice of several circuit ski routes using these trails. Another option is to start at Fern Park on South Shore Rd. and follow the town's Trail No. 6 (shown on the ADK map that accompanies this book as the end of trail 81 nearest Inlet) along the E side of the town's network to the DEC ski trail W of Limekiln Rd., and then continue as desired, perhaps all the way to South Shore Rd. near Third Lake.

✲ Trail in winter: DEC ski touring trails.

⚸ Distances: Vary by loops chosen.

(82) **Whites Pond Trail**

Map: D3, 4

A trail to a small pond and then over a ridge before a drop to Limekiln Lake.

▶ Trailhead: From the jct. of Moose River Rd. and Rock Dam Rd. (4.6 mi from the W entrance and 16.6 mi from the E entrance of the MRPWF), drive S on Rock Dam Rd. for 2.6 mi. The trailhead is on the R. There is a trailhead sign and parking for three cars. The trail is marked with DEC yellow markers. The route is well marked and generally not difficult to find.

One also may start from the Limekiln Lake end by renting a boat at the Limekiln Lake Public Campground or bringing one to launch there. The landing is not very prominent at the trailhead; it is a little bit W of the creek. ◀

FROM ROCK DAM RD. (0.0 mi), after a short lead-in section, the route follows an old road. It contours along pleasant but dense forest, crossing several creeks.

At 0.5 mi, the route turns L and climbs, going S at first, then generally W. It turns R at 0.9 mi and climbs, sometimes steeply, until 1.1 mi. Shortly beyond, the old road crosses a marshy meadow. The route then leaves the old road and becomes more rugged. After more ups and downs, the trail skirts a nice marsh-ringed pond on the L.

Whites Pond appears on the R at 1.7 mi. There was once a cabin on the spruce-covered island in the middle of the lake.

Continuing beyond the beaver dam at the outlet, the trail becomes more obscure as it goes up the hillside N of Whites Pond. The route turns N, still climbing, then follows a ridge NE to the high point at 2.2 mi. A long downhill section leads to a creek crossing at 2.8 mi and the shore of Limekiln Lake at 3.1 mi. There are some possibilities for camping on the hill above the trail L.

❋ Trail in winter: Not very accessible, except by snowmobile. The Limekiln Lake end is somewhat steep.

⋙ Distances: Rock Dam Rd. to Whites Pond, 1.7 mi; to Limekiln Lake, 3.1 mi (5.0 km).

(82A) East Shore Path and Snowmobile Trail

Map: D3

The East Shore Path gives access to the shores of Limekiln Lake below Fawn Lake Mt. Public access to this beautiful shoreline is via a snowmobile trail from Moose River Rd. The other end of the trail connects with Limekiln Rd. on the N, but as a private path going right through the front yards of many cottages along the E bay. Hikers who have not obtained permission should not use that route.

▶ Trailhead: From the W entrance to MRPWF, go E on Moose River Rd. for 3.0 mi. As the road takes a sharp turn to the L, an almost unnoticed snowmobile trail goes straight off the road, headed downhill. There is a slight clear spot for parking one or two cars 30 ft down the road at the road bend. ◀

THE TRAIL PASSES across the lower rear of the small clearing (0.0 mi), headed downhill L. This is a very pleasant old road, somewhat overgrown, with a green, soft-carpeted surface. It passes a wetland on the L, then goes over a slight hill before descending to cross Limekiln Lake inlet at 0.6 mi. From here on, the almost level trail follows the side of the inlet, which bubbles along rock ledges and under large boulders, until it reaches quiet meadowlands.

Continuing W, the width of the meadows grows, while the trail keeps on solid ground at its edge. The forest on the uphill side is of well-established open hardwoods. Soon after first glimpses of the lake appear, the wide old road ends abruptly at the lake's edge at 1.8 mi. There is heavy brush on either side of the trail, seeming to block all further travel. The view over Limekiln Lake is quite nice, with the prominent W peninsula dominating the scene.

About 30 ft back from the end of the snowmobile trail, there is an unmarked but maintained path on the R (N) side of the trail which continues on around the lake. This is the East Shore Path. Continuing on this path, there is an unofficial campsite above the lake shore at 1.9 mi. The path continues near the shore until it turns abruptly R at 2.1 mi and passes behind a slight hill at the tip of the E shore peninsula. This inland passage doesn't last long, and the lake shore is soon close on the L. Thereafter, the route stays close to the shore and its beautiful views.

State land ends at 2.7 mi, where a house is visible uphill R. From this point on, the path crosses right through the tiny front yards of side-by-side private cottages and is clearly not a public trail. The hiker should return by the snowmobile trail.

❋ Trail in winter: Snowmobile trail. Easy snowshoeing. Easy and pleasant skiing, but the beginner may find the first half mile a bit steep. Parking is no closer than the W entrance, 3.0 mi from the trailhead, unless you have a snowmobile.

🚶 Distances: Moose River Rd. to level ground at creek crossing, 0.6 mi; to end of snowmobile trail, 1.8 mi; to informal campsite, 1.9 mi; to end of state land, 2.7 mi (4.4 km).

(83) Rock Dam Trail

Map: D4

An easy trail to the confluence of the Red River and the Moose River, where a natural stone wall holds back much of the Moose.

▶ Trailhead: Start at the jct. of Moose River Rd. and Rock Dam Rd. (4.6 mi from the W entrance and 16.6 mi from the E entrance to MRPWF). Drive S on Rock Dam Rd. for 3.8 mi. The trailhead is on the L. Rock Dam Rd. is barricaded at private land about 0.4 mi S of the trailhead. ◀

LEAVING THE TRAILHEAD (0.0 mi), the route cuts over a minor hump, joins an old woods road, and loops gently NE on the old road through well-established forest. At about 1.0 mi, the route leaves the old road, turns around, and heads S. An unofficial cutover of perhaps 50 yd on this unnecessarily long loop cuts more than 0.1 mi off each way. This end of the trail is generally wetter and rougher, but easy to follow.

The trail ends at 1.4 mi at a slight opening on the South Branch of the Moose River. An unmarked path L upstream along the river bank will bring the traveler even with the "dam" or out on the rocks below it. In times of low flow, sturdy hikers wade out to the dam, which is a broad, smooth rock formation blocking the river from a small island to the far bank with deeper water behind it upstream. Others may prefer to gaze at the formation from the rocks downstream. The Red River joins just above the dam L.

❋ Trail in winter: Not readily accessible except by snowmobile.

🚶 Distance: to Rock Dam, 1.4 mi (2.3 km).

(84) Bear Pond Trail

Map: D4, E3

A remote pond with boggy edges and a so-called trail best left to experienced bushwhackers.

▶ Trailhead: Drive E for about 300 ft from the jct. of Moose River Rd. and Rock Dam Rd. (4.6 mi from the W entrance and 16.6 mi from the E entrance to the MRPWF), starting up a slight hill. The first road L goes to a gravel pit. Some 100 ft farther on, at the top of the slight rise, turn L onto a two-track dirt road. Go 0.7 mi along this side road to an overgrown parking area on the L with a barricaded road beyond. The two-track road continues E past this trailhead to rejoin Moose River Rd. in another 0.5 mi. ◀

BEYOND THE BARRICADE (0.0 mi), the trail follows an overgrown old road to a wetland at the SW tip of Bear Pond at 2.5 mi. It climbs a little at first, then contours along the flank of Mt. Tom before descending to the pond. It is not marked.

✽ Trail in winter: Far from a plowed road, and very thick.

🐾 Distances: To SW end of Bear Pond, 2.5 mi (4.0 km).

(84A) Benedict Creek Trail

Map: E3, 4

This is not a marked or maintained trail, even though it continues to appear as a snowmobile trail on the maps handed out at the entrance gates. It could serve as a wet nature walk into a celebration of old-growth forest with magnificent white pines and birch trees.

▶ Trailhead: From the jct. of Moose River Rd. and Rock Dam Rd., drive E for 2.6 mi, or from the jct. of Moose River Rd. and Otter Brook Rd., go N uphill toward Inlet for 1.1 mi to a sharp L turn in the road. Turn E to a campsite on the sharp turn on a steep hill. ◀

FROM THE BARRICADE at the campsite, the trail, going NE, heads gently downhill on an old road, passes along the lower edge of a small clearing L at 0.2 mi, and continues downhill straight ahead. It soon reaches the creek level and continues along the L edge of the marshy bottom. There is no particular end to the trail; it just becomes fainter and fainter.

✽ Trail in winter: Listed as a snowmobile trail, but no longer useable as such. Fine skiing and snowshoeing, but it is far from drivable roads.

ᴍ Distance: Your choice.

(85) **Mitchell Ponds Trail**

Map: D4

The Mitchell Ponds are beautiful remote waters, easy to reach on a pleasant path and offering some opportunities for camping. Robert West, a WWI veteran, set up camp here some years after the war, having been advised to spend time in the open air. He lived quite alone fishing, guiding sportsmen, and trapping in the area until WWII.

▶ Trailheads: To reach the E (main) trailhead, from the W entrance to the MRPWF near Limekiln Lake, go E for 7.9 mi. Turn R onto an old two-track road and park in the grassy space in about 50 ft ahead. From the E (Cedar River) gate, the trail is 10.3 mi from the entrance and 0.3 mi past the Otter Brook Rd. jct.

The W trailhead, unmarked, is 0.3 mi E of the Rock Dam Rd. jct. (which is 4.6 mi E of the W entrance to MRPWF). Park near the entrance to a camping area where a snowmobile trailhead continues through the back (S) of the campsite. ◀

FROM THE BARRIER AND PARKING AREA at the E trailhead (0.0 mi), the route follows an old road, in good condition, with views of lowlands L and a steep bank R. There are occasional yellow markers, but the road is obvious. At 1.3 mi, the valley narrows and the road comes close to a stream.

As the trail comes into the open in a grassy area at 1.8 mi, a slight but marked trail joins on the R. This is the continuation of the route. Straight ahead is a trail leading to the end of Upper Mitchell Pond, the higher of the two ponds.

(Continuing ahead on the side trail past the jct., the road almost disappears at the edge of the clearing, and a foot trail continues with yellow DEC markers. In another 100 yd this trail ends at a scenic picnic site near the edge of the water, which is not inviting, but views of a rock face R make it worth the trip.)

Back at the jct., from next to an 8 ft rock at the side of the clearing, the main trail continues on a lesser-noticed woods road going R, with yellow markers, across a small creek. The road soon reaches another trail jct. just as it turns uphill on a steady climb. The yellow trail turns

L at the base of the hill. (The road up the hill is a snowmobile trail leading in 1.7 mi to the N trailhead on Moose River Rd. This snowmobile trail is a generally pleasant and easy route, up and over a hill, except for a crossing of a beaver dam, marked with yellow and snowmobile markers.)

Continuing L (W) from the jct. at the base of the hill, the yellow trail follows the contour near Upper Mitchell Pond on a footpath. Coming even with Lower Mitchell Pond at 2.2 mi, the trail gets bumpier along the hillside but with views of the lower pond. It passes rock formations R, rounds the end of Lower Mitchell Pond, turns L, and ends at 2.8 mi at the outlet stream. To reach an informal campsite, cross the stream on rocks or logs and go up the hillside for 50 ft onto a point, which has a nice small picnic or swimming beach on the other side.

✳ Trail in winter: The MRPWF gates are closed to cars in winter. Snowmobiling area.

ᴁ Distances: To Upper Mitchell Pond, 1.9 mi; to far end of Lower Mitchell Pond, 2.8 mi (4.5 km). To alternate trailhead via snowmobile trail, 3.5 mi (5.6 km).

(86) Helldiver Pond Trail

Map: E4

Leads to a small pond that can be explored with a canoe or kayak and a brief carry.

▶ Trailhead: A small dirt road goes S from the Moose River Rd. at 8.1 mi from the W entrance, or 13.1 mi from the E entrance, to the MRPWF (0.8 mi E of the jct. with Otter Brook Rd.). Drive 0.2 mi down this road to a camping and parking area. ◀

FROM THE TRAILHEAD (0.0 mi), the trail goes briefly through open forest, then twists through dense forest on corduroy to the shore of the pond. The pond is pretty, but the only effective access beyond the trail is by boat. Its most likely use is for fishing or camping and lazily paddling about. It's held back by a beaver dam at the NW corner.

✳ Trail in winter: Far from drivable roads.

ᴁ Distance: To Helldiver Pond, 0.2 mi (0.24 km).

(87) Ice House Pond Trail

Map: E4

Early market hunters had an ice house here, in which they stored venison destined for the market in Saratoga. The plains here are notably open, and deer were no doubt easy to find.

▶ Trailhead: Start at the jct. of Moose River Rd. and Otter Brook Rd., 8.3 mi from the W entrance or 12.9 mi from the E entrance to the MRPWF. Drive S on Otter Brook Rd. for 0.8 mi. Trailhead is on the L (E), parking on the shoulder on the R (W). This point is 0.4 mi N of the Moose River. ◀

A GATE ON AN OLD ROAD is the trailhead (0.0 mi). The route goes through a large field of bushes, reenters the forest, and ends at a campsite by the edge of the pond. Generally wide, the trail is an easy canoe carry. The pond has nice scenery and appears to be popular with anglers.

❊ Trail in winter: Snowmobile trail.

𝔐 Distance: To Ice House Pond, 0.4 mi (0.6 km).

(88) Beaver Lake Trail

Map: D4, E4

This was once the Chapin estate, established about 1904. The lodge had seven buildings, now all gone. Chapin had stayed with the Kenwells before that, and apparently liked the area. Wellington Alexander Kenwell had a hotel on the Moose River near the trailhead from 1891 to 1901. This is presumed to be the Sportsmen's Lodge at Indian Clearing listed in S.R. Stoddard's 1894 tourist guide, *The Adirondacks Illustrated*. Stoddard warned that, "The way is rough, and the accomodations primitive...." Things in this area haven't changed much since then. Gerald Kenwell established a later public lodge about three miles up Otter Brook from the trailhead at a spot labeled "Kenwells" on older maps. The lodge was still in business in 1947, but is now gone. A state brochure on the area says the lake "is named for its odd shape which resembles a beaver."

▶ Trailhead: From the jct. of Moose River Rd. and Otter Brook Rd. (8.3 mi from the W entrance, or 12.9 mi from the E entrance to the MRPWF), drive S on Otter Brook Rd. for 1.2 mi to the bridge across the South Branch of the Moose River. The trailhead road is on the right (W) just S of the bridge. Drive 0.2 mi on the access road and park near the barricade, without blocking it. ◄

THE TRAIL STARTS at a bridge with a double sluice designed to handle a large flow (0.0 mi). It passes along the South Branch of the Moose River for a short ways, then swings inland through a dark forest of large trees. Starting at 1.2 mi a stand of white pines pokes majestically above the forest. Their limbs start where the other trees leave off.

Beyond the white pines, the trail tops out at the cleared site of an old sawmill at 1.9 mi. From there, a short road plunges diagonally downhill to the shore of the lake and another clearing at the site of a long-departed cabin at 2.1 mi. Informal campsites here and at another spot nearby give excellent lake scenery, although they are close to the water.

❋ Trail in winter: Snowmobile trail. Very far from drivable roads.

🐾 Distance: To Beaver Lake, 2.1 mi (3.4 km).

(89) Lost Ponds Trail

Map: E4

This trail passes a stillwater on Sumner Stream and then continues to another pond visited by anglers and picnickers.

Remote pond in the Moose River Plains Wild Forest. RICHARD NOWICKI

▶ Trailhead: From the jct. of Moose River Rd. and Otter Brook Rd. (8.3 mi from the W entrance, or 12.9 mi from the E entrance to the MRPWF), drive E on Moose River Rd. for 1.9 mi. Turn L (N) onto a dirt road, leading to a parking spot after 0.4 mi. ◀

STARTING AT THE BARRIER just beyond the parking area with two campsites (0.0 mi), the trail takes a jeep road N, passing a camping site on the R (E) just before bridging Sumner Stream. There is a path next to the campsite leading a short way R to the remains of a dam in the stream. The dam has backed up the picturesque stillwater, which has handsome conifers around it.

Beyond the bridge, the route L (W) leads to a picnic spot above the S shore of the eastern pond at 0.7 mi. The route beyond is an old logging road, now overgrown and choked off, although sporadic flagging may continue. The alternate route straight ahead from the jct. at the bridge leads around the N side of the pond to a fish barrier dam on the outlet stream. The rock ledge on the N shore of the pond is covered with poison ivy, the only place with that plant in the MRPWF. Plant researchers Brian and Eileen Keelan say there are several outcroppings of marble there, which is uncommon in the Adirondacks and usually has a distinct plant community. Because poison ivy is not a true calciphile—a species that grows exclusively on calcium carbonate substrates such as limestone, marble, and even artificial cement or mortar—its growth only there may be partly coincidental. Growing with it, also found nowhere else in the MRPWF, are early saxifrage, purple clematis, and slender wheatgrass.

❋ Trail in winter: Snowmobile trail. Far from accessible roads, but otherwise suitable for skis or snowshoes.

❖ Distance: To picnic spot on E Lost Pond, 0.7 mi (1.1 km); to outlet stream, 1.3 mi (2.1 km).

(90) Sly Pond Trail

Map: E4

A real wilderness experience is the climb through a col and down to Sly Pond at 2872 ft. Primitive camping might be possible a suitable distance (150 ft from stream and trail is the legal minimum) from where streams cross the trail for water access.

▶ Trailheads: From the jct. of the Moose River and Otter Brook Rds. (8.3 mi from the W entrance, or 12.9 mi from the E entrance to the

MRPWF), go S on Otter Brook Rd. 2.3 mi to a truck road on the L (NE), 1.1 mi beyond the Moose River. Parking is along the start of the trail off Otter Brook Rd., with spots for as many as five vehicles on the R and a couple of spots for a vehicle on the L (make sure not to block the roadway). A flat spot opposite the trail on Otter Brook Rd. is not suitable; it collects water.

To reach a summer trailhead, which requires wading the Moose River, from the jct. of Moose River Rd. and Otter Brook Rd. in the MRPWF, go E on Moose River Rd. for 3.8 mi. Take the side road R (S) for 0.1 mi to parking by a campsite. ◀

FROM THE BARRIER above Otter Brook Rd (0.0 mi), the trail starts uphill on a red-marked truck road with a gate. Soon a rock wall several feet high extending some 40 yd is seen L, but at 0.3 mi a more impressive rock formation, maybe 20 ft high, is on the R. After rising about 140 ft from the road to about 2100 ft, the trail drops to about the 2000 ft line and continues with slight grade changes, crossing a bridge at 2.6 mi and reaching a jct. at 2.7 mi.

(Ahead is a 0.6 mi access trail that requires crossing the Moose River. The river is within sight L soon after the jct. and parallels it to the site of a former bridge, but now fording, possibly 30 ft downstream, is required, unless one can find enough rocks.)

From the jct., the main trail turns R on a gradual uphill with mostly red markers and a roaring stream R. The trail crosses a small side stream before it bends around a hill, turning nearly E. Sand banks are crossed at 4.3 mi and 4.6 mi. At 5.1 mi there is a Y in the trail where hikers need to be sure to keep L. The trail bends R (SE) around another hill and at 6.2 mi reaches a beaver dam where the trail is flooded. At 6.3 mi it avoids some former beaver ponds, bending L and starting uphill, with far fewer markers and more blowdowns. The climb is moderate, with some views L, and then becomes steeper, reaching height of land (elevation 2940 ft) on the Little Moose Mt. range at 7.3 mi. From there the roadway becomes obscure, but in 20 yd (or more when there are more leaves) there are glimpses of water downhill as the route descends slightly. The trail goes through a wet area of spruce-fir to the edge of Sly Pond at 7.7 mi and about 1000 ft above the Otter Brook Rd. trailhead. This lofty pond, 2872 ft in elevation, is lined by conifers and has boggy edges. It is doubtless devoid of fish. From the pond's far end, the crest of Little Moose Mt. rises to a summit of 3620 ft.

❄ Trail in winter: Snowmobile trail. Far from accessible roads, but otherwise could be skied or snowshoed.

🐾 Distances: To trail jct., 2.7 mi; to first sand bank, 4.3 mi; to height of land, 7.3 mi; to Sly Pond, 7.7 mi (12.4 km). Ascent from Otter Brook Rd, 1000 ft (305m). Elevation (height of land), 2940 ft (896 m).

Short Trails on Indian River Rd.

▶ Trailhead: Start at the jct. of Moose River Rd. and Otter Brook Rd. in the MRPWF (8.3 mi from the W entrance and 12.9 mi from the E entrance). Drive S on Otter Brook Rd. for 1.3 mi to the crossing of Otter Brook. Take the R fork just after the brook. The road continues past several ponds and trails and ends at a barrier and trailhead next to Indian Lake, 5.2 mi from Otter Brook. ◀

(91) Squaw Lake Trail

Map: D4

3.2 MI FROM OTTER BROOK on the R side of the road. It is 0.3 mi downhill all the way on yellow markers to the E end of Squaw Lake, about 100 ft below, where an informal campsite lies. Three other campsites, reachable by boat, are on the SE shore of the lake. Reaching them, boaters will pass on the L a towering rock wall, visible only by boat.

(92) Muskrat Pond Trail

Map: D5

4.4 MI FROM OTTER BROOK, on the L. This 0.1-mi trail goes from the SE side of Indian River Rd. to narrow, boggy Muskrat Pond.

(93) Indian Lake Trail

Map: D5

5.2 MI FROM OTTER BROOK, at the end-of-road trailhead. This is a minor piece of trail going R (N) 0.1 mi to the SW corner of Indian Lake. Two informal campsites on the W shore are reachable by boat. The outlet is at the far NW end of the lake. At the SW end, near a beaver lodge, there are pitcher plants and other wetland varieties of plants. The Indian

River (Horn Lake) Trail (trail 94) begins at the same trailhead.

❄ Trails in winter: Snowmobile trails, far from drivable roads.

🦫 Distances: Squaw Lake Trail, 0.3 mi (0.5 km); Muskrat Pond Trail, 0.1 mi; Indian Lake Trail, 0.1 mi (0.2 km).

(94) Indian River (Horn Lake) Trail

Map: D5

Indian River Rd. formerly continued past Indian Lake as a private road extending to Canachagala Brook near the Moose River (now on private land). The old road is now an access route into a remote section of the West Canada Lakes Wilderness Area. After it crosses the Indian River, marked trails lead to Balsam, Stink, and Horn Lakes.

▶ Trailhead: Start at the jct. of Moose River Rd. and Otter Brook Rd. in the MRPWF (8.3 mi from the W entrance and 12.9 mi from the E entrance). Drive S on Otter Brook Rd. for 3.3 mi to the crossing of Otter Brook. Turn R at the next jct. Continue past several ponds and trails and park at a barrier and trailhead next to Indian Lake, 5.2 mi from Otter Brook. ◀

STARTING AT THE BARRIER at the Indian Lake trailhead (0.0 mi), the route goes SW through a gentle notch below Indian Lake Mt., passing beaver meadows first L and then R. At 1.9 mi, the road reaches the Indian River and turns R to follow along it. To the L at the turn, a clearing leads down to the banks of the river. This is a possible crossover spot for wilderness travel by experienced bushwhackers to the group of lakes near Mountain Lake; however, if the water is high, this may be quite dangerous.

Continuing on around the tip of Indian Lake Mt., the route turns N across a swampy low ground, and at 2.6 mi enters the first of several "hallways" along this route—a trail with conifers packed tightly along each side with visibility sharply limited. The trail climbs slightly along a shoulder of the mountain and descends again to the Indian River at 3.8 mi. An old bridge is long gone, and the river must be waded. The hiker can choose water that is ankle deep over slippery rocks, or nearly waist-deep water with firmer footing under a cable upstream. It can be dangerously high in wet times. A rock for changing back into boots about 50 yd beyond the river has a benchmark showing an elevation of 1899 ft. From here on, the main route is generally W.

Horn Lake provides the first side trail at 4.4 mi. Turn L (S) onto an old road. The yellow-marked trail, with little maples trying to impinge on the roadway, climbs continuously, but not too steeply, to a jct. at 1.9 mi. The Horn Lake trail goes L while another road goes R. After turning L at the jct., the trail crosses a creek and climbs again to reach an informal campsite on Horn Lake at 3.0 mi (7.4 mi from the trailhead). There is a jct. in the old road not far from Horn Lake. When going up, the branch to the R is an old logging road which leads W along the lower edge of Ice Cave Mt. This would give experienced bushwhackers a path to continue on to North Lake in the J.P. Lewis Tract. Refer to trail 108E. That route is among suggestions for the North Country Trail from North Dakota to Lake Champlain.

Continuing on the main trail past the Horn Lake turnoff, it is a short way to the Balsam Lake Trail R (N) at 4.6 mi. This trail goes N on yellow markers to the shore of boggy, pond-size Balsam Lake (4.7 mi from the trailhead) with a round-trip distance from the main trail of less than a quarter mile.

Past the Balsam Lake turnoff, the main trail parallels the Balsam Lake outlet R, now a beaver pond nearly 0.3 mi long, and then crosses the end of another beaver pond L, making travel wet, reaching a clearing with a trail jct. at 5.9 mi. The 0.4-mi side trail goes N on level ground to the SW end of pond-sized Stink Lake (6.3 mi from the trailhead). The old road continues but eventually crosses into posted private land of the Adirondack League Club, and is not recommended past the Stink Lake spur.

✳ Trail in winter: Extremely remote, accessible only by snowmobiles, which can legally go as far as the wilderness boundary at the trailhead. Otherwise, it is suitable for backcountry skiing and snowshoeing, taking into consideration the river crossing. Any group attempting this trip should be well prepared for winter wilderness conditions.

🪣 Distances: Indian Lake trailhead to Indian River crossing, 3.8 mi; to Horn Lake via spur, 7.4 mi (11.9 km); to Balsam Lake via spur, 4.7 mi (7.6 km); to Stink Lake via spur, 6.3 mi (10.2 km). ◆

McKeever–Woodgate Section

This section offers many trails to and along beautiful lakes and ponds as well as scenic views from the summit of Woodhull Mt. and a ledge overlooking Bear Lake. This region is frequented by hunters in the fall, many having their own traditional locations.

The waters of the region mostly feed the Black River. Several of the lakes are or were dammed to store water for the Black River Canal, which supplied water to the Erie Canal. Smaller dams were also used by lumbermen to supply water for log drives down the river. A dam and lumber mill existed on the Moose River just upstream of the NY 28 bridge until, rather late in life, it went out in a gala performance, leaving the downstream bridge lodged solid with cut timber. The dam and mill were owned by John Dix, former governor of New York State.

JOHN BROWN TRACT

The original John Brown Tract was a vast piece of the West-Central Region. A 1990 agreement between a paper company and New York State has named and opened this smaller piece of the original tract to public access for recreational use. The tract extends along NY 28 from the Moose River on the S to Gull Lake (near Minnehaha) in the N. The W boundary for most of the way is the Hamilton Herkimer county line, about 1.7 mi W of the highway at Gull Lake. The public may enter the tract for recreational use and camping, keeping in mind that the paper company may close any one of the five sections for timber harvesting for approximately two to four years. The DEC will eventually install three trails. At present, two trails are in place. Motorized vehicles and bicycles are not permitted. Snowmobiles are to be allowed only on a trail close to and paralleling NY 28.

The two trails now in place are the southern end of the Browns Tract Trail (trail 76) and the JBT Gull Lake Trail (trail 76A)—see the Old Forge–Thendara section. An access parking area is also located on the W side of NY 28, 1.6 mi N of the Moose River bridge. From there, a barricaded road leads a short distance N to an open area.

There is a stub of highway that can be used for the E side of NY 28 just N of the bridge over the Moose River by McKeever. Access on the tract W of this parking area is limited, since the easement mostly covers land in Herkimer and Oneida counties. The three-county boundary point is only about 0.3 mi from the highway.

SHORT HIKES:

◆ Gull Lake—6.8 mi round trip. This peaceful lake makes a beautiful setting for lunch. Return by the same route, or continue on the Gull Lake Loop, for a round trip of 7.8 mi. See trail 102.

◆ Bear Lake—4.0 mi round trip. Offers a modest amount of climbing, and the lake is a very rewarding wilderness experience. Return by the same route. See trail 104.

MODERATE HIKE:

◆ Woodhull Lake—9.0 mi round trip. The lake is large, and the lean-to is one of the largest in the Adirondacks. See trail 100.

HARDER HIKES:

◆ Sand Lake Falls—15.2 mi round trip. Pleasant trip on gentle terrain to the lean-to at Sand Lake Falls. The falls are modest, but the scene is pleasant. See trail 101.

◆ Woodhull Mt.—15.2 mi round trip. The view from the fire tower is very nice, with panoramic views and, surprisingly, no trace of the facilities of the Adirondack League Club to the SE. As of Autumn 2006, the tower could be ascended to just below the cab; however, there is no assurance that it will be climbable when you get there. See trail 98.

Woodhull Lean-to. NORM LANDIS

(95) **Round Pond–Long Lake Trail**

Map: A5

▶ Trailhead: From the NY 28 bridge over the Moose River near McKeever, take Moose River Rd. on the S side of the river, heading W, for 2.1 mi. The trailhead is an old woods road on the L (S), shortly before the high point on the road. Although marked, it is easy to miss. Park on the shoulder (almost room for one car) or on the S side at a wider spot at the top of the hill. ◀

FROM NY 28 (0.0 mi), the route follows the old road straight for 40 yd, then turns R and curves gently up a hill and over the top, curves R, and meets an unmarked trail jct. Ahead from the jct., and then to the R, an old road leads quickly to the beautiful shore of Round Pond at 0.3 mi. The marked trail leads L (E) away from the old road at the jct., climbing gently. It continues generally S along a ridgetop woods road. The forest here is nearly all hardwood. Ignore a road fork on the R at 0.9 mi.

The route finally comes down off the ridge in a couple of moderate descents. For the final quarter mile, the route follows S near the Lost Pond–Long Lake stream.

The trail ends at a jct. at 1.7 mi with the Brandy Lake Trail (trail 96). From here, to the L it is 1.0 mi to NY 28 via trail 96 and 1.3 mi to Lakeview Rd. along Otter Lake via trails 96 and 97. To the R, one may continue on trail 96 to Brandy Lake, 1.0 mi from the jct., and Round

Lake Rd., 3.4 mi. Round Lake, S on Round Lake Rd., should not be confused with Round Pond near the start of this trail.

❋ Trail in winter: State snowmobile trail, but not shown on Oneida County snowmobile map. Otherwise suitable for snowshoeing or skiing.

🐾 Distances: Moose River Rd. to Round Pond, 0.3 mi; to Brandy Lake Trail (trail 96), 1.7 mi (2.7 km).

(96) Brandy Lake Trail

Map: A5, 6

▶ Trailhead: From the bridge over the Moose River near McKeever, drive S on NY 28 for 3.6 mi. The snowmobile trailhead and woodsy parking for several cars are located in the trees to the R (W). Headed N, after passing through Woodgate, it's 3.6 mi from the Adirondack Park sign to the trailhead on the L.

It is also possible to canoe across Long Lake to reach a yellow-marked spur trail that connects to the main trail. From NY 28 at a 90-degree turn W of White Lake and Boy Scout Camp Russell, drive N, take the next L onto Round Lake Rd., then turn R onto Long Lake Rd. at 0.5 mi from NY 28. Go 1.1 mi NNE, passing Camp Nazareth, to a gravel parking lot on the R with DEC markers at the intersection of Capron Rd., a few yards from the lake L. Paddle N (R from the put-in) less than 0.4 mi past a couple islands (one behind the other) and turn L (NW) before the lake narrows, where the trail comes down to the shore on the L. ◀

THE ROUTE FROM NY 28 (0.0 mi) is an old woods road going gently down to Otter Lake outlet stream at 0.4 mi. On the other side, the trail climbs gently and meets a jct. on level ground at 0.5 mi. To the R is the Otter Lake Outlet Trail (trail 97), leading to trailheads at Otter Lake.

Turning L, the trail goes SW, swings around a hill, and heads N to cross an inlet creek of Long Lake shortly before the jct. with the Round Pond–Long Lake Trail (trail 95) at 1.0 mi. The route then heads L (SW) and starts a gentle climb, passing a rock pile perhaps 40 yd long. It soon levels out, continuing on easy terrain to a jct. at 1.4 mi. The route ahead looks better, but the marked trail turns abruptly L and begins a climb.

The trail crosses two snowmobile bridges, and at 1.7 mi where the wide snowmobile trail is rising and bending right, there is a footpath L with a handmade sign and an old faded arrow. This blue-marked trail heads uphill, turns right, and continues rising slightly, eventually dropping to an informal campsite at the E shore of Brandy Lake at 2.1 mi. It continues along the side of a hill, across a wet area, and climbs a ways into the woods until, at 2.3 mi, it reaches a large log across the trail. Although another log L is cut out, that is a trail to private land. The trail goes R, downhill, to the shore of Brandy Lake at 2.3 mi, passing a yellow-marked spur trail at L.

[This spur trail continues to Long Lake and can be used to reach the main trail by boat or canoe across Long Lake (see Trailhead, above). It can function also as a carry from Long Lake to Brandy Lake. It heads generally S, then bends R uphill, passing some side trails with flagging, apparently leading to private property. It then goes along a ridge with some glimpses of Long Lake and between rock walls 6 to 8 ft high and about 20 ft apart at 0.5 mi from the jct. At 0.6 mi the trail drops L to near Long Lake and then turns R along the lake to end at an overhanging tree with a yellow trail marker at 0.7 mi.]

The main trail continues as a snowmobile trail SW and then S to a trailhead on Round Lake Rd. near Masonic Home Camp, approximately 2.0 mi farther.

✻ Trail in winter: Part is snowmobile trail. Otherwise suitable for snowshoeing and skiing.

ᙏ Distances: Trailhead to Otter Lake Outlet Trail (trail 97), 0.4 mi; to Round Pond–Long Lake Trail jct. (trail 95), 1.0 mi; to Brandy Lake campsite, 2.1 mi; to Brandy Lake shore, 2.3 mi (3.9 km). To Long Lake via spur, 3.1 mi (5.0 km).

(97) Otter Lake Outlet Trail

Map: A5

▶ Trailhead: At the Otter Lake settlement on NY 28 S of the Moose River, take Lakeview Rd. 1.4 mi to its end. A dirt road continues on to a tiny dam on Otter Lake outlet. The snowmobile trail starts on the S side, near the dam. Alternately, from the highway take Woods Rd. on the S side of Otter Lake for 0.4 mi. The snowmobile trail starts on the S side at a bend in the road. At the other end, the trail may be reached via the Brandy Lake Trail (trail 96). ◀

FROM WOODS RD. (0.0 mi), go S a short way to a snowmobile trail jct. Turn R up the hill and continue in a gentle loop, to meet the trail from Lakeview Rd. at about 0.3 mi (0.1 mi from Lakeview Rd. to the R). That route goes S from the side of Lakeview Rd. about 50 ft before the dam.

The trail turns L and follows the Otter Lake outlet stream through hardwood forests and past huge boulders strewn about. At 0.8 mi, the route leaves creek bottomland and ascends to a broad shelf along a hillside. This easy surface allows the trail to remain almost level for the rest of the way to the jct. with Brandy Lake Trail (trail 96) at 1.1 mi. From here, trail 96 goes L to NY 28 in 0.5 mi; the route R goes around Brandy Lake and beyond to Round Lake Rd.

❋ Trail in winter: Snowmobile trail. Otherwise suitable for skiing and snowshoeing.

𝔐 Distances: Woods Rd. to jct. near Lakeview Rd., 0.3 mi; to Brandy Lake Trail (trail 96), 1.1 mi (1.8 km). (Lakeview Rd. trailhead to Brandy Lake Trail, 0.9 mi.)

(98) Woodhull Mt. Trail

Map: B5

This trail to a fire tower is long for a day trip (15.2 mi round trip) but it offers easy walking, much of it on an old RR bed with gentle grades. Some people make the trip as a combined bike/hike, mountain biking for approximately the first five miles, securing their bikes, and hiking to the top.

The recommended day hike for the area is a loop trip: take either trail 98 or 99 from its McKeever trailhead to the Bear Lake Trail (trail 104); follow this to Bear Lake; then take the Bear Lake–Woodhull Lake Trail (trail 100) to Woodhull Lake and its lean-to. Then use the Wolf Lake Landing Rd. (trail 99) N to the Woodhull Mt. Trail (trail 98), proceeding W to the starting point. Both lakes have fine scenery. Bear Lake has a nice sand and pebble beach, and Woodhull Lake has a grand lean-to. The full loop is 10.4 mi (16.8 km).

▶ Trailhead: Go to McKeever Rd., on NY 28 S of Old Forge. Turn E toward McKeever, just S of the Moose River bridge. Go 0.3 mi to a jct. The pavement turns L. Leave it and continue straight ahead on a dirt road past the old RR station. Cross the tracks and continue to the second parking lot, 0.8 mi from the highway. The first parking lot, at 0.6 mi, is for the Wolf Lake Landing Rd. (trail 99). ◀

FROM THE PARKING LOT AND TRAIL REGISTER (0.0 mi), the route continues beyond the barricade on a surprisingly smooth surface. This rebuilt roadway follows the roadbed of the former Moose River Lumber Company Railroad, which went to Number Four Camp near Woodhull Mt. You may notice the gentle slope of the route and the occasional cut needed to avoid sudden climbs.

At 0.7 mi, a trail R leads to Bear Lake and beyond (trail 104). At 2.6 mi, the yellow route crossing the trail leads L (N) to Remsen Falls and R (S) 0.3 mi to connect with the Wolf Landing Rd. about 100 ft before it turns R (S) on the way to Woodhull Lake.

[Remsen Falls, a 6.2 mi round trip via this route, is a popular day hike. From the jct., the Remsen Falls spur trail L goes generally N, descending almost continuously with a gentle slope. It passes several camping spots and reaches the South Branch of the Moose River near Remsen Falls at 0.5 mi. Crossing the river at times of high water is out of the question, but the usual crossing otherwise is above the falls, where the trail reaches the river at an old road ford. Some hikers wade the stream at the Remsen Falls lean-to (see trail 78), about 0.2 mi to the L, or just below it. In any case, the water may be more than knee deep. It becomes chest deep about 24 hours after a rain. The falls are not very high, but are still worth the trip.]

Continuing E from the four-way jct., the Woodhull Mt. Trail passes a small pond on the L at 2.9 mi. After some gentle climbing, the route levels off. It was in this area that the logging RR crew headed for Number Four Camp would uncouple the moving cars from the engine and race ahead to pull off to the L on a Y. After the cars rolled by on the main line, they would back the engine on the second leg of the Y, rejoin the main line going in reverse, catch up with the cars, and hook on before applying the brakes at Number Four Camp. The train was thus reorganized for the return trip.

As it starts down the gentle slope, the road finally leaves the RR bed and turns slightly L. The remains of the old RR bed continue on ahead. A short distance farther on, the route becomes slightly rougher and the road finally ends in a sharp R turn on a creek bank at 5.1 mi. The trail turns L at the end of the road on the creek bottom, and crosses over the creek. The route continues from the creek bank as a narrow foot trail, fairly well marked with a combination of red DEC markers, red painted can lids, red tape, and finally orange and red rectangular markers.

From here on, the trail climbs steadily with very few level parts. At 5.6 mi, a red-marked hunting trail goes R, and the trail takes a sharp L. The route climbs more steeply and zigzags somewhat randomly. It drops into a swampy creek bed at 6.1 mi, goes up steeply for a short distance, and reaches a trail jct. at 6.4 mi. (The route straight ahead shows the heaviest use. This is a hunting trail, marked occasionally with red paint blazes, that leads 0.3 mi to the Wolf Lake Landing Rd. Extension.)

The red DEC trail turns L and continues climbing. A creek at 6.6 mi provides a brief level section, followed by more climbing through thickets and blowdown. As the trail levels out, it becomes bumpier and somewhat overgrown, finally leading to the fire tower near a huge boulder at 7.6 mi.

The only view from the ground may be obtained by going E on the summit for 200 ft to the site of a burned cabin, where a limited opening to the E gives a glimpse of unending forest and hills. A better view by far can be gained by climbing the tower, which is open to just below the cab. (Care must be taken here. The steel tower seems in usable condition, but the wood steps are showing rot and boards are broken.) To the S, one can see part of Woodhull Lake, with Big Island visible at the near end. To the N, Nicks Lake is visible. Looking W, the South Branch of the Moose River appears nearby, passing through an interesting gorge on its journey W.

❁ Trail in winter: Snowmobile trail most of the way. Suitable for snowshoeing or backcountry skiing. Mountain section recommended only for experienced backcountry skiers.

🐾 Distances: To Bear Lake Trail jct. (trail 104), 0.7 mi; to Remsen Falls Spur and Wolf Lake Landing Rd. Link, 2.6 mi; to road end, 5.1 mi; to summit and lookout tower, 7.6 mi (12.2 km). Ascent, 812 ft (247 m). Summit elevation, 2362 ft (720 m).

(99) Wolf Lake Landing Rd.

Map: B5

There were once plans to abandon this trail, which had become terribly rutted. Vast improvements since have rehabilitated it for use by the disabled. It's quite smooth and suitable for bicycles as well—this being in a Wild Forest rather than a Wilderness Area, where bicycles are banned.

Funding from several sources, including a federal grant under the National Recreation Trails Fund Act, allowed improvements. One goal was to provide access to scenic destinations for the disabled on a multiuse trail. Improvements have made the trail into a road, open to the public with motor vehicles; however, ATVs are not allowed. The disabled can obtain permits to use gates for access to Remsen Falls (and a handicapped accessible privy, picnic table, and campsite) and the last several hundred yards to Woodhull Lake. For others, parking at the connecting trail to Remsen Falls would cut about five miles off a round trip hike to Woodhull Mt. via trail 98. Contact the DEC office in Herkimer (315-866-6330) well in advance to arrange for a permit.

Once used by the Adirondack League Club to reach the steamboat at Wolf Lake landing, it has effectively been replaced for that purpose by the private Bisby Rd.

▶ Trailhead: Go to McKeever Rd., on NY 28 S of Old Forge. Turn E toward McKeever just S of the Moose River crossing. Go 0.3 mi to a jct. The pavement turns L. Leave the pavement and continue straight ahead on a dirt road past the old RR station. Cross the tracks and continue to the first parking lot, on the R 0.6 mi from the highway. The automobile road continues ahead a short distance to another parking lot used for the Woodhull Mt. Trail, trail 98. ◀

FROM THE PARKING LOT (0.0 mi), the route turns R (S) and soon curves E. At 1.1 mi, a jct. is created by the crossing of the blue-marked Bear Lake Trail (trail 104), on its way uphill from trail 98 as it continues R to Bear Lake and beyond.

At a jct. at 3.1 mi, a road L leads N to the Woodhull Mt. Trail (trail 98). Just beyond the jct. Wolf Lake Landing Rd. turns R, passing some hunters' campsites. The road heads S in reasonably dry condition. An unmarked road L (E) at 4.8 mi is not a DEC trail but an abandoned old road that led to the region of the old Number Four lumber camp.

Beyond the jct., Wolf Lake Landing Rd. climbs over a minor hill and descends. At 5.0 mi, the L fork leads down to Wolf Lake Landing, a shoreline with a nice view, with the Woodhull Lake lean-to in sight on a point R. The landing was once a major transfer point for Adirondack League Club members going to camp. The R fork of the road continues S parallel to the lake.

A yellow-marked trail R at 5.5 mi is the Bear Lake–Woodhull Lake Trail (trail 100). Just beyond, the trail crosses a creek, and 50 ft beyond that there is a terribly muddy, red-marked spur trail L (E) to the Woodhull Lake lean-to, a doublewide: where the end would normally be, there are a couple of posts and the shelter continues to about twice the length of a normal lean-to. Beyond this jct., the old road becomes the Woodhull Rd. Trail (105).

❊ Trail in winter: Snowmobile trail. Suitable for skis and snowshoes, but the first segment should be bypassed by using trail 98 and the Landing Rd. link.

❧ Distances: McKeever trailhead to Bear Lake Trail (trail 104), 1.1 mi; to crossover trail to Woodhull Mt. Trail (98), 3.1 mi; to extension, 4.8 mi; to Wolf Lake Landing, 5.0 mi; to Woodhull Lake Lean-to and Bear Lake–Woodhull Lake Trail (trail 100), 5.5 mi (8.9 km).

(100) **Bear Lake–Woodhull Lake Trail**

Map: B5

This interior trail connects Bear Lake (see trail 104) and Woodhull Lake on the Woodhull Rd. Trail and the Wolf Lake Landing Rd. Trail (trails 105 and 99). It passes small Bloodsucker Pond near Woodhull Lake.

▶ Locator: The N end of the trail intersects trail 98, 0.7 mi from the McKeever trailhead; the S end is on trail 105, 7.5 mi from the Bear Creek Rd. trailhead. ◀

FROM THE BEAR LAKE TRAIL at the inlet to Bear Lake (0.0 mi), the yellow-marked trail goes E along the creek, then turns slightly S away from it to climb over the divide between Bear Lake and the much larger Woodhull Lake. At the top of the divide, there is a confusing turn to the R (S) along a wet area.

After the high point, the route is easier to recognize on an old road. It passes Bloodsucker Pond at 1.6 mi and reaches the Woodhull Rd. Trail (trail 105) at 1.7 mi, just 50 ft N of Bloodsucker Creek, which is itself 50 ft N of the side trail E to Woodhull Lake lean-to 0.2 mi away. The jct. with Woodhull Rd. is not marked. It is best located by its position just N of the creek and lean-to trail.

❊ Trail in winter: Suitable for snowshoers or good backcountry skiers.

❧ Distances: Bear Lake to Woodhull Lake, 1.7 mi (2.7 km).

(101) **Sand Lake Falls Trail**

This trail provides a through route from the Woodgate area, partly via trail 105, to North Lake. Sand Lake Falls is closer to the North Lake end, but the Woodgate trailhead leads to many other trails.

▶ Trailheads: From Woodgate on NY 28, take Bear Creek Rd. E. Cross the RR tracks and continue to the parking lot just over the line into Herkimer County, 3.1 mi from Woodgate, on the L. A badly rutted and rocky jeep road continues 3.7 mi to a small section of private land; this is trail 105, with which trail 101 shares the route at its start and also briefly midway.

The North Lake end of the trail is reached from Forestport on NY 28. Go E on North Lake Rd., cross the RR tracks at Forestport Station, and continue to the dam at Atwell at 15.4 mi. Turn L at the dam and go 0.3 mi to a snowmobile trailhead with a register where the trail heads immediately uphill L. ◀

FROM THE PARKING LOT and trail register on Bear Creek Rd. (0.0 mi), the trail shares its route with Woodhull Rd. (trail 105). The blue-marked Chub Pond Trail (trail 103) departs R at 0.25 mi. The yellow trail 101 turns L off of the deeply rutted and muddy Woodhull Rd. at 0.4 mi. (Woodhull Rd. continues straight ahead, rejoining trail 101 at 2.6 mi, compared to 3.1 mi by the trail; one can choose to follow the road, but it is rough going. See below.)

Turning L off the road and going past a barricade, the trail follows an old woods road N. After a gradual descent, the trail becomes nearly level. At 1.2 and 1.4 mi, old roads L lead in 50 yd to the banks of Bear Creek.

Continuing NE on the R fork, the old road is nearly level, but ATVs have made the next half mile into a chain of hogwallows. At 2.0 mi, after two tiny brooks, the red trail to Gull Lake (trail 102) goes uphill R, while the yellow trail continues on ahead. There is little change in elevation along this part of the trail, because it follows the contours.

The yellow (and snowmobile) route turns R, and heads SSE to a jct. with Woodhull Rd. at 3.1 mi. The route then turns L and follows the muddy jeep road, which soon heads E and tilts upward, leaving the mud behind. This climb is not very steep or long. After topping the hill, the route levels and comes to an inholding of private land at 3.9 mi. There are several private camps here, once labeled "Village of

Millbrook, population 0 (Dry town)." The road continues on past the cabin to the L as the red hiking (and snowmobile) Woodhull Rd. Trail (trail 105). At the corner in the road just before the Millbrook site the route heading R (E) is the blue hiking (and snowmobile) trail 101 to Sand Lake Falls.

After the wet Millbrook area, conditions improve as the trail climbs a slight hill, then drops. At 6.9 mi, the trail finally reaches a high point, turns almost S, and heads down. The downhill continues on a mostly gentle slope to a lean-to at 7.0 mi. Sand Lake Falls is just beyond the lean-to. The falls are in a very pleasant setting, with the water gliding over a smooth rock slab for a 10-ft descent. Smaller falls on the stream above and below this site make for pleasant exploring. In summer, the stream is small, but still high enough to top your boots (but no crossing is necessary). The blue-marked trail continues through woods past the lean-to, then emerges on the banks of the creek at a long beaver meadow at 7.3 mi.

Depending on the time of year, the next 0.7 mi can be soggy going. The trail follows the L edge of a vlei, crosses a point of land, continues along the edge, crosses another point of land, then proceeds on a snowmobile bridge over a tributary. Following the edge of a vlei again, the trail bends R and proceeds over a bridge (sometimes under water) of nearly 40 yd, crossing two streams. To the L, signs indicate the private property boundary of the Adirondack League Club as the trail heads uphill. It ascends, bends R and L and drops to Grindstone Creek at 8.9 mi. Grindstone Creek can be crossed on a bridge.

The next segment is pleasant walking on an old road in good condition, which is marked for snowmobiles. At 9.9 mi on the R (SW), the Little Woodhull Lake Trail (trail 107) leads to Little Woodhull Lake and North Lake Rd. Trail 101 continues SE, crossing several brooks, before finally descending to North Lake Rd. at 11.9 mi.

❊ Trail in winter: Snowmobile trail, probably lightly used. Suitable for strong backcountry skiers and snowshoers.

❀ Distances: Bear Creek Rd. trailhead to Chub Pond Trail (trail 103), 0.3 mi; to split from trail 105, 0.4 mi; to return to trail 105, 3.1 mi; to jct. at Millbrook site, 3.9 mi; to lean-to and falls, 7.0 mi; to Grindstone Creek, 8.9 mi; to Little Woodhull Lake Trail (trail 107), 9.9 mi; to North Lake Rd., 11.9 mi (19.2 km).

(102) **Gull Lake Loop**

▶ Trailhead: This interior trail begins at 2.0 mi on the Sand Lake Falls Trail (trail 101). Take Bear Creek Rd. E from Woodgate on NY 28. Cross the RR tracks and continue to the parking lot on the L, at 3.1 mi from Woodgate.

A badly rutted and rocky jeep road (trail 105) continues on for another 3.4 mi to a small section of private land. ◀

FROM THE PARKING LOT (0.0 mi), follow trail 101 past its jct. with the blue Chub Pond Trail (trail 103) on the R at 0.3 mi (a loop trip returns to this jct.), being sure to follow it L off Woodhull Rd. (trail 105) at 0.4 mi. The red-marked Gull Lake Loop leaves this trail at a jct. R at 2.0 mi.

Heading SE, the red-marked trail goes gently uphill for 0.3 mi to a crossing of Woodhull Rd. (trail 105). Past Woodhull Rd., 4WD vehicles occasionally mangle the route, an old woods road, on their way SE to Gull Lake. It is marked as a snowmobile trail in red, and as a red foot trail.

The route is easy going to a jct. at 1.0 mi. To the L, a yellow foot trail follows an old woods road for a short ways, then continues across rougher terrain to the lean-to at 1.4 mi. It is well located on a point of land, with fine views of a peaceful wilderness lakeshore and clean water. A return to the trail takes only a few minutes. (Total trip distance from the trailhead to this point is 3.8 mi.)

The trail briefly skirts the lake near an unofficial boat landing, plunges into the woods with little ups and downs, and then crosses the lake outlet stream on a snowmobile bridge. The route continues generally W. A short herd path leads through the woods to the swampy S shore of Gull Lake.

The main trail bends R (S), and finally SW, continuing through open woods to a jct. with the blue-marked Chub Pond Trail (trail 103) at 4.2 mi. From here, the loop trip follows the blue trail R (W) on a smooth, pleasant woods road, reaching the trailhead at 7.8 mi.

❋ Trail in winter: Snowmobile trail. Suitable for backcountry skiing and snowshoeing.

🐾 Distances: Parking lot/trailhead to trail via Sand Lake Falls Trail (trail 101), 2.0 mi. Sand Lake Falls Trail to Gull Lake lean-to spur, 1.0 mi; to lean-to, 1.4 mi; to Chub Pond Trail, 4.2 mi (6.8 km). Full loop to parking lot, 7.8 mi (12.5 km).

(103) **Chub Pond Trail**

Map: B6, p. 223

▶ Trailhead: See trail 102. ◀

FROM THE PARKING LOT and trail register (0.0 mi), the route follows Woodhull Rd. for 0.3 mi, then turns R on another old road marked as a blue foot trail (and snowmobile trail). At 1.2 mi, a trail on the R with two old paint blazes leads past a beaver pond on Gull Lake Outlet stream and into unknown territory. Shortly afterward, the trail turns R and crosses Gull Lake Outlet stream on a snowmobile bridge. The stream meanders quietly beside grass hummocks.

At 2.0 mi, the Gull Lake Loop (trail 102) joins on the L. Continuing past this jct., at 2.2 mi the route crosses a stream and turns L, the snowmobile route following the old road through a miserably wet section, and the foot trail paralleling it on the hillside.

At 2.6 mi, the routes rejoin. At 3.0 mi, a short path leads R to the open marsh at the upper end of Buck Pond.

The trail splits at 3.7 mi. The L fork is marked for snowmobiles and as a red foot trail; the R fork continues as a blue foot trail only (see below). The L fork (red) leads down a mostly gentle hill to the shore of Chub Pond at 4.2 mi. A spur trail leads L to a lean-to, Chub Pond 2, on the shore of the lake at 4.4 mi. The setting is idyllic. The pond is gravel-bottomed, and lined with evergreens.

The snowmobile trail continues around the shore of the lake, passing lean-to #1 (see description below) in the midst of old blowdown on the S side, and ending on the S shore of the lake.

The blue trail continues from the jct. at 3.7 mi as a foot trail. At 4.0 mi, the route starts down gently, then steeper, to a jct. with the snowmobile trail around the lake at 4.3 mi. Continuing R (SW) around the lake, the trail reaches a bridge across an old dam at the outlet at 4.8 mi. A tornado in 1984 took down nearly every tree in this area. The debris is now hidden by fields of ferns, bushes, and young trees.

At 5.2 mi, the yellow trail to Stone Dam Lake (trail 106) joins on the R (S). It may be difficult to find in the heavy bushes. The snowmobile trail continues ahead and ends in woods at the S shore of the lake. A side trail R at 5.3 mi leads a short distance to Chub Pond Lean-to 1. The lean-to has to be seen to be believed. It was built in 1961 (DEC lean-to permit #193, according to a sign) by a private group as a sort of wilderness palace, with bunks, tables, shelves, and skylights (normally covered to prevent damage). It was refurbished in 1986 with a porch added for stability after the structure was damaged by trees falling on it during the 1984 tornado. Nonetheless, its setting is deep in the woods, while Chub Pond Lean-to 2 overlooks the lake.

Gull Lake Outlet was reportedly dammed by canal authorities in the early part of this century, to store water for the Black River Canal. Most of the earthen parts of the very small dam remain.

[For travelers continuing on to Stone Dam, the yellow trail, trail 106 at 5.2 mi, near Chub Pond Lean-to 1, leads S over a small hill and across rolling terrain to Stone Dam Lake at 7.8 mi. The route is marked with yellow foot trail markers. It provides a real sense of wilderness, and offers a through hike from Black Creek Rd. to North Lake Rd. The trail does not stop at Stone Dam Lake, or at Stone Dam, which is washed out. Be alert for the water seen through the trees L at 7.8 mi (2.6 mi from Chub Lake). Stone Dam Lake Camp, listed on the North Wilmurt USGS Quad map, is now no more than detectable foundations (10 x 12 ft) hidden in the woods. After crossing Woodhull Creek at 10.3 mi, the route follows a smooth and broad woods road, with obviously greater usage. The end of the trail, at 11.4 mi, is on North Lake Rd. (see trail 106).]

❄ Trail in winter: Snowmobile trail. Suitable for snowshoeing or backcountry skiing. The descent to Chub Pond on the N side has some steep parts, but the trail via Chub Pond Lean-to 2 is gentle.

🚶 Distances: Trailhead to split from Woodhull Rd., 0.3 mi; to Gull Lake Loop (trail 102), 2.0 mi; to Buck Pond spur, 3.0 mi; to Chub Pond Lean-to 2, 4.4 mi; to Lean-to 1 near Chub Pond, 5.3 mi (8.5 km). Continuation to Stone Dam Lake, 7.8 mi; to North Lake Rd., 11.4 mi (18.4 km).

(104) **Bear Lake Trail**

Map: B5

The Bear Lake Trail connects the Woodhull Mt. Trail (trail 98) on the N with the Woodhull Rd. Trail (trail 105) on the S. It passes Bear Lake, which is remote and beautiful, and has a connecting trail in its middle for access to the lean-to on Woodhull Lake. A very nice loop trip can be had by taking the Woodhull Mt. and Bear Lake trails from McKeever to Bear Lake, the Bear Lake–Woodhull Lake Trail to the lean-to on Woodhull Lake, the Wolf Lake Landing Rd. to connect on the N, and the Woodhull Mt. Trail to return (trails 98, 104, 100, 99, and 98). Longer loop trips can be made using all of Woodhull Rd.

▶ Locator: This interior trail's N end is on trail 98, 0.7 mi from the McKeever trailhead, and its S end is on trail 105, 7.5 mi from the Bear Creek Rd. trailhead. ◀

THE YELLOW-MARKED BEAR LAKE TRAIL begins (0.0 mi) on the R (S) at 0.7 mi on the Woodhull Mt. Trail (trail 98). It heads S, crossing Wolf Lake Landing Rd. (trail 99) at 0.2 mi. After the road, the route crosses some marshy ground and begins a mild climb while weaving a bit. At 0.8 mi, after descending a little, the route turns L and starts more steeply downhill. There is a lookout next to the corner giving a view through the trees of Bear Lake and the hills beyond.

At the bottom of the descent, at 1.2 mi, the trail comes close to the lake at an enjoyable sand and pebble beach. A little farther E around the lake, an unofficial campsite makes a good place to stay. Continuing beyond that, the route turns gradually S and meets the main inlet stream at 1.7 mi. A spur trail R leads to an unofficial campsite at the lake near the inlet stream.

On the S side of the bridge over the stream, the yellow-marked Bear Lake–Woodhull Lake Trail (trail 100) goes L (E). To the S beyond this jct. the Bear Lake Trail passes through an old lumber clearing, strikingly bordered by fir trees at 2.1 mi. The trail turns L, climbs a hillside, goes sharply L, and continues uphill to a saddle below Neejer Hill, where the trail joins the Woodhull Rd. Trail (trail 105) at 3.4 mi. To the R, it is 4.7 mi to the Bear Creek Rd. trailhead.

❅ Trail in winter: Suitable for snowshoeing or intermediate-level backcountry skiing. There are some ups and downs, including a rather steep descent to Bear Lake.

🐾 Distances: McKeever trailhead via trail 98 to Bear Lake Trail, 0.7 mi. Trail 98 to Bear Lake, 1.2 mi; to Bear Lake–Woodhull Lake Trail (trail 100), 1.7 mi; to Woodhull Rd. Trail (trail 105), 3.4 mi (5.5 km).

(105) Woodhull Rd. Trail

Map: B5, 6

This old road once gave access to the landing on Woodhull Lake for travel to Adirondack League Club land as well as later access to the dam on the lake. The dam is on private, posted land, but the route still allows access to state land on Woodhull Lake (not the shortest route) and to many other backwoods lakes and streams. The road is still used by 4WD vehicles to reach a private plot of land on Mill Brook, about halfway to Woodhull Lake.

▶ Trailhead: From Woodgate on NY 28, go E on Bear Creek Rd. Cross the RR tracks at 0.8 mi, and continue to the end of the good road and a DEC parking lot at 3.1 mi. ◀

BEGINNING AT THE REGISTER by the parking lot (0.0 mi), the route starts on a jeep road. In a short distance, the blue-marked Chub Pond Trail (trail 103, used also for the Gull Lake Loop) joins on the R. Woodhull Rd. continues straight.

At 0.4 mi, the Sand Lake Falls Trail (trail 101) goes L as the road continues ahead. They rejoin later; the hiker can avoid the muddy road by taking trail 101, although the trail is 0.5 mi longer.

At 1.9 mi, a trail on the R leads to Gull Lake (trail 102). At 2.6 mi, trail 101 rejoins the road. After climbing E up a hill, the road turns L and a not-too-prominent blue-marked trail connects on the R at 3.7 mi. This is the continuation of the Sand Lake Falls Trail (trail 101) to the E.

The Woodhull Rd. Trail continues N on the L branch, through "Village of Millbrook, Population 0 (Dry town)." This is a collection of private camps on a private plot surrounded by state land. Beyond the camps, the trail crosses Mill Brook and begins a long gentle climb along the flank of Neejer Hill. After ascending, the trail turns E across a broad hilltop. At 4.7 mi, the Bear Lake Trail (trail 104) joins on the L.

At 6.2 mi, the trail meets an old road jct. (Straight ahead, the old road heads E, then curves to the SE, headed for Woodhull Dam. It reaches private posted land 1.1 mi from the jct.) The trail continues L (NW) from this jct. with some muddy areas.

At 7.4 mi, a spur R leads to the gigantic Woodhull Lake Lean-to in 0.2 mi. The view from this lean-to and from rocks on the shoreline is very good. The old road continues on past the jct. toward Wolf Lake Landing (reaching trail 100 in 0.1 mi) and returns to NY 28 as the Wolf Lake Landing Rd. (trail 99).

✽ Trail in winter: Snowmobile trail. It is an easy ski route, with the hill before Millbrook and a few modest slopes in the Mill Brook area.

❧ Distances: Bear Creek Rd. trailhead to second jct. with Gull Lake Loop (trail 102), 1.9 mi; to Sand Lake Falls Trail (trail 101), 3.4 mi; to Bear Lake Trail (trail 104), 4.7 mi; to Woodhull Lake lean-to, 7.6 mi (12.2 km). ◆

West Lake. JAMES APPLEYARD

NY 8 and North Lake Road Section

The West Canada Lakes Wilderness Area covers a vast area N of NY 8 from Nobleboro to Piseco Lake. There are only four official trails into the wilderness from the S, but several additional access points allow extensive possibilities for the experienced wilderness traveler.

The remainder of the area, between NY 8 and North Lake Rd., is mostly state land in the Black River Wild Forest. Hikers here need to be a bit more self-reliant, with a sense of direction and expectations for close forest scenery rather than sweeping views. This is the country of Adirondack French Louie, Nat Foster, Jock Wright, Atwell Martin, and a host of ragged, rugged lumberjacks, trappers, and hermits who tangled with the upper reaches of the Black River. It is the home of several of the earliest sportsmen's clubs in New York State.

The importance of the waters in this section may have been a principal factor in the creation of the Adirondack Park. The water fed the Erie Canal, which was chronically short of water in the summer. The larger lakes in this section still store and supply water for the canal. The water is tapped off from Kayuta Lake at Forestport and sent down the old Black River Canal, past Boonville to Delta Lake and on into the high point of the Erie Canal at Rome. West Canada Creek sends water into storage in the Hinckley Reservoir and then on to the canal at Herkimer.

Access to some trailheads is difficult along NY 8. Anyone expecting to drive Haskell Rd. N of Nobleboro should be aware of its sometimes rough condition, best suited to jeeps and pickups. G Lake Rd. is best used in good weather. The road to North Lake, however, is in reasonably good condition most of the year, with trailheads to Stone Dam, Twin Lakes, Little Woodhull Lake, North Lake, South Lake, and Sand Lake Falls readily accessible to passenger cars.

J.P. LEWIS TRACT

In 1990, the Nature Conservancy helped arrange a New York State-owned conservation easement on this 11,490 acre tract of land formerly posted by the Adirondack League Club. It surrounds the N end of North Lake and contains the former ALC exclusive, Ice Cave Mt. The owner has the right to continue to manage the forest for timber harvest. The easement allows the owner to close any of the seven zones within the tract while timber harvesting is in progress.

Otherwise, the tract is open to public recreational use with the exception of motorized vehicles such as motorcycles, ATVs, and snow-mobiles. Cars are allowed only on the loop road extending into the heart of the tract, but they must give way to lumber trucks as necessary. Camping is "first come, first served," including the designated camping sites along North Lake. Trails 108A thru 108K—all logging roads—are located within this tract. These are not DEC trails. The agreement allows the DEC to mark and maintain seven trails, but they may or may not follow any of these routes. Updated information may be obtained from DEC foresters in the Herkimer office (315-866-6330).

PRATT–NORTHAM MEMORIAL PARK
This land, given to the state as a park, provides recreational access to South Lake. There is a small, informal picnic site just S of South Lake Rd. where it first meets South Lake. This site can also be reached by a side trail from trail 109 (South Lake Trail) shortly after the trailhead.

PRATT–NORTHAM MEMORIAL TRACT
This tract, which surrounds Pratt–Northam Memorial Park, was given to the state as silviculture (tree-cutting) land. It is currently managed in the same manner as the surrounding Wild Forest lands. The South Lake Trail (109) passes through this tract.

SHORT HIKES:
◆ G Lake—0.1 to 1.8 mi. Short walk to picnic at the lake; 1.0- or 2.0-mi walk around to W side of lake. See trail 115C.
◆ Keegans Trail to Ledge Mt. Overlook—1.5 mi round trip. Short, well-marked trail with moderate grades to small lookout over West Canada Creek and forest. See trail 111A.

MODERATE HIKES:
◆ Echo Cliff—1.2 mi round trip. Short but somewhat steep climb to a great view over Piseco Lake. See trail 116A.

◆ Twin Lakes—6.0 mi round trip. Easy walking, but sometimes wet. Crosses through a small swamp, and ends near the remains of a small dam once used to impound water for the Erie Canal. See trail 108.

HARDER HIKE:
◆ Little Salmon Lake—12.6 mi round trip. An old road and old logging road lead to a pleasant, remote lake. See trail 113.

(106) **Stone Dam Trail**

Map: B7, p. 223

Initially gentle, this route becomes somewhat rough and is apparently less used after it crosses Woodhull Creek. Pay careful attention to the yellow markers. Fairly open older hardwoods give way in places to evergreens, with only an occasional muddy spot. The trail does not reach any reliable landmarks until it passes Stone Dam Lake (seen through the trees on the R). Keep a careful watch for the lake, or you may go much farther than intended. The lake and dam site must be reached by bushwhack. The route ahead goes to Chub Pond and can be used as a through trip to Bear Creek Rd. at Woodgate or the McKeever trailhead.

▶ Trailhead: From the highway jct. at Forestport, on NY 28, take North Lake Rd. E to the RR tracks at Forestport Station. Continue straight ahead (E) on North Lake Rd. The trailhead is on the left (N) just after a bend in the road, 6.5 mi from Forestport Station. Park in a three-car parking lot just off the road (somewhat lower than the road), or on the shoulder beside the trailhead. ◀

FROM THE TRAILHEAD on North Lake Rd. (0.0 mi), the yellow-marked route heads N on an old road with a soft, broad pathway. At 1.0 mi, the trail crosses Woodhull Creek on a nice log bridge with a cable for a handrail. Beyond this, the trail becomes rough, and is less used.

At 1.8 mi, a thick group of large spruce trees dominates the trail, but doesn't last long. Open hardwoods again prevail. A particularly magnificent birch sits right by the trail at 3.2 mi, at the top of a climb. A modest downhill slope after that should encourage attention to Stone Dam Lake through the trees R at 3.5 mi. A short bushwhack through the forest will reveal the shore. On a slight peninsula of the N shore is the site of the former Stone Dam Lake Camp, one of the smallest imaginable sportsmen's camps.

The yellow trail continues past Stone Dam Lake, climbing a little before crossing an inlet brook. The route winds over small bumps and crosses several little creeks, often passing through open, well-established forest. It finally takes a distinctly downhill trend and joins the blue-marked Chub Pond Trail (trail 103) at 6.2 mi. Trail 103 goes R for 0.3 mi to Chub Pond Lean-to 1, and L 1.4 mi around the lake to Chub Pond Lean-to 2. Lean-to 2 has by far the better scenery.

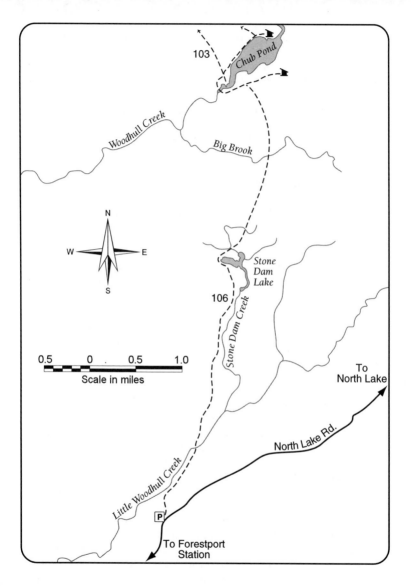

Stone Dam Trail (106)

For continuation to Bear Creek Rd., see the Chub Pond Trail (trail 103).

✴ Trail in winter: Suitable for backcountry skiing and snowshoeing. The trail is lightly marked, and the country is remote. Trailhead parking may be a problem.

𝕞 Distances: North Lake Rd. trailhead to Woodhull Creek, 1.0 mi; to Stone Dam Lake, 3.5 mi; to Chub Pond Trail, 6.2 mi (10.0 km). To Bear Creek Rd. trailhead, 11.4 mi (18.4 km).

(107) **Little Woodhull Lake Trail**

Map: B6

▶ Trailhead: From the highway jct. at Forestport, on NY 28, take North Lake Rd. E to the RR tracks at Forestport Station. Continue straight ahead (E) on North Lake Rd. Check the distance carefully. The trailhead is an old road on the L (N) at 14.0 mi from NY 28. Park in the snowmobile trailhead on the R just beyond. The other end of the trail is on trail 101, 2.1 mi from its trailhead on North Lake Rd. near North Lake; this trailhead is 1.8 mi farther on the road. ◀

FROM THE TRAILHEAD on North Lake Rd. (0.0 mi), the route heads NW on an old road with an easy pathway under yellow DEC markers. It gradually turns N, gently climbing up a ridge. At 1.0 mi, the trail tops out, turns L, and goes somewhat downhill.

At 1.2 mi, the old road (with blue markers) goes straight ahead into the brush and blowdown, but the yellow-marked trail follows another old road turning sharply R. The path is mostly easy and pleasant, if not always well marked. There is an occasional old snowmobile marker and a foot path on the old road, which heads N, then swings W.

The trail finally curves W and reaches Little Woodhull Creek at 2.4 mi. At the creek, the vlei ahead seems to be the expected direction, but as it emerges, the trail instead turns L and follows along the margin of the woods in tall marsh grass. At the end of the soggy meadow, the trail turns inland L on a boulder-strewn, moss-covered old road (obscure; look carefully for markers). The route turns L off this old road at 2.5 mi. Look carefully for the markers, some of which are homemade.

The route soon becomes more obvious and follows Little Woodhull Creek, just S of it but not within sight of it. At 3.0 mi, the trail turns R and crosses the creek at the site of a former snowmobile bridge. The path straight ahead along the creek leads to an informal campsite in approximately 175 yd. There is a path W to the lake, which is pretty and has a strong sense of remoteness.

Continuing N from the creek, the now red-marked trail continues on gentle ground. In about 100 yd, the lake comes into view through the open woods to the L. At the first tiny creek crossing, there is an obscure trail L to the lake.

The trail continues on easy ground and then climbs gently up a hill. The route is faint here but has red DEC, and red paint markers as well as homemade markers. The hill is fairly open. The trail skirts to the R of its broad hilltop and meets the Sand Lake Falls Trail (trail 101), an obvious old road, at 4.9 mi. To the L, it is 0.7 mi to the crossing of Grindstone Creek on the way to Sand Lake Falls, and to the R it is 2.1 mi to North Lake. To complete a round-trip hike, go R to North Lake at 7.0 mi, turn R and walk to the dam at 7.4 mi, then turn R and walk down the road to your car at 8.8 mi.

✤ Trail in winter: Snowmobile trail, probably not used. Suitable for backcountry skiing and snowshoeing. This trail is far from civilization. Prepare well for your trip.

⚐ Distances: Trailhead to Little Woodhull Lake, 3.0 mi; to Sand Lake Falls Trail (trail 101), 4.9 mi (7.9 km). To Sand Lake Falls, 6.2 mi; to North Lake, 7.0 mi; complete loop trip via North Lake, 8.8 mi (14.2 km).

(108) Twin Lakes Dam Trail

Map: B7

▶ Trailhead: From NY 28 at Forestport, go E to Forestport Station. Continue straight ahead across the RR tracks on North Lake Rd. The road narrows at 5.1 mi from the RR tracks. At 10.0 mi from the tracks, turn R on the gravel road to North Wilmurt. The trailhead is 0.4 mi down this road on the L (E). There is parking for three cars. ◀

THE ROUTE BEGINS at the DEC-marked trailhead in a hardwood forest (0.0 mi). An old woods road is used for this section, marked now and then by DEC snowmobile trail markers. An occasional mudhole and adjacent bog make the route more interesting.

At 2.1 mi, the route leaves the smooth old road and ascends slightly through evergreens before dropping again to a beaver meadow at 2.5

mi. This crossing may muddy your feet slightly. If the beavers return, you will probably have to make a bushwhack detour around the pond, going R.

The trail continues from an enormous stump at the E side of the meadow, through evergreens and over another small hill to the Twin Lakes outlet at 3.1 mi. The dam rotted out many years ago, but the remains can be inspected just a little ways down from the trail's end. The rock and concrete frame for the gate is still in place, and the rotten stub ends of the wooden dam can be seen sticking out from the bank on the opposite side of the creek. This dam was used to store snowmelt, which could be let out later in the summer to maintain a sufficient water level in the Erie Canal (by way of the Black River Canal). Beavers have dammed the stream here in the past, and no doubt will return when enough small trees reappear in the meadow to provide food for them.

❄ Trail in winter: Snowmobile trail. Otherwise suitable for snowshoeing or backcountry skiing.

🦌 Distances: To departure from woods road, 2.1 mi; to Twin Lakes, 3.1 mi (5.0 km).

(108A) **Grindstone Creek Trail** (unmaintained)

Map: C6

Note: "Trails" 108A–108K are old logging roads and not DEC trails. Open for public use, they have no markers and are not maintained. Signs should be posted on the road along the N shore of North Lake if logging is under way, restricting access.

▶ Trailhead: Starting from Forestport on NY 28, go E on North Lake Rd., cross the RR tracks at Forestport Station, and continue to the dam at Atwell at 15.4 mi. Turn L at the dam and travel 3.3 mi to the first parking lot on the L. The trailhead is 0.2 mi S of the parking lot. ◀

THIS LOGGING ROAD is now grass-covered, and very easy walking. From the trailhead (0.0 mi), it follows the course of Mud Pond Outlet for the first 0.5 mi, until the creek turns S and the road continues W up the mild slope of the hill. There is a 40 ft wide dugout pit on the L at 0.9 mi. This is a useful landmark for locating the start of the Mud Pond Trail (108B), which is another 0.1 mi ahead on the L at 1.0 mi.

The main road continues over a gentle high point and descends very slowly. Numerous narrower old logging roads go L and R along the route.

At 2.2 mi, the road turns R while a lesser road continues straight ahead. After the turn, the route is downhill to a turnaround at 2.4 mi. A less prominent old road continues ahead to cross Grindstone Creek in another 100 ft. That road turns L and continues downstream along the creek. Another older road turns R at the turnaround and goes 300 ft upstream along the upper edge of a grassy marsh. After emerging from the wet grassy area, the road crosses a small creek and continues up the end of Golden Stair Mt. The creek just crossed is fed by a two-ended marsh to the E; it sends water E to Golden Stair Creek and W to Grindstone Creek. Back at the turnaround, still another easy old logging road goes L from the end of the road to follow downstream along Grindstone Creek.

❄ Trail in winter: Suitable for backcountry skiing and snowshoeing. The trail is not marked, but the roadway is prominent. The loop road along the length of North Lake is not plowed, thus adding 3.3 mi to the trip. Trailhead parking may be a problem.

⚶ Distances: Trailhead to jct. of Mud Pond Trail (108B), 1.0 mi; to turnaround, 2.4 mi (3.9 km).

(108B) **Mud Pond Trail** (unmaintained)

Map: C6

Mud Pond is a scenic but shallow lake surrounded by a boggy shoreline. Thick and treacherous bogs at the N and S ends make access difficult; a stroll around the lake is out of the question. Adventurous bushwhackers can approach the lake from the W side by taking the R uphill branch on the road at 0.4 mi.

▶ Locator: On trail 108A. ◀

STARTING FROM THE JCT. on trail 108A (0.0 mi), the route is nearly level, heading SW. At 0.4 mi, at a Y jct., the route bears L, going downhill. At 0.6 mi, the old road reaches a small clearing and turns sharp R. Beyond that, it continues S over a slight hill at 0.8 mi.

The best route to Mud Pond is from this slight hilltop. Turn sharp R and bushwhack 0.1 mi through the evergreens to the rim above Mud Pond. The old road continues beyond the hilltop, down across Mud Pond Outlet creek, turns R at 1.0 mi, and continues onto the tabletop behind Sugarloaf Mt., which overlooks North Lake.

❋ Trail in winter: Suitable for backcountry skiing and snowshoeing. The trail is not marked, but the roadway is prominent. The loop road along the length of North Lake is not plowed, thus adding 3.3 mi to the trip. Trailhead parking may be a problem.

❧ Distances: Trail 108A to Mud Pond bushwhack turnoff, 0.8 mi (1.3 km). To Mud Pond, 0.9 mi (1.5 km).

(108C) **Canachagala Trail** (unmaintained)

Map: C5, 6

▶ Trailhead: See trail 108A. From the dam, go 3.6 mi to the second parking lot on the L, where the road makes a sharp R bend. The trailhead is on the E edge of the parking lot. ◀

FROM THE ROAD CORNER in front of the parking lot (0.0 mi), the old road goes NW past a gate on nearly level ground, then begins a gentle climb to the terrace above a creek. Once on the terrace, the route wraps around Canachagala Mt. A small pond on the L at 0.6 mi is the E end of the extensive swamps surrounding Golden Stair Creek.

After a mild climb, the trail reaches Golden Stair Mt. Trail (trail 108D) on the L at 1.2 mi. Continuing N, the trail parallels the unnamed creek, turns uphill at 1.4 mi, and reaches the boundary of Adirondack League Club land at 2.0 mi. There is a high point in the valley just ahead. Canachagala Lake is on the other side, and does not contribute to the creek followed by this trail.

❋ Trail in winter: Suitable for backcountry skiing and snowshoeing. The trail is not marked, but the roadway is prominent. The loop road along the length of North Lake is not plowed, thus adding 3.6 mi to the trip. Trailhead parking may be a problem.

❧ Distances: Parking lot to Golden Stair Creek swamp, 0.6 mi; to Golden Stair Mt. Trail (trail 108D), 1.2 mi; to boundary of Adirondack League Club, 2.0 mi (3.2 km).

(108D) **Golden Stair Mt. Trail** (unmaintained)

Map: C6

This area is of special interest for its extensive flower fields.

▶ Locator: On trail 108C. ◀

FROM TRAIL 108C (0.0 mi), the trail heads W across the lay of the land, drops down once to cross the nearby creek, crosses over a slight hill at 0.4 mi, drops down again to cross Golden Stair Creek, and finally proceeds up Golden Stair Mt. The primary road ends at 0.9 mi on the lower slopes of the mountain, where the steep hillside begins.

❋ Trail in winter: Suitable for backcountry skiing and snowshoeing. The trail is not marked, but the roadway is prominent. The loop road along the length of North Lake is not plowed, thus adding 3.6 mi to the trip. Trailhead parking may be a problem.

♨ Distances: Trail 108C to end of road at Golden Stair Mt., 0.9 mi (1.5 km).

(108E) **North Branch Trail** (unmaintained)

Map: C6

This trail leads to an interesting backcountry section of the upper Black River, and provides the shortest access to Ice Cave Mt. The Ice Cave is actually a 96 ft deep trench on the SW end of the mountain which collects winter snows and remains icy into the summer months. Ice Cave Mt. seems to have a severe case of fracture throughout its length. The summit is mostly a jumble of boulders covered by a thin quilt of soil which doesn't quite fill the gaps. There are many boulders standing along the ridge where they have broken away and begun to slide off. One gigantic boulder stands precariously on the very steep W slope about 0.4 mi NE of the cave. For another approach to the cave, see trail 108F.

▶ Trailhead: See trail 108A. From the dam, go 4.5 mi to the third parking lot on the R at the end of the road. The trailhead is the straight continuation of the road at the end of the parking lot. (The Eastside Trail, trail 108G, turns R at the same location.) ◀

LEAVING THE PARKING LOT (0.0 mi), the old road heads due N, then climbs gently as it curves to head NE. There is a jct. with trail 108F on the L at 0.5 mi. At 1.2 mi, the road crosses a small creek. This seems to be the most popular spot to begin bushwhacking up Ice Cave Mt.

(Ice Cave: Turning L off the road, this is the shortest Ice Cave route, but it is very steep. To reach the Ice Cave, go due N to the summit, then turn L in the middle of the ridge and make your way cautiously to the SW tip. The Ice Cave is on the W side of the tip. It is deep and dangerous. Be careful when you lean out to look.)

Past the creek and turnoff for the Ice Cave, at about 1.4 mi, an old road joins on the L, faintly marked by ancient red blazes. This is overgrown, but leads NW along the base of Ice Cave Mt. A L branch near the start may have been an ancient route to the Ice Cave. With a half-mile bushwhack where the R branch gives out, one could reach the W end of the old Gould lumber road, which continues along the valley of the North Branch of the Black River to join trail 94 near Horn Lake.

Beyond the old road, the North Branch Trail continues along easy terrain until crossing a creek in a culvert at 1.6 mi. After the creek, the road becomes rough and overgrown, and finally ends beside the North Branch of the Black River at 1.8 mi, where the river splashes as it tumbles over boulders and slight cascades.

❋ Trail in winter: Suitable for backcountry skiing and snowshoeing. The trail is not marked, but the roadway is prominent. The loop road along the length of North Lake is not plowed, thus adding 4.5 mi to the trip. Trailhead parking may be a problem.

⚹ Distances: Parking lot to trail 108F, 0.5 mi; to take-off point for Ice Cave bushwhack, 1.2 mi; to North Branch of the Black River, 1.8 mi (2.9 km).

(108F) Ice Cave Creek Trail (unmaintained)

Map: C6

There is a large clearing at the end of this road where one could camp and explore the area. It also provides a second and not-so-steep access route to the ice cave on Ice Cave Mt. (see introduction to trail 108E above). The Ice Cave Mt. area is mentioned by David Beetle in *Up Old Forge Way*, when he describes tractors being used for the first time to replace horses in large-scale logging operations.

▶ Locator: On trail 108E, 0.5 mi NE of the parking lot. ◀

FROM THE JCT. with trail 108E (0.0 mi), the old road goes W uphill for 0.2 mi, then levels off and passes the S tip of Ice Cave Mt. At 0.4 mi, the route crosses Ice Cave Creek near a beaver dam and turns N. The grassy old road passes a tiny waterfall dripping over bare rock L along the lower edge of Canachagala Mt. A little farther on, the road enters a large lumber clearing along its upper edge at 1.3 mi.

[To reach the "cave" on Ice Cave Mt., go downhill across the clearing and locate the lumber road crossing Ice Cave Creek (no bridge). Follow it SE up the hill. At 0.2 mi from the creek, another old tote road goes uphill L, possibly marked with red tape on a tree overhead. Follow it uphill, approximately 60 degrees by compass. This takes you up the gentlest slope on the end of Ice Cave Mt. As it nears the top, it goes into a slight notch to the L of the cliffs on the end of the mountain. Follow along the nearly level ground below the cliffs for another 0.1 mi until the cliffs disappear and you can climb onto the summit ridge with ease. Turn R and go along the middle of the ridge until you reach the ice cave at the end, approximately 2.7 mi from the trailhead. (The route along the edge of the cliffs is annoyingly uneven and difficult going, not to mention dangerous.) Take care with your footing on the summit. It is a jumble of broken rock, half covered by soil. You can drop a leg into many a crevice. The Ice Cave is a vertical cleavage in the rock of the mountain, no doubt being slowly forced apart by expansion of the ice at its bottom in winter. It is about 96 ft deep. A careless visitor could be killed by a fall into what seems at first glance to be only a slight gap in the rock. The safest view is from the far (SW) end.]

❃ Trail in winter: Suitable for backcountry skiing and snowshoeing (the Ice Cave Mt. part is hard to follow and sometimes a bit steep for skiing). The trail is not marked, but the roadway is prominent. The loop road along the length of North Lake is not plowed, thus adding 4.5 mi to the trip. Trailhead parking may be a problem.

❃ Distances: Trail 108E to Ice Cave Creek, 0.4 mi; to clearing on Ice Cave Creek, 1.3 mi (2.1 km). To Ice Cave, 2.7 mi.

(108G) Eastside Trail (unmaintained)

Map: C6

Overnight campers may find this route very much to their liking for its eight primitive campsites and two lean-tos along the E shore of North Lake.

▶ Trailhead: See trail 108A. From the dam, go 4.5 mi to the third parking lot on the R at the end of the road. The trailhead is the gate on the R at the N end of the parking lot. ◀

FROM THE GATE (0.0 mi), continue along the loop road extension. At 0.3 mi, this crosses the North Branch of the Black River and turns SW to follow the river along its upper bank. At 1.1 mi, the Black River

Middle Branch Trail (trail 108H) curves L and starts gently uphill, while the Eastside Trail road turns R off the main road and continues SW along level ground above the N end of North Lake.

The Middle Branch of the Black River crosses under the road at 1.4 mi. At 1.5 mi, the trail passes within 200 ft of the lake R. A slight two-track road R leads to a campsite with a steel fire ring.

At 1.9 mi, the trail crosses Jocks Brook, named after Jonathan "Jock" Wright. The road going uphill on the L is trail 108I, the Jocks Brook Trail. Continuing S past the jct., the old road becomes overgrown for a short distance. At 2.2 mi, the road crosses a culvert. There is another campsite with a fire ring 200 ft R at the edge of the lake.

The haul road ends at 2.3 mi, but a rutted skid road continues on. At 2.6 mi, the skid road passes a private cabin downhill by the lake. There is another camping site slightly farther S, at 2.7 mi. This the end of the trail. (If one is willing to bushwhack another 0.5 mi along the steep slope above the lake, two lean-tos are set on state land. The state land boundary is at 3.0 mi, but the old road goes only as far as the last campsite at 2.7 mi.)

❄ Trail in winter: Suitable for backcountry skiing and snowshoeing. The trail is not marked, but the roadway is prominent. The loop road along the length of North Lake is not plowed, thus adding 4.5 mi to the trip. Trailhead parking may be a problem.

🚶 Distances: Parking lot to Black River Middle Branch Trail (trail 108H) jct., 1.1 mi; to Jocks Brook Trail (trail 108I), 1.9 mi; to campsite at end of trail, 2.7 mi (4.4 km).

(108H) **Black River Middle Branch Trail** (unmaintained)

Map: C6

▶ Locator: On trail 108G, 1.1 mi from parking lot. ◀

AT THE JCT. (1.1 mi on trail 108G), where the Eastside Trail (trail 108G) turns R and goes downhill to cross the Middle Branch, the Black River Middle Branch Trail curves L (E) and starts gently uphill. At 0.6 mi, the Hardscrabble Lake Trail (108J) starts R. At 0.8 mi, the Middle Branch Trail starts up more steeply, then alternates down and up as it crosses streams and climbs hillsides. It meets a corner of Adirondack League Club land on a hilltop at 1.9 mi and ends on another hillside at 2.5 mi. There is a small pond on the Black River just a little S of the end of the trail. Private land is only a little farther on the S, E, and N.

❋ Trail in winter: Suitable for backcountry skiing and snowshoeing. The trail is not marked, but the roadway is prominent. The loop road along the length of North Lake is not plowed, thus adding 4.5 mi to the trip. Trailhead parking may be a problem.

⋈ Distances: From jct. with Eastside Trail (trail 108G) to Hardscrabble Lake Trail (trail 108J) jct., 0.6 mi; to end of trail, 2.5 mi (4.0 km).

(108I) **Jocks Brook Trail** (unmaintained)

Map: C6

▶ Locator: On trail 108G. ◀

THIS OLD ROAD LEAVES the Eastside Trail (108G) near the Jocks Brook inlet into North Lake (0.0 mi) and heads uphill parallel to the brook. There is a Y jct. at 0.4 mi. The R fork, which once went all the way to Honnedaga Rd., disappears in the brush. The L fork goes downhill to Jocks Brook at 0.5 mi and continues across the brook and up the slopes of Hardscrabble Mt., into many branches that end at various points on the slope.

❋ Trail in winter: Steep, but otherwise suitable for experienced backcountry skiers and snowshoers, although very remote. The trail is not marked, but the roadway at the beginning is prominent. The loop road along the length of North Lake is not plowed, thus adding considerable distance to the trip. Trailhead parking may be a problem.

⋈ Distance: Trail 108G to Jocks Brook, 0.5 mi (0.8 km).

(108J) **Hardscrabble Lake Trail** (unmaintained)

Map: C6

▶ Trailheads: W trailhead on the Black River Middle Branch Trail (trail 108H), 0.6 mi from trail 108G (1.7 mi from parking lot).

To reach the E trailhead, start from Forestport on NY 28, go E on North Lake Rd., cross the RR tracks at Forestport Station, and continue to the dam at Atwell at 15.4 mi. Continue on across the dam and along the gravel road, now called South Lake Rd. Pass South Lake and continue on Honnedaga Rd. to the locked gates at a Y in the road at 19.4 mi. The loop road extension is on the L (NW) side of the road about 200 ft back from the Y jct. ◀

STARTING AT THE W TRAILHEAD, the trail leaves the Black River Middle Branch Trail (108H) on the R, goes downhill, and crosses the Middle Branch of the Black River. A long, gentle, but steady climb leads past a slight view of Hardscrabble Lake end-on (L) to a saddle at 0.5 mi in the hills above Hardscrabble Lake (downhill L). At 0.7 mi, the road makes a sharp R turn where a side route goes L to private land at Honnedaga Lake. From here, the route is downhill to Jocks Brook, where the culvert is washed out. Once across the brook, it is an easy trip around the headwater swamp and up to Honnedaga Lake Rd. (1.7 mi) just W of the gates that halt public access to the private lands around Honnedaga Lake.

❋ Trail in winter: Suitable for backcountry skiing and snowshoeing. The trail is not marked, but the roadway is prominent. The loop road along the length of North Lake is not plowed, thus adding 4.5 mi to the trip. Trailhead parking may be a problem.

⚕ Distances: Black River Middle Branch Trail (108H) to saddle overlooking Hardscrabble Lake, 0.5 mi; to Jocks Brook, 1.1 mi; to Honnedaga Lake Rd., 1.7 mi (2.7 km).

(109) South Lake Trail

Map: C6, 7

The major portion of this trail lies within the Pratt-Northam Memorial tract donated to the state with the condition that it not be part of the Forest Preserve. The land surrounding South Lake is a park (Pratt–Northam Memorial Park), while the remainder is silviculture land, currently treated in the same manner as Wild Forest land.

▶ Trailhead: From Forestport on NY 28, go E on North Lake Rd., cross the RR tracks at Forestport Station, and continue to the North Lake Dam at Atwell in 15.4 mi. Continue across the dam past private homes and into the woods again. At 17.6 mi, just before reaching South Lake, park in the weedy open space beside an old road R. This road is the trail. The main road continues on to South Lake in 0.1 mi, becomes Honnedaga Lake Rd., and enters barricaded private land in about two miles. There is a nice picnic spot in the Pratt–Northam Memorial Park on the R, just as the main road reaches South Lake. ◀

FROM NORTH LAKE RD. (0.0 mi), the route, marked with DEC snowmobile markers, heads S near the W end of South Lake. A branch to the L goes to the picnic spot on the lake nearby. About 350 yd past this branch, an unmarked trail joins on the R. That trail is on private land.

Continuing straight ahead on the main trail, at 0.6 mi there are some wet dips as the old road curves L around the corner of the lake (out of sight). Modest ups and downs continue, still following the S shore, out of sight of the lake. A small bridge across an outlet creek crosses near a low spillway holding back the water of South Lake at 2.5 mi. Because of the artificial damming, South Lake has two outlet streams which join a little farther downstream.

At the top of the climb from the creek, an unofficial trail goes L 375 ft to the shore of the lake beside the outlet arm. There is a good view of the lake. Back on the main trail, another side trail L at 2.6 mi leads L 450 ft to the main dam (of modest size).

The main trail soon crosses the outlet stream on a snowmobile bridge. Shortly beyond, at 2.8 mi, an old road goes L, while the trail goes R (S). Following along the flatlands of the South Lake Outlet, the road passes through an old lumber clearing. Beyond the clearing, one road in fairly good condition goes S, but the snowmobile trail takes a L fork at 3.2 mi and starts uphill, curving E. By 3.5 mi, the route has turned to the NE and reached a jct. The route straight ahead soon disappears, while the trail takes a sharp R turn and continues uphill a little farther.

The trail reaches another old road at 3.9 mi and turns R on that road, heading S. Jones Brook (one of many by that name) is crossed near the bottom of the hill, followed soon by Little Salmon Outlet at 4.6 mi. Just beyond, the remains of an old cabin in a clearing signal a R turn and a short diversion to the W. After this short excursion on level ground to another jct. at 4.8 mi, the old road ahead leads along Little Salmon Outlet, while the trail goes uphill on the L branch.

At 5.2 mi, the snowmobile trail turns uphill L while the old road straight ahead leads over the top of a small hill and to a jct. L at 5.5 mi. Both branches soon disappear into thick undergrowth. Continuing on the snowmobile trail, the route heads SE, going steadily upward on an old road. As it curves L and heads NE, the trail levels off. After another 0.3 mi, the route curves R and heads steadily but gently uphill across a wet hillside, finally leveling out to meet the Little Salmon Lake Trail

(Trail 113) at 7.1 mi. Summit Camp (private) is straight ahead through the woods, but not visible from the jct.

The Baby Lake Falls Trail (trail 115), extending another 2.8 mi to Baby Lake Falls, can be reached by going about 300 ft R (S) on trail 113 and then taking an unmarked primitive road L past Summit Camp. Continuing S on trail 113 leads to Cement Bridge at 2.5 mi and Haskell Rd. at 5.2 mi. From the jct. of trails 109 and 113, a turn to the L (N) leads to Little Salmon Lake in 1.1 mi. See Little Salmon Lake Trail (113) for details.

❅ Trail in winter: Easy skiing most of the way, suitable for intermediate skiers familiar with wilderness travel. Expect some snowmobile usage, and keep out of the way.

⚹ Distances: North Lake Rd. to South Lake Dam, 2.6 mi; to Little Salmon Outlet, 4.6 mi; to Little Salmon Lake Trail (trail 113), 7.1 mi (11.4 km). To Haskell Rd. via trail 113, 12.3 mi (19.8 km).

(110) **Middle Branch Marsh Trail** (unmaintained)

Map: B, C8

The Middle Branch Marsh Trail does not have markers and is not a DEC trail. It is used by owners of a private camp S of Middle Branch Marsh.

▶ Trailhead: From the jct. of NY 8 and NY 365, 28 mi NE of Utica, go W on NY 365 for about 300 ft to Hooper Dooper Rd. Turn N on that road and go 1.1 mi to a snowmobile trailhead R. ◀

TAKE THE ROAD W at the jct. near the trailhead. Continue on the most heavily used route for approximately 0.4 mi W from the jct. The principal route turns N and continues through private land, finally reaching state land at about 1.4 mi. The old road reaches a private camp at about 4.5 mi, and Middle Branch Marsh at about 5.2 mi. The scene is quite remote and the region beyond the marsh is said to be very wild and beautiful. There are no special lakes or viewpoints; this trip would appeal mostly to wilderness explorers.

❅ Trail in winter: Not a DEC trail, but may have snowmobile traffic. Suitable for snowshoeing and backcountry skiing, if a parking place can be found farther down Hooper Dooper Rd.

⚹ Distance: To state land, 1.4 mi; to Middle Branch Marsh, approximately 5.2 mi (8.4 km).

(111) **Mad Tom Trail** (unmaintained)

Map: C8

This trail leads along the ridge above Mad Tom Brook to provide access to Mad Tom Lake (tiny, but nice), Mill Creek Lake, Black Creek Lake, Crosby Vlei, and Burp Lake. Black Creek Lake, 0.5 mi long, is the largest of the lakes reached directly from NY 8.

▶ Trailhead: From the jct. of NY 8 and NY 365, 28 mi NE of Utica, go E on NY 8 for 1.1 mi to Remonda Rd. (This is 4.2 mi W from Haskell Rd. at Nobleboro near the West Canada Creek scenic overlook.) Turn L (N) and go 0.2 mi to the end of the road, where there is a snowplow turnaround and parking (except in snowplow season). The Mad Tom Trail is the old and narrower continuation of this road. ◀

FROM THE END OF THE PAVED ROAD (0.0 mi), the route goes N on the old road and passes an old cabin at 0.4 mi. Owners of the cabin have retained the right to drive past the open gate, but all others must park on state land on Remonda Rd.

The trail continues N on the old road, climbing gently until reaching the hill W of Mad Tom Lake at 1.6 mi.

Descending gently from the hill, the trail passes through a small clearing, crosses a stream, and reaches a jct. at 2.1 mi. The route to the R is a side trail leading to Mad Tom Lake at 2.3 mi.

The main trail forks L and continues on easy terrain. At 3.1 mi, there is a T jct. with the old Black Creek Lake Rd. To the R, the Mill Creek Lake Trail (112) leads to Mill Creek Lake (about 1.0 mi), which has two private plots on its E end. (Trail 112 continues on past Mill Creek Lake to a trailhead off NY 8, making a loop hike possible with a car spotted at the S trailhead for 112.)

To the L, the Mad Tom Trail follows Black Creek Lake Rd. uphill past a jct. with the Milk Can Trail at 3.2 mi. (The Milk Can Trail leads to the private Shanty Mt. Camp in another 1.3 mi.) From the jct., the Mad Tom Trail climbs NE, gaining about 400 ft in the next half mile. After a level section, it goes up again to follow the hillside above Little Black Creek, crossing it at 4.7 mi. A slight additional climb leads to a broad hilltop and later a relatively gentle downhill run to Black Creek Lake.

The trail reaches a private land boundary at 5.4 mi. The old road goes downhill inside that boundary, which is prominently posted. To avoid the posted private land, turn L and bushwhack through open forest WNW to the lake at 5.7 mi. Partway along this bushwhack route, you will encounter a well-worn path leading WSW across the S end of the pond at Crosby Vlei. Privately maintained trails also lead around Black Creek Lake to give access to Burp Lake. The private landholding on Black Creek Lake is approximately the middle third of the lakeshore on the S side.

❊ Trail in winter: Snowmobile trail.

ᗰ Distances: Trailhead to Mad Tom Lake, 2.3 mi; to Black Creek Lake Rd., 3.1 mi; to Black Creek Lake, 5.7 mi; to Burp Lake, 6.9 mi (11.1 km).

(111A) Keegans Trail to Ledge Mt. Overlook

Map: C8

Formerly a bushwack, this spot is sure to become popular now that a trail has been built. Keegan Roberts, now a guide, built this route as an Eagle Scout project. It provides a pleasant climb with gentle to moderate grades to a small ledge overlooking mixed forest and part of West Canada Creek. (The ledge has a big drop, so don't get too close).

▶ Trailhead: From the jct. of NY 8 and Haskell Rd. in Nobleboro, go 2.0 mi W on NY 8. Turn R just before the entrance to a gravel pit. Or northbound from the jct. of NY 365 on NY 8, go 2.1 mi E to a dirt road just beyond a gravel pit. On that dirt road go in 0.3 mi, staying L at a Y, through brush and small trees to a parking area on the L, suitable for about four vehicles. Note that the road may be "tight"; brush may scrape the side of your vehicle. If you enter forest, you've gone too far. Signs are planned and the road may be improved over time. ◀

FROM THE PARKING LOT (0.0 mi), until signs are installed, look for flagging on the N end (avoiding a more obvious trail on W side). In about 20 yd, yellow foot trail markers start, and the trail drops through a gully to near a property boundary (keep L), then climbs to a small ridge and bends L. There are many slight bends along the trail to keep grades gentle and prevent the erosion that occurs on steeper trails, so users should look ahead for markers and not take shortcuts.

At 0.2 mi, a moderate climb starts. The trail crosses a one-step stream, bends around a rock pile at 0.4 mi, and in another 100 yd passes a 7 ft high boulder, the only one seen this low on the mountain, and crosses a three-step stream on rocks. A steeper section at 0.5 mi leads to the back side of the end of a ridge where slippery moss-covered rocks may be hidden by ferns at 0.6 mi, then there are generally easy grades W with the trail crossing WSW to the "front" (S) of the ridge, and another 35 yd later dropping to the small lookout at 0.75 mi (1.2 km).

Caution should be used along the edge: the drop-off is large—higher than the trees below—and the trees along the edge don't have much soil to hold onto, and so may not hold hikers.

❄ Trail in winter: Possible snowshoe. Park on NY 8 as best one can manage, adding another 0.3 mi distance and 40 ft elevation.

⚕ Distance: Road to ledge, approximately 0.75 mi (1.2 km). Ascent from parking lot, 130 ft (39.6 m). Elevation (high point of trail), 1776 ft (541 m).

(112) Mill Creek Lake Trail

Map: C8

▶ Trailheads: To reach the N trailhead, from NY 8 at Nobleboro, go N on Haskell Rd., which becomes a gravel road, for 1.4 mi. The trail starts on the L with grassy parking for at most a couple of vehicles. The former snowmobile trail is an old road heading NW, with no trailhead sign, but there is a sign prohibiting vehicle travel. After a while, there are a few snowmobile markers, then flagging.

To reach the S trailhead, go 1.5 mi E from the jct. of NY 365 and NY 8 on NY 8 (or 0.8 mi W from Haskell Road at Nobleboro by the scenic overlook at West Canada Creek) and look for a utility pole that has a guy wire going over a dirt road, with the pole on the E side and the guy wire anchored on the W side. There is a faded, homemade sign on the pole saying "Mill Creek Lake" (2005). The dirt road leads 0.7 mi to parking in a clearing next to a small pond. Alternatively, there is a wide spot near the start of the road for possible parking; be careful not to block the road. ◀

FROM THE N TRAILHEAD, go N on the old road. The route climbs around a hill, heads NW along a creek, then goes briefly W away from the creek to reach level ground. From there, it heads generally W on gentle ground. Starting at 0.7 mi, there is a series of four old snowmobile bridges (or the remnants thereof). To 1.0 mi, the way is somewhat thick and boggy. After that, it is decently dry but more obscure, even though the forest is fairly open. There is flagging, however, the rest of the way to Mill Creek.

At 1.8 mi, the trail turns R on a very old road and soon comes to the red blazes of a privately marked trail. To the L on that trail it is about 200 yd to a small, home-built footbridge (with two sections each side of an island) over Mill Creek. Continuing on the marked snowmobile route, the path is open and fairly easy to follow. It curves around and over the slight hill L, and reaches Mill Creek at 2.0 mi. There, two creeks, one the outlet from the lake and another coming in from the NE, join and flow SE. The beaver meadow is flooding well away from the creeks. Crossing the section flowing SE may be possible on a beaver dam, or hikers can work their way back downstream to the narrow footbridge.

Across the creek, there are two routes S. The old snowmobile route goes SW to a jct. with a red trail (see below), where it turns L along the creek for about 100 yd before curving R and climbing the hillside. There are few markers and this route may be difficult to follow. Also, it goes through the woods and does not offer any view of the lake. The route winds S uphill to a road at 2.4 mi. Following this private road to the L, it is only a short distance to the main dirt road. Turn L to reach the S trailhead. To the R, this road leads W past side trails to private camps on Mill Creek Lake and goes on to meet the Mad Tom Trail (111) in another 1.3 mi.

From the footbridge (or farther W if the beaver dam crossing is used closer to where the creeks merge), blazes indicate a privately marked trail on public land heading SW along Mill Creek to the outlet of Mill Creek Lake. Views of the lake are easiest here, but there is no convenient access. A trail going R across an impressive bridge over the outlet leads to a private camp on the NE corner of the lake.

The red trail continues along the E side of the lake, eventually reaching a private camp on the SE side. Turn L near that camp to reach the main dirt road at 2.5 mi. (Northbound travelers may have difficulty finding a turnoff R (N) from the private road to the camps. If you miss it, continue down the road until you approach the house. Turn R, staying away from the private land, and then go L again to Mill Creek Lake until you reach the red-blazed trail.)

On the road to the R, it is about 1.2 mi to the Mad Tom Trail (111). To the L, the trail follows a rocky snowmobile road (which may have vehicle traffic to the camps) SE and then S downhill, dropping about 300 ft in 1.4 mi to reach the S trailhead. At that pond, the snowmobile route goes E, reaching Haskell Rd. in 0.8 mi, but a portion crosses private land; the new S trailhead was created so hikers no longer need to use that route.

❋ Trail in winter: N section is no longer used or maintained as a snowmobile trail, but S portion along the old road is used. Easy backcountry skiing and snowshoeing. Haskell Rd. may not be plowed to N trailhead and the 0.7 mi dirt road to S trailhead probably will not be plowed.

⚲ Distances: N Trailhead to Mill Creek, 2.0 mi; to Mill Creek Lake via red trail, about 2.3 mi; to main dirt road via red trail, 2.5 mi; to S trailhead, 3.9 mi (6.3 km).

(113) Little Salmon Lake Trail

Map: C7, 8

This old road dates from the 1800s, when it was used to bring the public to the privately run Forest Lodge on Honnedaga Lake. That was a grueling carriage trip with an overnight stop at Nobleboro. The hotel was taken over as a private facility by the Adirondack League Club after the club's formation in 1890. Access from the S was eventually abandoned, and the club uses a short private road at the end of North Lake Rd. The remains of the sturdy concrete bridge (known as Cement Bridge) across Big Brook attest to continuing use of the Herkimer Landing Rd. through WWII, when a USGS survey marker was placed on the bridge.

The more recent extension of Haskell Rd. along West Canada Creek beyond Herkimer Landing Rd. was used for lumbering, but is now falling into disrepair. Two private camps still stand along the Little Salmon Lake Trail route, and several more along the Haskell Rd. extension N.

▶ Trailhead: From NY 8 at Nobleboro, go N on Haskell Rd. This becomes a gravel road. Continue for 2.6 mi to the end of the gravel road at an open field known as Haskell Place. You may wish to park your car here; the remainder of the road is rough. Continue on the dirt road for another 0.9 mi to the trailhead on the L. Haskell Rd. continues along West Canada Creek for another 6.0 mi to private land in Miller Park, but is exceedingly rough and suitable only for high-clearance 4WD. The Honnedaga Brook Trail (trail 114) is near the end of this road. ◄

AS HASKELL RD. TURNS R and descends past the trailhead, the trail turns L (0.0 mi) and climbs a slight hill on a rocky old road, gradually turning W. At 0.6 mi, the old road levels off and turns N to follow the contour of the hill. A side trail R (N) at 1.2 mi leads down steeply to a private camp on Big Brook.

After a moderately steep descent, a small creek at 2.4 mi must be crossed by wading (or push upstream 30 ft and step across). Beyond that, some gentle ups and downs lead to the site of the Cement Bridge, a landmark at Big Brook at 2.7 mi. This formerly sturdy concrete bridge makes it clear that this was once a well-used road.

Just before the bridge there is a jct. The trail L is the Round Top Trail (trail 113A). Just 370 ft N of the bridge on the R, a road leads a short distance to a clearing L and a camping location R.

The trail soon starts uphill, with mild climbing to a high point on the hill above Whiskey Spring Vlei at 4.3 mi. On the next hilltop, above Threemile Vlei, the trail proceeds on a less used track at 5.2 mi, while the road R shows more use. It goes to Summit Camp, a private camp on the edge of the hill. The Baby Lake Falls Trail (trail 115) starts at the rear (NE) corner of the clearing at Summit Camp. When using that trail, please do not disturb the private camp or use its facilities.

Trail 113 continues N through grass. The South Lake Trail (trail 109) comes in on another old road L; it leads NW around the S shore of South Lake to South Lake Rd. and Atwell (7.1 mi to the road). Just beyond this jct., on the R at 5.4 mi is a second road R leading to Summit Camp.

The trail continues NE downhill, crosses a creek, and ascends slightly. Just after it levels off, a faint trail L is the route to Little Salmon Lake at 5.9 mi. It is an unmarked, unofficial cutoff. The official trail connection is 300 ft farther down the hill, just at the flats before a creek. There is a snowmobile trail sign pointing L, but there is absolutely no trace of a trail and the trail markers are difficult to spot. If you reach this point and want to visit the lake, go back 300 ft to avoid a thick bushwhack.

The well-worn road continuing N from this jct. leads to a crossing of a wetland shown on the map as a pond, but is currently just a soggy bog. Beyond that, the road goes onto posted private land of the

Adirondack League Club, headed for Herkimer Landing on Honnedaga Lake.

The cutoff trail L (NW) leads down the hill 200 ft to level ground. The official trail route connects on the R at this spot, but that 200 ft section is not usable. From here, the trail heads W, winding through the woods with a slight footpath and sufficient markers. Just before the lake, a hill on the L with semilevel ground provides some possibilities for camping.

The trail ends on the E end of Little Salmon Lake at 6.3 mi. This lake is pleasant and remote, with a fairly abrupt shoreline but thick surrounding growth. The S side has many magnificent trees in a long-established and fairly open forest. Possible campsites are more numerous on the S side, especially toward the W end of the lake. Hikers wishing to bushwhack W to the South Lake Trail (trail 109) should keep well above the creek on the S side. The other side is reported to have an ATV trail to the lake, but if you don't find it, the way is thick and wet.

❋ Trail in winter: Snowmobile trail. Haskell Rd. is not plowed. Easy backcountry skiing and snowshoeing, with one somewhat steep slope, but the remoteness of the region and the long distance to the lake make this trail best suited for groups with strong backwoods winter experience. On the return ski, there are two long glide slopes.

🐾 Distances: Haskell place (winter trailhead) to trailhead, 0.9 mi; trailhead to Round Top Trail (trail 113A) and Cement Bridge, 2.7 mi; to South Lake Trail (trail 109), Summit Camp, and Baby Lake Falls Trail (trail 115), 5.2 mi; to Little Salmon Lake, 6.3 mi (10.2 km). To Baby Lake Falls via trail 115, 8.0 mi. To South Lake Rd. via trail 109, 12.3 mi.

(113A) **Round Top Trail**

Map: C8

This is a woodsy cutover trail that connects the Little Salmon Lake Trail (trail 113) and the Mad Tom Trail (trail 111), both snowmobile and ATV trails. However, ATVs are not allowed on this one because it crosses private land. It is shaded nearly the entire route. A snowmobile trail, it is fairly easily followed.

▶ Locator: On trails 113 (E) and 111 (W). ◀

AT THE 2.7 MI POINT on trail 113, just before the Cement Bridge (0.0 mi), trail 113A bears L, passes a "motorized vehicles prohibited" sign, and climbs uphill, generally SW, crossing a few rocky areas that make it interesting for hikers, although they wouldn't concern snowmobilers. There are a couple of switchbacks, but stumps several inches high reveal where the route was cut.

In less than half a mile the trail becomes much more moderate and flattens out after climbing about 660 ft to skirt N of the top of Round Top. The trail crosses private land and then a couple of wet spots as it gradually descends to the Mad Tom Trail (trail 111) about 0.8 mi S of where that trail hits the private land boundary, which hikers must bypass for access to Black Creek Lake and Burp Lake. A trail is planned to replace the WNW bushwhack to Black Creek Lake.

❋ Trail in winter: Remote trail far from trailheads. Marked as a snowmobile trail. Suitable for snowshoeing or use by advanced skiers.

⚲ Distance: Little Salmon Lake Trail to Mad Tom Trail, 2.8 mi (4.5 km).

(114) **Honnedaga Brook Trail** (unmaintained)

Map: D7

This trail goes up Honnedaga Brook, past Beaverdam Pond, and continues to a jct. The R branch goes along Jones Brook to private land in Miller Park. It seems most suitable for fishermen from the private land nearby. The L branch goes along Honnedaga Brook to Falls Camp and Baby Lake Falls. Access by road is too difficult for casual day hiking, but the region is clearly remote and this may be a good starting place for hardy adventurers. The Baby Lake Falls Trail (trail 115) is a longer but better maintained and more accessible route to Baby Lake Falls.

▶ Trailhead: From NY 8 at Nobleboro, go N on Haskell Rd., which becomes gravel. Continue for 2.6 mi to the end of the gravel road at an open field. Parking is allowed here. This is the end of the town-maintained road. From here on, the road gets progressively rougher, passable by 4WD vehicles, preferably with high clearance. Continue through rock and mud for one hour. At 7.8 mi, the road crosses a stream bridge, with a house uphill L just before the stream. On the N side of the stream, an old road goes L (the trail). Park near the entrance to that side road. This is an unofficial trail with no markers. ◀

STARTING UPHILL on the old road NW from Haskell Rd. (0.0 mi), the route soon levels off, crosses an outlet stream, and loops around Beaverdam Pond on the hillside above. The view is pleasant through the trees.

The old road turns R at 1.0 mi to continue N along Jones Brook to private land at 1.7 mi. At the turn, the Honnedaga Brook Trail goes straight (NW). It is much fainter than the trail to the R. This somewhat obscure old road continues parallel to Honnedaga Brook (100 yd L) to the confluence of Honnedaga and Jones brooks at 1.2 mi. The route crosses Jones Brook (no bridge and rather deep water) and continues on the N side of Honnedaga Brook, finally crossing that brook at 2.1 mi to join the Baby Lake Falls Trail (trail 115) at Falls Camp (a clearing). Baby Lake Falls is 0.6 mi to the R on that trail.

The old road beyond Jones Brook is now very obscure; travel is for experienced bushwhackers. Jones Brook is wide and has fairly deep water.

❋ Trail in winter: The winter trailhead is at Nobleboro, 7.8 mi S of the summer trailhead. Easy traveling as far as Jones Brook. Shortest route to Baby Lake Falls (10.5 mi). The one-mile section from Jones Brook to Falls Camp is a bushwhack. The entire route is otherwise easily skied.

❀ Distances: End of town road to trailhead by jeep road, 5.2 mi; trailhead to Beaverdam Pond, 0.3 mi; to trail jct., 1.0 mi; to crossing of Jones Brook, 1.2 mi; to Falls Camp, 2.1 mi; to Baby Lake Falls, 2.7 mi (4.4 km).

(115) Baby Lake Falls Trail

Map: D7

These beautiful falls are located on Honnedaga Brook, which is the outlet of Baby Lake and Honnedaga Lake. Although the falls are not straight down, and the highest cascade is only about 30 ft, the entire 200 ft of descending water forms an exceptional scene, flanked by moss-covered giant boulders. The shorter Honnedaga Brook Trail (114) also goes to the falls, but its trailhead is reachable only by 4WD vehicles; 1.0 mi of the trail is very obscure; and a wide, deep stream must be crossed without a bridge.

▶ Trailhead: See Little Salmon Lake Trail (trail 113). The Baby Lake Falls Trail starts at Summit Camp on the Little Salmon Lake Trail near

Little Salmon Lake. There are no trail markers to Baby Lake Falls. ◀

FROM TRAIL 113 (0.0 mi), the trail continues from the L rear corner (NE) behind Summit Camp, a private cabin. (Please do not disturb the cabin or use the facilities.) The way is slightly obscure, but recognizable in the beginning as an old road going downhill. Do not confuse it with another trail heading NW from the same spot, which goes on level ground to rejoin the Little Salmon Lake Trail.

After a short descent, the trail climbs slightly to pass along the hill above Threemile Vlei. There are no markers, but the route is easy to follow. At the SE end of the hill, at 0.9 mi, a long descent begins, with a steady, moderate grade. At 1.8 mi, the trail levels briefly and passes a small bog on the R.

The route goes briefly L and then NE down the hill, before the trail bottoms out at a clearing on Honnedaga Brook at 2.2 mi. This is the site of the former Falls Camp, now just a slight clearing. The Honnedaga Brook Trail (trail 114), coming from the E, crosses the brook here.

On the N side of the clearing there is a trail continuing to the falls. It is overgrown at the start. Search carefully for a slight footpath in open woods. It goes N along the base of the hillside L until it crosses a side stream. After crossing, it turns R and descends to a wet grassland. Stay L around the edge of the grassland to avoid water in the middle. At this point, the falls can be heard ahead.

The trail heads NE into the woods for another 200 ft to the bottom of Baby Lake Falls, 2.8 mi from Summit Camp and 0.6 mi from Falls Camp. If you wish to see the flume and the peaceful meadow at the top of the falls, climb the hill 30 ft on the L, away from the stream, to avoid destroying the beautiful moss covering the rocks at the side of the falls. Take care at the top. If you slip into the fast-running flume, your body will be recovered at the very bottom.

✳ Trail in winter: The winter trailhead is at Nobleboro, 3.5 mi before the summer trailhead. Most of the route is a lightly used snowmobile trail. The distance is definitely pushing the limits for winter day trips, even for strong groups, but the trail is otherwise suitable for snowshoeing. The Little Salmon Lake Trail is suitable for backcountry skiing, but the steepness of some hill sections makes it most suitable for intermediate skiers. The return trip has two long glide sections. The Baby Lake Falls Trail has a long downhill section with thick undergrowth, suitable only for snowshoers or very good skiers.

※ Distances: Trail 113 to descent, 0.9 mi; to Honnedaga Brook, 2.2 mi; to Baby Lake Falls, 2.8 mi (4.5 km).

(115A) Morehouseville Wilderness Access

Map: p. 249

There are no trails in this region, but the road crossing the South Branch of West Canada Creek at Morehouseville provides access to the trailless interior of the West Canada Lakes Wilderness Area.

▶ Locator: From the center of Morehouseville on NY 8, turn N on a gravel road and head downhill across a bridge and uphill again for about 0.5 mi. The road turns W upon reaching level ground and soon enters private land. Park along the road just after it reaches the high ground. ◀

(115B) South Branch Trail

Map: p. 249

This trail along the South Branch of West Canada Creek gives access to the S part of the West Canada Lakes Wilderness Area. There is a trail register at the start, and the path is cleared for a considerable distance, but the trail is not marked. It is intended for experienced sportsmen and wilderness hikers.

▶ Trailhead: From Piseco Lake, go W on NY 8 through Hoffmeister to a jct. with Mountain Home Rd. 1.6 mi W of Hoffmeister. From Nobleboro, go E on NY 8 for 4.8 mi to a road jct. on the L. Turn onto Mountain Home Rd. Go past Wilmurt Lake Rd. at about 1.3 mi. At 2.1 mi there is a wide turnaround. If your car has a low center, and also in wintertime, park as far as you can to the side of this turnaround. Others can proceed beyond the gate (in season) through a section of private land to an old road on the L at 3.3 mi. Park out of the way on the L. If you go too far on the main road, it is only 0.1 mi farther to a ford across West Canada Creek. The road on the other side leads to private land at Pine Lake. This is a DEC trail, but it is not marked. ◀

THE TRAIL L leads in 200 ft to the trail register (0.0 mi) at the crossing of a small creek (Mad Tom Brook, but not the one referenced in trail 111 description). The trail climbs gently for the first 0.8 mi, then levels out and goes parallel to West Canada Creek. Some minor downhill travel leads to Roaring Brook at 1.0 mi and a minor creek at 1.3 mi. The Roaring Brook crossing is 20 ft wide, but the creek in midsummer is typically very small.

The path continues on easy ground to the crossing of Wagoner Brook at 1.8 mi. The trail goes modestly uphill after Wagoner Brook, then levels out. Shortly after, at 1.9 mi, an obscure trail goes L on an old road. This is the High Trail. The Low Trail continues straight ahead.

LOW TRAIL

The route straight ahead from the trail jct. leads mostly downhill for another 0.8 mi to West Canada Creek at 2.7 mi. The old road crossed the creek on a long-gone bridge and headed uphill along Twin Lakes Outlet. (These twin lakes are near Piseco Lake and are not the ones described in trail 108.) The route is still discernible, but requires some expertise to use. Several branches of the old logging road lead to slopes and hilltops in the region of L–D Pond. This access to the L–D Pond area is not a marked hiking trail, but is intended to give hunters a route to the interior.

Bushwhackers intending to walk upstream on West Canada Creek are in for a very bad time. The lowland is mostly choked with viburnum and heavy bushes and is a nightmare to navigate. If you are determined to use this route instead of the High Trail, the best travel in the circumstance is somewhat up the hillside on the W.

HIGH TRAIL

This route turns L at the obscure jct. at 1.9 mi and starts gently uphill. The route is mostly a very old road, but only the most experienced hikers would believe it when they see the trail. The footpath is used just enough to make the route easy to follow in most places. In others, the hiker must be careful not to lose the known trail while searching for the continuation on the other side of old blowdowns. (The trail is maintained, and blowdowns are cut away, but occasional massive trees are simply bypassed.)

The route goes N up the slope, then turns NE to follow along the contour for another half mile. At 2.8 mi, the trail turns NW uphill and climbs to the summit of a hill. The route along the hilltop is open and easy, but still not used enough to let the hiker dream on without watching the footpath. After a gentle downhill slope, the trail reaches Beaudry Brook at 3.6 mi. The hiker is right to wonder how a brook can

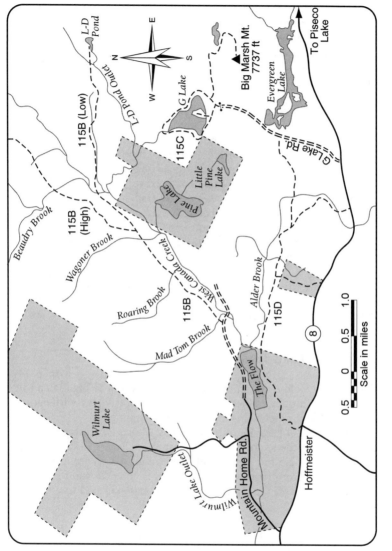

Big Marsh Mt. 7737 ft

L-D Pond

L-D Pond Outlet

115B (Low)

Beaudry Brook

115B (High)

Wagoner Brook

Roaring Brook

West Canada Creek

115B

Mad Tom Brook

G Lake

115C

Little Pine Lake

Pine Lake

Evergreen Lake

G Lake Rd.

To Piseco Lake

Alder Brook

115D

8

The Flow

Wilmurt Lake

Wilmurt Lake Outlet

Mountain Home Rd.

Hoffmeister

Scale in miles

0.5 0 0.5 1.0

South Branch Trail (115B), G Lake Trail (115C), and Alder Brook Trail (115D) go sideways along the top of a hill. In fact, the hill is just the shoulder of a somewhat level area of Buck Pond Mt.

The trail crosses Beaudry Brook. There is no obvious footpath at this point, but one can see a former lumber clearing just above on the far side. The trail continues its N course from the far corner on the N side of the clearing. It is not very obvious for the first 100 ft, but does go through the most open part of the evergreen thicket. After that, it again becomes a noticeable footpath on an old logging road. After traversing easy open summit forest, it comes to Jones Brook at 4.7 mi. This brook was mislocated on the old quad maps. The location was corrected on the new quad, but the name was dropped.

On the other side, another old logging camp includes pipe frames, various debris, and a logging camp barrel stove. This seems to be used by present-day sportsmen in season. The trail and old road continue NE past the lumber camp. It becomes too difficult to follow within the next half mile, but the forest is quite open.

❋ Trail in winter: Suitable for skiing or snowshoeing. The High Trail may be too difficult to follow in winter, but the Low Trail makes a fine day's outing.

🏔 Distances: Trailhead to jct. of High and Low trails, 1.9 mi; to West Canada Creek by Low Trail, 2.7 mi; to lumber camp on Beaudry Brook, 3.6 mi; to lumber camp on unnamed creek, 4.7 mi (7.6 km).

(115C) G Lake Trail

Map: p. 249

Except for the old roads around the shore and a spur to Big Marsh Mt., G Lake is essentially trailless. It is, however, a pretty lake with various spots suitable for picnicking and primitive camping.

▶ Trailhead: G Lake Rd. is easy to miss. Measure highway distances carefully. From the jct. of NY 8 and West Shore Rd. on Piseco Lake, go W on NY 8 for 2.5 mi. Turn R and go downhill steeply from the highway shoulder. From Hoffmeister, go 3.8 mi E on NY 8 and turn L (N) onto G Lake Rd. Go 2.1 mi on this rocky seasonal road to a parking spot at a barrier. ◀

FROM THE PARKING LOT (0.0 mi), the old road continues for 0.1 mi to the somewhat obscure first jct. in a small clearing. To the L, an unmarked old road leads most of the way around the W side of the lake. At 0.2 mi down this side road, an obscure old road leads R to the peninsula which forms the center cutout of the "G". The peninsula road is now obscure and overgrown, but one can't get very lost on the pleasant, tiny peninsula. The road continuing around the W side is fairly easy to follow in open forest. Views from the W side are pleasant.

Continuing ahead on the main trail, there is another small clearing and jct. on the R at 0.2 mi. That old road to the R leads past a small pond below Big Marsh Mt. It is not maintained, but is fairly easy to follow (see Big Marsh Mt. below).

At 0.5 mi, a branch goes L at 0.5 mi to a former house site on the lake. There is a beautiful picnic area in the pines near the lake and camping possibilities nearby. From this jct., the trail continues on around the lake to the R, but becomes obscure and essentially useless by the time it reaches the end of the lake.

BIG MARSH MT.

This side route on an unmaintained old road passes through some small clearings and a large clearing at 1.0 mi. Just after the large clearing, the old road crosses a small stream and curves L to go along the hillside parallel to the stream. At 1.2 mi, the route forks. The L branch goes down through soggy terrain to the pond N of Big Marsh Mt. The R branch continues on drier ground above the pond and reaches another large clearing at 1.4 mi.

The former route up Big Marsh Mt. starts from the high point of this clearing on an older woods road. The old road is reasonably easy to follow, but is not suitable for hikers who are not experienced with map and compass. To reach the summit, follow the old road N for 0.1 mi and take the R branch, which starts more steeply uphill. The old route is obvious until the long hilltop at 1.9 mi, where it suddenly ends. From here it is fairly easy walking on open ground, but the forest has regrown nicely, with scant views.

❋ Trail in winter: Remote trail at the end of a seasonal use road; would add more than four miles to round trip in winter. Otherwise, suitable for snowshoeing.

𝖒 Distances: Trailhead to peninsula tip, 0.5 mi. Trailhead to homesite on E side, 0.6 mi; to end of either trail around lake, 1.3 mi (2.1 km); to summit of Big Marsh Mt., 2.3 mi.

(115D) **Alder Brook Trail**

This snowmobile trail extends into a pleasant region of open hardwood forest along Alder Brook. It is a piece of a trail network extending from Ohio to Speculator, but parts of the network are on private land, which may not be open to hikers. There are three other trailheads in this region, all shown on the map, but the one on G Lake Rd. is the only usable one on public land. (The trailhead on NY 8 near Alder Brook Rd. is on state land, but very boggy, and would be severely damaged by foot traffic.)

▶ Trailhead: On G Lake Rd., which is easy to miss. Measure highway distances carefully. From the jct. of NY 8 and West Shore Rd. on Piseco Lake, go W on NY 8 for 2.5 mi. Turn R and go downhill steeply from the highway shoulder. From Hoffmeister, go 3.8 mi E on NY 8 and turn L (N) onto G Lake Rd. Go 1.1 mi on this rocky seasonal road to a slight parking area and snowmobile trail signs on the L. ◀

THE TRAIL BEGINS on level ground at the rim of the marsh just W of Evergreen Lake (0.0 mi). The path is easy, but can be somewhat wet. At 0.5 mi, it turns S and crosses a brook on a small bridge. After climbing out of the bottomland, the trail turns W again and continues along the rim through easy, open, hardwood forest.

At 1.0 mi, the old trail continues straight ahead (W) while the new route turns R and descends the hillside. At the bottom, the trail turns L and follows Alder Brook for a short distance before meeting the former trail route at a bridge across the brook. This is a very pleasant region, with opportunities for camping along the brook just a little downstream.

From the bridge, the trail continues W along the gentle hillside to a jct. with the Alder Brook Rd. trail at 1.5 mi. This side trail is not difficult to follow, but is rougher underfoot and passes through extensive boggy sections. These bogs do not have bridges or corduroy, and will become dreadful hogwallows if used by hikers when the ground is not frozen.

The main trail continues along Alder Brook and passes above the S shore of The Floe; however, state land ends just as the trail reaches The Floe (3.4 mi). The remainder of the trail up to NY 8 (4.9 mi) at Hoffmeister is on private land. Another side trail up to NY 8 at 2.4 mi also passes through private land on its way to the road.

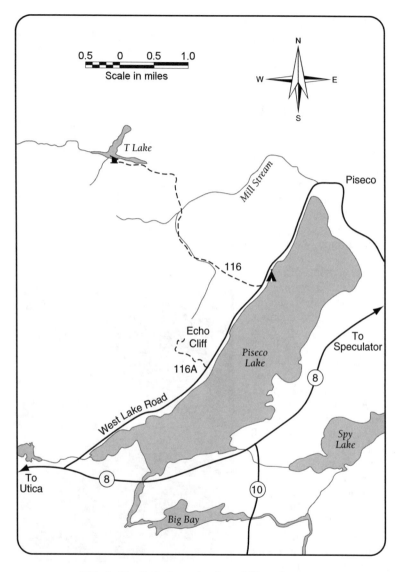

T Lake Trail (116) and Echo Cliff Trail (116A)

❋ Trail in winter: Snowmobile trail.

🐾 Distances: G Lake Rd. to Alder Brook Rd. trail, 1.5 mi; to second side trail, 2.4 mi; to end of state land at The Floe, 3.4 mi (5.5 km). (Through private land to end of trail, 4.9 mi.)

(116) T Lake Trail

Map: p. 253

T Lake is a readily accessible and quite scenic lake in the West Canada Lakes Wilderness Area. It has a genuine T shape, although the T section is not readily recognized from the S shore. A lean-to is up the hill with the lake barely visible through foliage.

▶ Trailhead: From NY 8 at the S end of Piseco Lake, go N on West Shore Rd. for 4.0 mi. The trailhead is on the L (W), just before the Poplar Point Campground. Park at the trailhead, or if necessary at the campground, where a day-use fee is charged. ◀

LEAVING THE HIGHWAY (0.0 mi), the blue-marked trail follows up the L bank of a ravine. The first mile of the trail continues in this manner, often steeply up. After 1.25 mi, the path heads down, sometimes steeply, to cross Mill Stream before going back up.

At 2.6 mi, the trail turns L onto the route of an older trail. The trail R leads to posted private land. Going L, the trail goes up fairly steeply, then levels out and goes above the long arm of T Lake, finally reaching the T Lake lean-to at 3.5 mi. The lake is quite scenic from the lean-to, and even better if you go a

T Lake Falls. ELEANOR FRIEND

short distance W along the shore.

Note: The former trail to T Lake Falls has been closed by the DEC. The area around T Lake Falls is deceptively dangerous, and several people have been killed in falls from the steep slopes.

❄ Trail in winter: Campground parking is not available and the parking lot may not be plowed. Suitable for snowshoes. The initial climb is too steep for all but expert skiers.

❧ Distances: West Shore Rd. to first height of land, 1.2 mi; to T Lake Lean-to, 3.5 mi (5.6 km).

(116A) Echo Cliff Trail

Map: p. 253

This is a short but steep climb to a nice view over Piseco Lake.

▶ Trailhead: From NY 8 at the S end of Piseco Lake, go N on West Shore Rd. for 2.6 mi. The trailhead is on the L (W). Park along the side of the road. ◀

LEAVING THE ROAD (0.0 mi), the trail goes up somewhat steeply on the L slope of a ravine. It levels out in a col at 0.5 mi, then turns R and goes uphill with a small creek on the L. The route soon turns R and heads up a steep slope, staying more or less on the ridge until leveling out on a narrow hilltop. The extensive view from the cliff includes Piseco Lake in the foreground, with Higgins Bay on the L and Spy Lake in the background.

❄ Trail in winter: Short and steep, a possibility for accomplished snowshoers.

❧ Distance: To hilltop and Echo Cliff, 0.6 mi (1.0 km).　　　　◆

Cedar River. C. B. MOORE

Cedar River Section

The Cedar River section forms a natural border for the West-Central Region. It is almost equally accessible from both the Central and West-Central regions, and it is traversed by the Northville–Placid Trail. ADK's *Central Region* and *Northville–Placid Trail* guides also address parts of this section. The coverage in this section is intended to describe only the trails that have the most immediate connection with the Moose River Plains Wild Forest (MRPWF).

The trails of this section are located just off the E edge of the west-central topo maps, and are covered by individual page maps. Access to them is either by the Cedar River Rd. (E entrance to the MRPWF) or by the Otter Brook–Indian Lake Rd. within the MRPWF.

There is a great difference in usage of the trails on these two roads. The Cedar River Rd. gives quick access to somewhat shorter trails, suitable for an interesting day hike, while the longer trails reached by Otter Brook Rd. are much more suitable for overnight trips far into the West Canada Lake Wilderness. Refer to ADK's *Northville–Placid Trail* for discussion of the colorful "French Louie" who lived in the backwoods of this region.

MODERATE HIKE:

◆ Cellar Pond—2.6 mi (4.2 km). A backcountry lake on an old logging road; fairly easy, but with a sense of adventure. See trail 118.

HARDER HIKES:

◆ Wakely Mt.—3.0 mi (4.8 km). A vigorous hike to the summit (1635 ft ascent) and the base of a fire tower. See trail 117.

◆ West Canada Lakes Loop—24.4 mi (39.4 km). This overnight (or multiple overnight) trip combines travel in the West Canada Lake Wilderness Area with lean-to or tent camping and a host of side trips to wild lakes. See trail 120.

(117) **Wakely Mt. Trail**

Map: p. 259

(Adapted from a description in ADK's *Adirondack Trails: Central Region.*)

Wakely Mt. is only 256 ft short of being a 4000 ft peak. The hiker ascends 1194 ft in the last 1.1 mi. It has the second tallest fire tower in the state (70 ft), but it is closed, limiting views.

▶ Trailhead: From the village of Indian Lake, drive W on NY 28/30 for 2.2 mi to a R bend in the highway. Turn L (S) on Cedar River Rd. and proceed 11.6 mi. The trailhead is on the R with a large parking area.◀

FROM THE TRAILHEAD (0.0 mi), walk NW along a gravel road. The red DEC trail markers are rare. A brief view of the summit can be had at 0.3 mi. The remains of an old lumber camp are found over a bank L at 0.7 mi. There is a private side road R, then a bridge over a creek at 1.1 mi. The trail register is at the crossing. Beyond the bridge, the route parallels the stream for a short time before veering away.

The trail crosses two more streams before the Wakely Mt. tower sign on the R at 1.9 mi. The clearing R of this jct. is the site of an old beaver pond and is worth a brief visit.

The trail turns R off the road and climbs steeply to the summit. There are yellow and red markers. Several unmarked trails branch off. A survey marker is located at 2.5 mi. The fire tower can again be seen at 2.7 mi, and 240 ft from the summit a side trail to the R leads to a helipad site.

The summit fire tower is at trail's end, 3.0 mi from the trailhead. Ground views are limited to the SE toward Cedar River Flow.

✣ Trail in winter: Suitable for snowshoeing, with a steep climb, but Cedar River Rd. is not plowed this far in winter, making this a combined snowmobile-snowshoe trip.

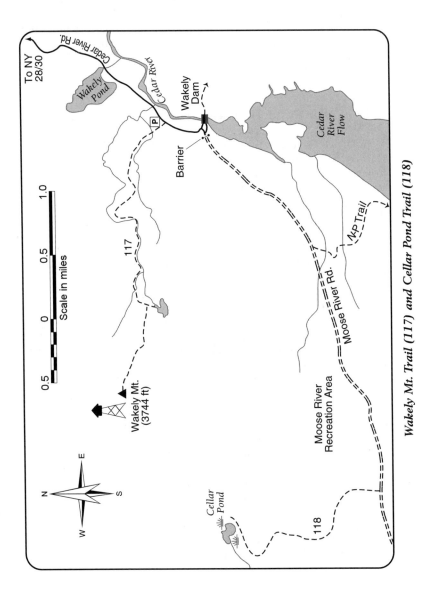

Wakely Mt. Trail (117) and Cellar Pond Trail (118)

🐾 Distances: To first view of summit, 0.3 mi; to old logging camp, 0.7 mi; to trail register, 1.1 mi; to start of steep climbing at trail sign, 1.9 mi; to summit, 3.0 mi (4.8 km). Ascent, 1635 ft (498 m). Elevation, 3744 ft (1141 m).

(118) **Cellar Pond Trail** (unmaintained)

Map: p. 259

▶ Trailhead: From the E entrance gate to the MRPWF, near Wakely Dam, go SW, then W on Moose River Rd. for 3.3 mi. The trail is an old logging road on the R. Park in a cleared area along Moose River Rd. just W of the logging road. Distance to this point from the jct. of Moose River Rd. and Otter Brook Rd. is 8.6 mi. This is an unofficial trail, and there are no trail markers. ◀

FROM MOOSE RIVER RD. (0.0 mi), the first 0.8 mi of the logging road was used for logging in 1984, and there can be little doubt of the route. Starting N, it curves around Cellar Mt. until it heads nearly W. Turning N again, the road climbs steadily across the slope.

At 0.8 mi, the evidence of logging ceases, but the route continues steadily upward. At 1.2 mi, the road turns L in a saddle, on level ground. From here on, thick growth covers much of the old road, with only occasional clear sections. The route heads gently downhill and slowly curves to the R.

At 2.3 mi, the road forks. The L fork (straight ahead) leads a short distance to Cellar Brook. Take the R fork (mag. 350 degrees), which is more overgrown than the L. Thick young fir trees cover the old road for most of the remaining distance. A small clearing on the R at 2.6 mi was the site of wooden cabins. The pond can be seen in the distance through trees to the N. Continue down the overgrown road for another 100 ft, then through the trees L to the edge of the pond. There are no obvious beaches or clear access points. The mountains across the pond are parts of the W extension of Wakely Mt. Both the inlet and outlet of the pond are on the far side.

✳ Trail in winter: Snowshoes or good skiing ability, but the MRPWF is closed in winter. Practical access by snowmobile only.

🐾 Distances: To saddle, 1.2 m; to fork, 2.3 mi; to Cellar Pond and old camp, 2.6 mi (4.2 km).

(119) Cedar Lakes Trail

Map: E4, pp. 264–265

▶ Trailhead: Start at the jct. of Moose River Rd. and Otter Brook Rd. in the MRPWF (8.3 mi from the W entrance and 12.9 mi from the E entrance). Drive S on Otter Brook Rd. for 3.3 mi to the crossing of Otter Brook, turning L immediately after crossing the bridge. This L branch is the continuation of Otter Brook Rd. (The main road R continues as Indian River Rd.) Go 0.6 mi above and parallel to the brook until you reach a barrier and trailhead. ◀

FROM THE BARRIER (0.0 mi), the yellow-marked trail heads E on a logging road on the N boundary of the West Canada Lakes Wilderness, crossing a number of streams, then turns R into the wilderness area on a logging road and goes generally SE. It crosses Jimmy Creek on a bridge at 1.7 mi. It descends sharply at 3.3 mi (offering views not available earlier) and crosses a stream at 3.4 mi via wading, rocks, or fallen trees to an informal campsite on the other side. Avoid the trail E from a clearing with a large machine, apparently a piece of old logging equipment, L at 5.8 mi, where a sign erroneously lists the distance from the trailhead as 6.0 mi. It's another 0.2 mi S to where a spur trail, also yellow marked, at the actual 6.0 mi mark leads L (E) 0.5 mi to Lost Pond.

The route changes to a footpath, ascends 300 ft, and crosses the divide between the St. Lawrence and Hudson River basins. The trail then descends, passes around the NE end of Beaver Pond, and ends at the blue-marked Northville–Placid (N–P) Trail near the N end of Cedar Lakes at 8.4 mi. See ADK's *Adirondack Trails: Northville–Placid Trail*.

To the L (E) on the N–P Trail it is 0.7 mi to a lean-to at the N end of First Cedar Lake. A little beyond it is the dam in the outlet of Cedar Lakes, which is the beginning of the Cedar River. The beautiful Cedar Lakes are a single body of water two miles long, divided into three segments. At 2442 ft, it is one of the highest of the Adirondacks' larger lakes.

Going R (SW) on the N–P Trail from the end of the Cedar Lakes Trail, at 0.3 mi there is a lean-to 100 yd to the L of the trail by the Beaver Pond outlet and First Cedar Lake.

If you wish to make a circuit backpacking hike rather than a round trip, continue SW on the N–P Trail, passing a side trail on the L at 2.3

mi leading 0.5 mi to a lean-to on Third Cedar Lake. Later the trail goes W, passing Mud Lake and reaching a jct. with the red-marked West Canada Lakes Trail (trail 120) at 6.3 mi, near the site of the former caretaker's cabin on the E shore of beautiful West Lake, one of the West Canada Lakes. From there it is 8.2 mi on the West Canada Lakes Trail (trail 120) NW to Indian River Rd., and another 1.5 mi on the Indian River and Otter Brook Rds. back to the Cedar Lakes trailhead, for a total distance of 24.4 mi (39.4 km), not including any side trails taken.

❋ Trail in winter: This trail is very remote. It is 20 mi from the nearest winter trailhead, the end of snowplowing on Cedar River Rd. Access to the West Canada Lakes is more reasonably done via the Northville–Placid Trail.

⚹ Distances: To Jimmy Creek bridge, 1.7 mi; to stream ford, 3.4 mi; to Lost Pond spur, 6.0 mi; to Northville–Placid Trail jct., 8.4 mi (13.5 km). To first Cedar Lake lean-to N of jct., 9.1 mi; to Beaver Pond Outlet lean-to S of jct., 8.7 mi; to West Canada Lakes Trail (trail 120), 14.7 mi; to loop back to Indian River Rd. by West Canada Lakes Trail, 22.1 mi; to loop back to trailhead, 24.4 mi (39.4 km).

(120) West Canada Lakes Trail

Map: E5, pp. 264–265

This trail offers visits to several bodies of water, including Falls Pond, Brooktrout Lake, and West Lake, that are beautiful and remote. The trail lies wholly in the West Canada Lake Wilderness Area. It starts from Indian River Rd. as a yellow trail and goes SE 5.6 mi to the lean-to at the E end of Brooktrout Lake. Then, as a red-marked trail, it continues E to the lean-to at the NE end of West Lake at 8.0 mi and goes S a short distance to end at 8.2 mi at the N–P Trail by the foundation of a former caretaker's lodge on the E shore of the lake. (Another lean-to is located 0.2 mi S on the lake.) The trail provides the closest access to West Lake from a drivable road.

Along the first 2.2 mi of the trail there are side trails leading to three ponds: Falls Pond, Deep Lake, and Wolf Lake. The first is especially worth a visit.

There are various ascents and descents along the trail, the principal change in elevation being a 500-ft ascent along easy or moderate grades in the first 1.5 mi.

West Canada Lake

▶ Trailhead: Start at the jct. of Moose River Rd. and Otter Brook Rd. in the MRPWF (8.3 mi from the W entrance and 12.9 mi from the E entrance). Drive S on Otter Brook Rd. for 3.3 mi to the crossing of Otter Brook. Continue past the Cedar Lakes Trail (trail 119) road on the L just after the bridge. After another 1.0 mi (4.3 mi from road jct.), park on the L in an area with a trailhead sign where the road bends R. There are yellow DEC markers to Brooktrout Lake, then red DEC markers to the N–P Trail. ◀

HEADING SE (0.0 mi), the old logging road gradually ascends through small tree growth. At 1.5 mi, a yellow side trail goes R (W) to Falls Pond.

[The yellow-marked Falls Pond Trail goes W. At 0.3 mi from the main trail, where conifers begin to prevail, the trail crosses a wet area and the pond's outlet and then traverses a stand of spruce-fir. The trail reaches the pond next to its outlet and continues another 70 yd, going R in a muddy section along the water's edge and ending at an informal campsite at a N corner of the pond. By following a narrow path R (W) near the rock-lined water's edge, you will arrive at a point of land with an informal campsite and a better view of the pond. Small, rocky

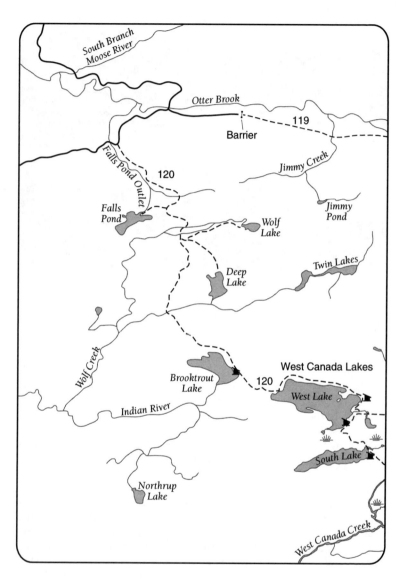

Cedar Lakes Region

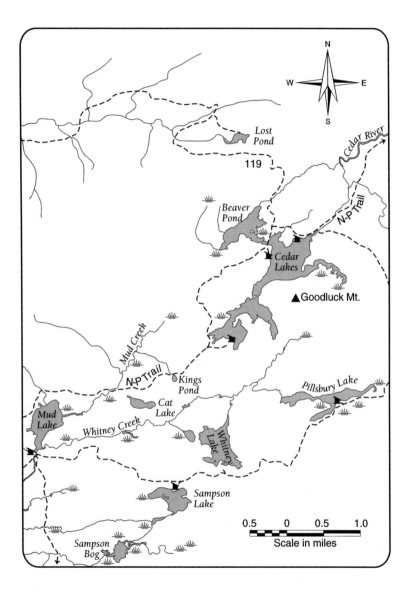

N

W E

S

Lost Pond

119

Cedar River

N-P Trail

Beaver Pond

Cedar Lakes

▲ Goodluck Mt.

Mud Creek

N-P Trail

Kings Pond

Pillsbury Lake

Cat Lake

Mud Lake

Whitney Creek

Whitney Lake

Sampson Lake

0.5   0   0.5   1.0

Scale in miles

Sampson Bog

islands—including one rock split by freeze-thaw cycles over the years—lie off the shore here. The pond is an attractive, conifer-lined body of water at an elevation of 2500 ft.]

The West Canada Lakes Trail, after further ascent and a descent, spans Wolf Creek on a bridge at 2.2 mi, where an open area has the remains of a logging operation. Some 140 yd beyond, in an open area of bedrock, a yellow side trail goes L and soon forks into two trails leading to Deep Lake and Wolf Lake. These bodies of water are at high elevation and devoid of fish owing to acid rain.

The combined yellow-marked trail goes E as a woods road with mudholes, splitting at 0.1 with Wolf Lake L and Deep Lake R. The Deep Lake Trail ascends over 200 ft to an elevation of 2800 ft. The trail narrows and descends approximately SE the rest of the way. It enters a spruce-fir forest and ends at an informal campsite at the N end of Deep Lake, 1.0 mi from the West Canada Lakes Trail. Typical of the region, the pond is conifer-lined and partly boggy on the shoreline. Despite its name, it's shallow from the inlet stream next to the end of the trail out to a large rock R.

[The Wolf Lake Trail is for wetland devotees who don't mind getting their feet wet. From the fork with the Deep Lake Trail, it goes N and E at first as a grassy avenue through a new growth of trees, reaching the wetland of Wolf Creek on the L with nice views of a beaver pond at 0.3 mi from the W. Canada Lakes Trail jct. (0.2 mi from the Deep Lake split). This is a good turnaround point. The trail is flooded—not because of beavers as it's higher than the beaver pond—and it goes through wet, marshy sections interspersed with areas of bedrock. The route narrows, and at 1.0 mi from the West Canada Lakes Trail one has to wade through a flooded marsh to reach an adequate view of Wolf Lake. It is 2600 ft in elevation, lined by wetlands and conifers.]

Beyond the Deep/Wolf side trail at 2.2 mi, the main trail continues as a wide route, much of it stony, with some bedrock. It reaches its highest elevation of about 2650 ft and after 2.5 mi becomes narrower, often stony or grassy, with many wet places. At 3.0 mi there is a beaver pond and a long curving beaver dam with an old moss-encrusted beaver house in view. Larger tree specimens begin to appear. At 3.4 mi, the formerly logged-over area ends and the trail becomes a footpath in a mature forest.

The outlet of Twin Lakes and Deep Lake crosses at 3.8 mi. The trail descends moderately steeply past stately yellow birches to go parallel to the NE side of Brooktrout Lake, visible through the trees. After some ups and downs, it passes an informal campsite on the R at 5.5 mi, and at 5.6 mi a spur trail leads 25 yd R to the Brooktrout Lake Lean-to.

The lean-to faces a rock wall that serves as backing for the fireplace. A few yards by trail through dense spruce brings one to the E corner of this attractive lake, 2369 ft in elevation. It has a rocky shoreline fringed with conifers; a bluff rises from the far end. Walk L along the rocks at the edge of the lake for a fuller view of it.

The West Canada Lakes Trail continues SE with the yellow markers replaced by red ones. Between Brooktrout Lake and West Lake it crosses the inconspicuous divide between the St. Lawrence and Hudson drainage basins. At 6.3 mi, 40 yd beyond a great boulder on the R, a spur trail goes R 30 yd to an informal campsite on the westernmost corner of beautiful West Lake. Beyond the far end of the lake one sees Pillsbury Mt., 3597 ft in elevation.

After a short steep climb, the trail parallels the N side of the lake. This is an especially attractive section with some large yellow birch and several open glimpses of the lake. There is a short stretch of open wetland with a view L of a steep ridge (Twin Lakes Mt.).

At 7.9 mi, West Canada Lake Lean-to 2 is located in the woods, with the nearby lake visible through the trees on the R. Just beyond, the trail passes the edge of the lake's NE corner. A shallow sandy bottom, a nearby island, and a view of South Lake Mt. rising from the far side of the lake are attractive features of this location, just off the N–P Trail and so possibly not used as much as the next lean-to 0.5 mi S.

The trail goes S on the E side of the lake, passing through a stand of spruce-fir and crossing the lake's broad outlet. There is an informal campsite nearby. At 8.2 mi (13.2 km) the trail ends in a field at a jct. with the N–P Trail, which makes a sharp turn here. On the R is the site of the former caretaker's lodge and French Louie's fireplace, with a fine view overlooking the lake.

Going straight ahead (S) on the broad, blue-marked N–P Trail, one reaches a side trail leading to West Canada Lake Lean-to 1 at 0.2 mi from the jct. This nice shelter on the E shore has a good view of the lake with its clean-cut, conifer-lined shores fringed by highlands. There are rocks along the edge here and a small island nearby to complete the idyllic scene.

From the end of the West Canada Lakes Trail, and turning L (E) on the N–P Trail, one reaches an informal campsite L in 115 yd. To make a circuit hike rather than a round trip, continue E and NE for 6.3 mi on the N–P Trail, passing Mud Lake and two separate lean-tos located off to the R on Cedar lakes. Turn L on the yellow-marked Cedar Lakes Trail (trail 119) and follow it 8.4 mi NW and W to Otter Brook Rd., from where it is 1.5 mi W and S along Otter Brook and Indian River roads back to the West Canada Lakes trailhead. This makes a total of 24.4 mi for the circuit hike, briefly described in the reverse direction in the description of the Cedar Lakes Trail (trail 119). For more information on the Northville–Placid Trail, see *Adirondack Trails: Northville–Placid Trail*, published by the Adirondack Mountain Club (Volume IV in the Forest Preserve Series).

❄ Trail in winter: This trail is very remote. It is 20 mi from the nearest winter trailhead, the end of snowplowing on Cedar River Rd. A more practical access for winter backpackers is via the Northville–Placid Trail.

⚹ Distances: Indian River Rd. trailhead to Falls Pond, 1.5 mi; to Deep Lake and Wolf Lake, 3.2 mi; to Brooktrout Lake Lean-to, 5.6 mi; to West Canada Lake Lean-to 2, 7.9 mi; to N–P Trail, 8.2 mi (13.2 km). To West Canada Lake Lean-to 1, 8.4 mi; to Cedar Lake Trail, 14.5 mi; to trailhead via Cedar Lakes Trail (119) and roads, 24.4 mi (39.4 km). ◆

Cedar River bridge. Norm Landis

Beaver River Section

The lands around Stillwater Reservoir are mostly state-owned, and tend to be used by the public for canoe and motorboat camping. Weekend use has increased greatly in recent years, with campsites filled to capacity. Even so, the reservoir is reputed to be the largest loon breeding area in the state.

The reservoir was once a collection of small ponds along the Beaver River. New York State erected a small dam in the Stillwater area in 1864 for logging purposes. In 1882–86, the Department of Transportation built a larger dam to serve the Black River Canal and the mills along the lower reaches of the Black River. A still higher dam was built in 1922–24 to serve water-powered mills downstream. Today the reservoir is part of a series along the Beaver River used to generate electric power. Besides the DEC forest ranger station, the community near the dam at Stillwater offers boat rentals, a store, a restaurant-hotel, and a bed and breakfast.

Several hiking trails are accessible from the lake. The Red Horse Trail and the trails at Beaver River Station must normally be reached by boat, and the Wilderness Lakes Trail is next to the outlet dam. Farther W, the Pepperbox Wilderness Area is reached by a bridge across the Beaver River at Moshier Falls or the bridge below Stillwater Dam. Some of the trails are also described in ADK's *Adirondack Trails: Northern Region*.

Beaver River Station can be reached overland via the Beaver River Trail from Twitchell Lake (6.6 mi) or the old RR bed from Big Moose Station (8.2 mi). The latter is listed as a snowmobile trail but walking on the tracks may not be legal. Beaver River Station can also be reached by boat from Stillwater (approximately 6.0 mi by water, or 1.2 mi by water and 5.6 mi on Flow Rd.). The Norridgewock, a lodge at Beaver River Station, operates water taxis and scheduled summertime cruise boats between Stillwater and Beaver River Station. Boats can also be rented at Stillwater. The Beaver River Hotel is also located there.

The old Carthage Military Rd. along the Beaver River passed close to the contemporary community of Beaver River Station, but the earliest occasional homes and camps were mostly nearer the river. The community owes its formal existence to W. S. Webb, builder of the Mohawk & Malone Railroad, which became the Adirondack & St. Lawrence Railroad (Adirondack Division of the New York Central). A lumber mill was established at Beaver River Station in 1893 by Firman Ouderkirk to process timber from Webb's land in the area. Webb had sued the state, contending that the 1886 dam on the river had blocked lumbering in the area and that the RR was not a feasible means of shipping the timber. After he won, the lumber was, of course, shipped on Webb's RR. Cutting was completed by 1904, Webb sold the surrounding land to the state, and the community shrank to just a few remaining families.

The Carthage Rd.—the remains of which is now called the Six Mile Rd.—once gave access by car from the W, but the rising waters of newly enlarged Stillwater Reservoir cut off that route by 1924. At the same time, the new and higher dam required the clearing of all the land to be flooded. Beaver River Station again became a booming lumber town from 1922 to 1924, then declined again. The railway station was closed in 1943, and the RR itself ceased all Adirondack operations in 1971.

This compact 0.6 square mi piece of private land is again reduced to a full-time population of only a few people, but it is chock full of summer cottages. Dilapidated old trucks without license plates ply the short road from the center of town to the boat landing at Grassy Point; the community has no road access to the outside world.

State lands N of the Beaver River are likely to remain nearly trailless, with the exception of the Wilderness Lakes tract. Private landholders at Raven Lake still use the old timber company road from Stillwater.

Canoe carry on the Beaver River.
BETSY TISDALE

This road—the Raven Lake Primitive Corridor—is not open to other vehicle traffic, and serves as an access route for foot travel to reach the E part of the Pepperbox Wilderness Area and W part of the Five Ponds Wilderness Area. It separates the two Wilderness Areas. The road is barricaded at the S tip of Raven Lake where maintenance ends. There are old roads beyond that. Canoe carries between Stillwater Reservoir, Raven Lake, Lyon Lake, and Bear Pond are marked and signed.

SHORT HIKE:
◆ Colvin Rock Trail—0.1 mi (0.16 km). A short walk 600 ft from Grassy Point landing with 300 ft of trail to a rock with some faint markings from the Colvin Survey Party. (Note: Not to be confused with Colvin Memorial, a rock with a plaque at the N end of Norridgewock Lake.) See trail 125.

MODERATE HIKE:
◆ Norridgewock Lake Trail—1.8 mi (2.9 km). Easy walk around the lake and across the causeway passing Colvin Memorial. However, may not be possible in times of high water as it involves a stream crossing at S end. See trail 129.

HARDER HIKE:
◆ Red Horse Trail—5.0 mi (8.1 km). A remote trail accessible by boat on the N side of Stillwater Reservoir with a lean-to at its start. The trail passes Salmon and Witchhopple lakes, and ends at Clear Lake. See trail 124.

TRAIL DESCRIBED	TOTAL MILES		PAGE
	(one way)		
Pepperbox Wilderness Access and			
Moshier Falls Trail	0.3	(0.5 km)	272
Sunday Creek Trail	0.3	(0.5 km)	273
Raven Lake Primitive Corridor	4.0	(6.5 km)	273
Red Horse Trail	5.0	(8.1 km)	275
Colvin Rock Trail	0.1	(0.16 km)	278
Bathtub Trail	1.0	(1.6 km)	278
Burnt Mt. Trail	2.0	(3.2 km)	279
Beaver River–Twitchell Trail	6.6	(10.6 km)	280
Norridgewock Lake Trail	1.8	(2.9 km)	282

(121) Pepperbox Wilderness Access and Moshier Falls Trail

Map: A1

▶ Trailhead: Go to Moshier Rd., which is 2.1 mi E of Number Four on the Stillwater Rd. and 5.9 mi W of the jct. of Stillwater Rd. and Big Moose Rd. Turn N on Moshier Rd. for 0.6 mi. As you approach the power station water surge tower, there is a DEC parking lot on the R. The trail starts just across the road. ◀

FROM THE ROAD (0.0 mi), the blue-marked trail goes down a bank between the road and Sunday Creek, then turns R and follows the creek a short ways to a bridge over the creek. At the far end of the bridge, at a T, the L fork is a canoe carry to Beaver River. (This spur turns L in a short distance, goes to a private road, turns R on the road, crosses a bridge without handrails, and turns L to the put-in at 0.3 mi from the main trail. This is a nice grassy area, perfect for a picnic.)

The Pepperbox Trail turns R at the spur jct., follows the stream, then curves to meet a second bridge across the Beaver River. On the second bridge, one can view the power station outlet and the final cascades of Moshier Falls.

The trail then plunges into the woods to reach a powerline route, now quite overgrown. The trail sticks to the edge of the "clearing" parallel to the powerline. When the powerline makes a L turn, the trail crosses the powerline path and ends at a trail sign on the other side at 0.5 mi. This puts the hiker onto state land at the border of the Pepperbox Wilderness Area. There are no official trails beyond this point. You are on your own, and should certainly know how to use your map and compass.

To view Moshier Falls, follow the herd path N past the powerline for about 100 ft, then bushwhack R (E) to the water's edge. This water is fast-flowing, powerful, and dangerous, and the banks are treacherous. Do not attempt to reach the very edge. Stay safely back and enjoy the view.

❋ Trail in winter: Suitable for wilderness experts on skis or snowshoes. There are no trails in the Pepperbox Wilderness Area. The parking lot may not be plowed in winter.

🏃 Distances: To Wilderness Area boundary, 0.3 mi (0.5 km). To Moshier Falls, 0.4 mi (0.7 km).

(122) **Sunday Creek Trail**

Map: A1

▶ Trailhead: See trail 121, the Pepperbox Wilderness Access and Moshier Falls Trail. ◀

THE ROUTE STARTS in the NE corner of the parking lot (0.0 mi) and goes over a small rise. It continues E along the N bank of Sunday Creek until reaching the state land boundary at 0.3 mi. A sign indicates that this is the Pepperbox Wilderness; however, it is the Independence Wild Forest. The trail ends abruptly, leaving one to wonder why; it allows anglers to reach state land along the creek without trespassing.

❋ Trail in winter: Suitable for wilderness skiers or snowshoers, but the trail is very short. Only expert skiers or snowshoers should enter the wilds beyond the trail.

🐾 Distances: To state land boundary, 0.3 mi (0.5 km).

(123) **Raven Lake Primitive Corridor**

Map: p. 273

The former Wilderness Lakes Tract is now the Raven Lake Primitive Corridor between the Five Ponds Wilderness Area N of Beaver River and lands next to the Pepperbox Wilderness Area. A network of logging roads from the 1980s is shown in approximate detail on the map. Hikers must verify exact details on their own. The only trailhead is at Stillwater, 0.2 mi below the dam, on Stillwater Reservoir. There is a sign-in/trail register here. A former logging access road is still in use to reach a private parcel of land on Raven Lake. Other vehicle traffic is prohibited. Hikers must use the road bridge to get across the Beaver River, and will most likely want to use the road (Raven Lake Primitive Corridor Trail) as a route to reach the wilderness interior.

▶ Trailhead: From Lowville, go E on Number Four Rd. and Stillwater Rd. At the jct. with Big Moose Rd., go L to Stillwater. From Eagle Bay on NY 28, go W on Big Moose Rd. to Stillwater Rd. Turn R to Stillwater. Just before the buildings at the boat launch site, turn L on a gravel road. Go 0.8 mi to a parking lot below the dam. A gate at the bridge across Beaver River bars vehicles, but the way is open for foot travel. There is also a trail register at the bridge. There are no trail markers. ◀

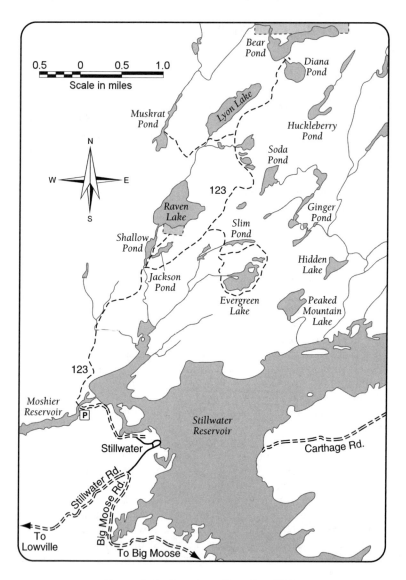

Raven Lake Primitive Corridor (123)

FROM THE FAR END OF THE BRIDGE (0.0 mi), the road heads gener-ally NNE for 2.0 mi to the outlet stream of Shallow Pond. (After it crosses the stream, a side road goes L, N, for 0.7 mi to a small plot of private land on Raven Lake.) The old main haul road is blocked to vehicle traffic just after the side road. It continues NE for another 1.0 mi before reaching the next jct. The R fork goes SE to Evergreen Lake and the L fork leads NE to Lyon Lake, Muskrat Pond, and Bear Pond. These are old, abandoned roads, not official trails. They are neither marked nor maintained. Hikers must realize this is wilderness travel and be prepared with map (the 7.5' x 15' Stillwater quadrangle) and compass.

❅ Trail in winter: The old logging roads are suitable for skis or snow-shoes until they become clogged with new growth. This is true back-country; be prepared for wilderness conditions. The road to the dam may not be plowed, so an additional 0.8 mi would be added with the use of the parking lot at the Stillwater boat launch.

⚹ Distances: Bridge over Beaver River to Shallow Pond outlet, 2.0 mi; to road jct., 3.0 mi; to Evergreen Lake, 4.0 mi (6.5 km).

(124) Red Horse Trail

Map: p. 276

The trail starts at Trout Pond on the N shore of Stillwater Reservoir (this point must be reached by boat) and passes several impressive medium-sized glacial lakes on its way to Clear Lake. It also gives access to the S portion of the Five Ponds Wilderness Area. Its name comes from the Red Horse Chain (including Clear, Witchhopple, and Salmon lakes). Supposedly, in times of high water, the outlet stream resembled galloping red horses. The trail was first cut by the superintendent at Nehasane Park in 1896 to provide a public way from the Beaver River to the Oswegatchie River that would bypass the private land at Nehasane Park.

▶ Trailhead: To reach the boat landing at Stillwater from Lowville, go E on Number Four Rd. to Number Four, turn R onto Stillwater Rd., and continue to the jct. with Big Moose Rd. Bear L to Stillwater. From Eagle Bay on NY 28, go NW on Big Moose Rd. Continue past Big Moose Station to the jct. with Stillwater Rd. Turn R into Stillwater. Park at the boat launch site by the ranger station. ◀

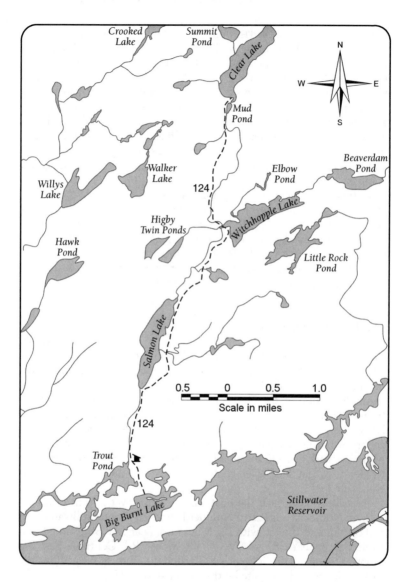

Red Horse Trail (124)

GOING BY BOAT to the N shore of the reservoir, the normal landing is on the NE shore of Trout Pond (0.0 mi). If the water level of the reservoir is low, boats cannot make the passage into Trout Pond. In that case, the alternate trailhead is at Burnt Lake, approximately 0.3 mi before Trout Pond. (Turn in next to the tip of the thin island on the E end of the lake.) Trout Pond and Big Burnt Lake, both formerly interior lakes, are now flooded bays of Stillwater Reservoir.

The trail N along the E shore of Trout Pond meets the alternate trail from Burnt Lake at a lean-to by the mouth of Red Horse Creek at the head of Trout Pond. Care should be taken when landing along the E shore, because of submerged stumps. A path leads along the shore to a register, with the lean-to 50 yd beyond.

From the register (0.0 mi), the trail proceeds along the bank of Red Horse Creek, until turning E to reach Salmon Lake at 0.9 mi. The magnificent stand of climax spruce, hemlock, and yellow birch encountered along the way is dwarfed by the occasional gigantic white pine on the shores of the creek.

The trail leaves the lake and passes through a continuous stand of impressive climax forest before crossing, on an 18-ft split spruce log (installed 2003), an extensive beaver-created wetland at 1.9 mi. The trail then gradually begins to ascend a modified esker with large spruce and hemlocks again present. It descends from the low ridge to cross several parallel wetlands before reaching Witchhopple Lake at 3.2 mi. There is no footbridge across the Witchhopple Lake outlet, but it can be crossed either downstream from the former footbridge site on a beaver dam, or possibly on a large hemlock blowdown. Return E along the N shore to get back on the trail.

The trail leaves Witchhopple Lake and proceeds through the same impressive climax forest as before, eventually going up along the outlet of Mud Pond, passing the pond, and reaching its ultimate destination on the shores of Clear Lake at 5.0 mi. The trail cut in 1896 to Crooked Lake and beyond is now just a memory. From here on, it's all wilderness travel.

❋ Trail in winter: The trail is very remote, but could be reached across the ice. In the unlikely event that this is attempted, the trail is suitable for backcountry skiing and snowshoeing.

🐾 Distances: N shore of Stillwater Reservoir to Salmon Lake, 0.9 mi; to Witchhopple Lake, 3.2 mi; to Clear Lake, 5.0 mi (8.1 km).

(125) **Colvin Rock Trail**

Map: p. 281

This is a very short trail at Beaver River Station, going to a witness rock carved by the Verplanck Colvin survey party. Colvin led a state survey of the Adirondack region in the late 1800s and is credited with pushing the creation of the Adirondack Forest Preserve and Park. On its side facing the trail, various initials and data are carved. The survey mark is on the survey line which separates the Totten and Crossfield Purchase from John Browns Tract.

▶ Trailhead: See Red Horse Trail (124) for directions to reach Stillwater. Obtain a map of Stillwater Reservoir at the registration booth in front of the ranger station. Go by boat to Grassy Point near Beaver River Station. Beach your boat; the docks are private. Go 600 ft up the road toward Beaver River Station. The trail starts on the L (E) and is 0.7 mi from Beaver River Station. ◀

LEAVING THE ROAD (0.0 mi), the trail goes gently up a slight hill heading NE. At a bit under 0.1 mi, there is an exposed rock on the L with some faint carving on it. This is the Colvin Rock. The trail continues on past the rock, gradually dimming from an ATV trail to a faint herd path. It arrives at the reservoir on the point of a small peninsula. If the water is high, you may not see the meadow ahead strewn with large boulders.

❋ Trail in winter: Gentle terrain, but hardly worthy of a winter trip.

🚶 Distances: From Grassy Point to trailhead, 600 ft; from Beaver River Station to trailhead, 0.7 mi; from trailhead to Colvin Rock, 0.1 mi (0.16 km).

(126) **Bathtub Trail** (unmaintained)

Map: p. 281

"The Bathtub" is a rock pool of cold water on the South Branch of the Beaver River. The trail is mostly used by anglers ("sports" from the big city) brought over by local guides. According to the etiquette described in Bill Marleau's *Big Moose Station*, if you (the outsider) are fishing this area when the local guide comes in with his "sport," you are decently expected to move on promptly.

▶ Trailhead: See Red Horse Trail (124) for directions to reach Stillwater. Obtain a map of Stillwater Reservoir at the registration booth in front of the ranger station. Go by boat to The Culvert near Beaver River Station. Cross the causeway and continue ESE to a tiny inlet in the middle of the almost straight shoreline. The trail is a continuation of the old Carthage Rd. ◀

FROM THE INLET (0.0 mi), follow the route of the old Carthage Rd. heading ESE on almost level terrain. The trail, which is not maintained by the state, ends at 1.0 mi when the old road reaches the South Branch. There is a modest-sized deep pool called The Bathtub, where hardy souls can take a dip.

  ❋ Trail in winter: Suitable, if unlikely, for skiing and snowshoeing.
  ᴁ Distance: Trailhead to Bathtub, 1.0 mi (1.6 km).

(127) **Burnt Mt. Trail** (unmaintained)

Map: p. 281

Burnt Mt., near Beaver River Station, was supposedly made bald by a fire, but this may be no more than someone's guess. In any case, it offers a rare opportunity to view the reservoir and surrounding territory. A former trail used the RR tracks; this trail is no longer available to hikers since the RR has been officially reactivated. However, a new trail has been flagged leaving from approximately the SW corner of Beaver River.

  ▶ Trailhead: See trail 125. After debarking at Grassy Point, go up the landing road for 0.8 mi to Beaver River Station, but not quite to the RR. Just before the old white hotel, turn R onto a small dirt lane. Pass an old gravel pit (probably with old trucks still in it) and a couple of camps on the right. Look for a larger camp with vertical bark siding on the L. At the foot of the driveway for this camp is the beginning of an old road R (don't enter the camp's dooryard), which is the trail; it begins in a briar patch. ◀

PASSING THROUGH THE BRIAR PATCH (0.0 mi), follow a path that bends L and reaches a state land boundary in less than 0.1 mi. The well-worn path, with gentle ups and downs, leads to the top of a steep hill at 0.6 mi. At the bottom the higher of a couple beaver dams (upstream) provides a crossing. The flagged trail then climbs up a gully, becomes more gradual at the top, and crosses a stream at 0.9 mi. It follows upstream, passing a series of beaver dams, bends L uphill and crosses another stream at 1.5 mi, and from 1.8 mi follows a ridge up to a rock outcropping at 2.0 mi.

Beaver River may not be in sight when leaves are out, but much of Stillwater Reservoir and mountains N and NE are visible. After the first open rock slab, it may be worth exploring SW where more rocky clearings give views to the W.

✸ Trail in winter: Suitable for mountaineering snowshoes if you are already in Beaver River.

✹ Distances: Beaver River Station to summit of Burnt Mt., 2.0 mi (3.2 km). Ascent, 629 ft (192 m).

(128) **Beaver River–Twitchell Trail**

Map: C1 and p. 281

The trail goes from Beaver River Station on Stillwater Reservoir to Twitchell Lake near Big Moose. The S trailhead at Twitchell Lake is accessible by car, but the N trailhead at Beaver River Station is accessible only by boat from Stillwater. A "water taxi" is available from Stillwater to Grassy Point and a barge goes from Stillwater to the W end of Flow Rd., the old Carthage Rd., so you can take your vehicle to Beaver River (with barge reservations—no set schedule—through Norridgewock III). The former use of RR put-put from Big Moose is no longer allowed because the RR, formerly abandoned, is now classed as active.

Beaver River, as noted in the introduction to this section, is interesting to visit in its own right. Hardy travelers who start early could walk the 6.6-mi Beaver River–Twitchell Trail from Twitchell Lake, visit Beaver River Station, perhaps have lunch at The Norridgewock or hotel, and return to Twitchell Lake by nightfall. This is a fairly long hike. For the less hardy, a two-car trip can be arranged by taking the cruise boat from Stillwater to Beaver River, then continuing on to Twitchell Lake via the Beaver River–Twitchell Trail, or the other way around.

▶ Trailheads: To reach the trail at its S end, drive NW from Eagle Bay on Big Moose Rd. to Big Moose (Station). At 7.3 mi from NY 28, just before the road crosses the RR tracks, turn R onto Twitchell Rd. and drive 2.0 mi to a parking lot on the lake at the end of the road. The trail starts on the L (W) end of the parking lot and is marked with blue markers. After debarking at Grassy Point, go up the landing road for 0.8 mi to Beaver River Station.

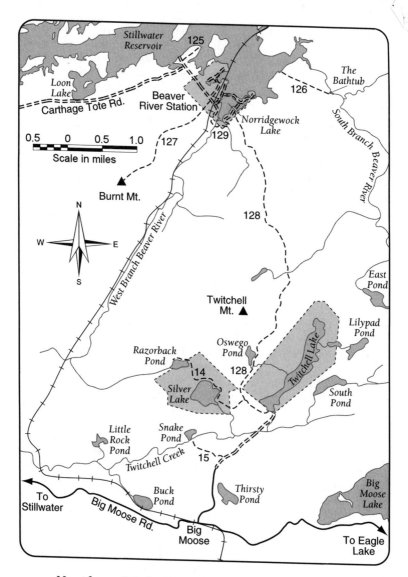

Norridgewock Lake (129) and Twitchell Pond Trails (128)

To reach the trail at its N end in Beaver River Station, start at the center of town in front of Norridgewock III, a combination inn, restaurant, and store. Proceed N along the tracks for 0.1 mi, turn R on a road, cross the causeway, and continue along the road. At 0.3 mi, there is a rock with a plaque honoring Verplanck Colvin. Turn R at the jct. at 0.5 mi. At 0.7 mi, the road makes a R turn, while the trail goes straight ahead along the edge of lawn for a cottage R. There is a sign on the tree pointing to Twitchell Lake. ◄

STARTING AT THE S TRAILHEAD PARKING LOT, the trail follows a woods road W on level ground. (This is also trail 14, the Razorback Pond Trail.) At 0.5 mi, the trail turns R onto a footpath and starts steeply up a hill. The hilltop at 0.8 mi is sharply pointed, and the trail starts steeply down again. This steep maneuver is necessary because the trail manages to squeeze in between the corners of two private tracts of land, without which there would be no public access. The trail continues on a much easier grade and crosses the outlet stream for Oswego Pond at 1.3 mi.

The route continues on fairly easy terrain to the pointed N end of Twitchell Mt. at 2.7 mi. The trail follows the base of the mountain, heads W for 0.3 mi to bypass a swampy creek bottom, then crosses the creek near its upper end. Signs at 3.2 mi mark a sharp L turn.

The route is low for a while but then climbs steadily on mostly gentle grades to the high point at 4.0 mi. The way from here is down, gently at first, until 5.0 mi, where a somewhat steep descent begins.

The trail reaches the register at 5.9 mi and then civilization on level ground at 6.0 mi. Turn R on trail 129 and follow the road to a T intersection. Then turn L to cross over the causeway to reach the RR tracks at 6.5 mi. Turn L into the center of town, reached at 6.6 mi.

❉ Trail in winter: Snowshoe and ski experts only. The remoteness of the trail and the strenuous, steep climbs make this a real challenge.

🏔 Distances: S trailhead to turnoff onto footpath, 0.5 mi; Oswego Pond outlet, 1.3 mi; Twitchell Mt., 2.7 mi; jct. with trail 129, 6.0 mi; center of Beaver River Station, 6.6 mi (10.6 km).

(129) Norridgewock Lake Trail

Map: p. 281

This is a loop trail, circling Norridgewock Lake. It is an easy stroll, best suited for those staying in Beaver River Station.

▶ Trailhead: Located at the center of town at Beaver River Station. To reach Beaver River, see trail 125. After debarking at Grassy Point, go up the landing road for 0.8 mi to Beaver River Station. ◀

STARTING AT THE TRACKS in front of the hotel known as Norridge-wock III (0.0 mi), go N along the tracks for 0.1 mi and turn R (E) on the road. Cross the causeway, passing a plaque commemorating Verplanck Colvin. Turn R at a jct. at 0.5 mi and go along the E shore of the lake. At 0.7 mi the road meets a T jct. The Beaver River–Twitchell Trail (trail 128) goes straight ahead at this jct., headed for Twitchell Lake 6.0 mi away.

Turn R and continue on the dirt road, which ends at 0.9 mi. Turn sharp L around a red building and follow the footpath. A private footpath turns R just after the building and crosses the creek to a private camp. Continue ahead (SE) on the less used footpath for another 300 ft, where it finally turns W to cross the creek on a small bridge. The footpath is marked occasionally with DEC markers, and is easy to follow. It winds among old forest, crosses the W branch of the Beaver River (a creek), and swings N to meet an old road at 1.5 mi. Continue along this road to the jct. at 1.6 mi. Turn L, go to the next jct., and turn R. This returns you to the center of town at 1.8 mi.

❃ Trail in winter: Ski or snowshoe.

⚹ Distances: Norridgewock III to center of causeway, 0.3 mi; to trail 128, 0.7 mi; to end of village roads, 0.9 mi; complete circuit, 1.8 mi (2.9 km). ◆

Appendix 1

Glossary of Terms

Azimuth A clockwise compass bearing swung from north.

Bivouac Camping in the open with improvised shelter or no shelter.

Bushwhacking To make one's way through natural terrain without the aid of a formal trail.

Cairn A pile of stones marking a summit or route.

Chimney A steep, narrow cleft or gully in the face of a mountain, usually by which the mountain may be ascended.

Cobble A small stony peak on the side of a mountain.

Col A pass between two adjacent peaks or between high points of a ridgeline.

Corduroy A road, trail, or bridge formed by logs laid side by side transversely to facilitate crossing swampy areas.

Cripplebush Thick, stunted growth at higher elevations.

Dike A band of different-colored rock, usually with straight, well-defined sides, formed when igneous rock is intruded into the existing rock. Dikes can manifest themselves either as gullies, if the dike rock is softer (as in the Colden Trap Dike), or as ridges.

Duff Partly decayed plant matter on the forest floor. Duff's ability to burn easily has started many forest fires.

Esker A long, winding ridge created by water running under or upon an Ice Age glacier. Prevalent in northern region. Soils layered and quite dry. Tops of ridge usually crowned with conifers.

Fire ring A rough circle of stones used as a site in which to build small fires.

Lean-to A three-sided shelter with an overhanging roof on the open side.

Logging or Lumber road A crude road used to haul logs after lumbering.

Summit The top of a mountain.

Tote road A road constructed in connection with logging operations and used for hauling supplies. Often built with corduroy, many of these roads are still evident after eighty years and are often used as the routes for present-day trails.

Vlei A low marsh or swampy meadow (pronounced *vly*).

Appendix II

State Campgrounds in the West-Central Region

Public campgrounds have been established by the DEC at many attractive spots throughout the state. Listed below are campgrounds that might be useful as bases of operations for hiking in the West-Central Region. Fees are charged for camping and use of these areas, except for the Moose River Plains Wild Forest.

A listing of all campgrounds is contained in the DEC brochure, "Breathe in...Camp out," and a listing online can be found at http://www.dec.ny.us/website/do/or2top.htm. Brochures are available at DEC regional offices (see www.dec.state.ny.us). Campground information is also available from DEC, 625 Broadway, Albany, NY 12233, and from most tourist information offices in the area. For campground information, call 518-457-2500. For campground reservations call 800-456-2267 (or go to www.reserveamerica.com). Private campgrounds in the area are listed in the *I Love NY* booklets generally available from the tourist information centers in Old Forge and Inlet.

Brown Tract Pond, on the E side of Lower Pond, with access from Uncas Rd., 2 mi W of the hamlet of Raquette Lake.

Eighth Lake, between Seventh and Eighth lakes, with access from NY 28 on the E.

Forked Lake, off North Point Rd., 3 mi W of Deerland on NY 30.

Golden Beach, on the E side of Raquette Lake's South Bay, with access from NY 28, 3.8 mi E of Raquette Lake village.

Lake Durant, on the E end of that lake and its adjacent S side, with access from NY 28, 2.5 mi E of Blue Mt. Lake village.

Limekiln Lake, on the N side and NW corner of that lake, with access from Limekiln Rd. S of Inlet.

Little Sand Point, on the W shore of Piseco Lake.

Nicks Lake, on the E side of that lake, with access from Bisby Rd. a little S of Old Forge.

Point Comfort, on the W shore of Piseco Lake.

Poplar Point, on the W shore of Piseco Lake.

The **Moose River Plains Wild Forest** SE of Inlet, beyond Limekiln Lake, contains eight primitive tent camping areas with 145 sites open from Memorial Day through Labor Day. It remains open through November, weather permitting, but 4WD or tire chains are required.

Special-Purpose Facilities of Interest

Tioga Point campground, on Tioga Point of Raquette Lake. Reachable only by boat on the lake or trail 49. 15 lean-tos, 10 tent sites. Reservations should be made well in advance.

Fourth Lake Picnic Area, on E side of Fourth Lake. 0.35 mi N of the W trailhead of trail 80.

Hinckley Reservoir Picnic Area, off NY 365, 5 mi W of Hinckley.

Acknowledgments

It's a little strange being the third editor of a book two other men have written. I wish to thank Robert J. Redington and Arthur W. Haberl, who researched the history of the region and compiled the trail list over the course of the first three editions. Their work relieved me of the burden of being inside checking books or microfilm for history, allowing me to be outside with my measuring wheel, GPS, and tape recorder checking the trails. I'm especially indebted to Art Haberl, who offered tips on GPS use and some trail updates even after he retired from the job. Also thanks to those who accompanied me on hikes and were distracted by my talking to my (note-taking tape recorder) self, thinking I was pointing out something to them.

About the Editors

NORM LANDIS has been an ADK member for more than twenty years. He served as trips chair for ADK's Iroquois Chapter and then for five years as chapter chair. He has led trips and participated in trail work and Adopt-A-Lean-to projects for the chapter in the Ha-de-ron-dah Wilderness as well as assisting on trail projects elsewhere.

A state-licensed outdoor guide, he is also DEC certified in Basic Wildlands Search and as a Basic Wildlands Search Crew Boss, and has assisted forest rangers as a searcher and search crew boss. His photos have appeared in the ADK calendar and in ADK's *Classic Adirondack Ski Tours*.

He holds an associate's degree from SUNY at Morrisville and two bachelor's degrees from SUNY Institute of Technology at Utica/Rome, which has honored him as a Distinguished Alumnus. He works as a copy editor and "Today's Living" pages editor at the *Daily Sentinel*, of Rome, New York. Originally from Albion, New York, he started work in Oneida after graduating from SUNY Morrisville and took the job at the Rome paper nearly ten years later.

NEAL BURDICK, a native of Plattsburgh, New York, first climbed Armstrong Mt. and the Wolf Jaws with members of the Algonquin Chapter when he was fifteen years old. He began his employment with ADK as a teenage hut crew member at Johns Brook Lodge more than thirty years ago, and continues that relationship today as editor of ADK's Forest Preserve Series and editor-in-chief of *Adirondac* magazine since 1984.

In 2001 Burdick received the Eleanor F. Brown ADK Communication Award for his many contributions. His column in *Adirondac*, "Random Scoots," was described by ADK member and author David Trithart as "a masterpiece in short, apt, and often entertaining communication."

As an acknowledged expert on the Adirondacks and the New York State Forest Preserve, Burdick has written many articles for a wide variety of publications. He edited ADK's *Adirondack Reader* (third edition); *With Wilderness at Heart*, an ADK history, and *Our Wilderness*, a young people's history of the Adirondacks. He is a frequent contributor to *Adirondack Explorer* and *Adirondack Life* and he provided the Adirondacks entry in Fodor's *National Parks and Seashores of the East*. He is a member of the Steering Committee of the Adirondack Center for Writing, a commentator for North Country Public Radio, and past juror for the New York Foundation for the Arts nonfiction writing competition.

Burdick is a graduate of St. Lawrence University and at his "day job" is St. Lawrence's associate director of University Communications and university editor. He is a member of ADK's Laurentian Chapter.

Adirondack Mountain Club

Information Centers

The ADK Member Services Center in Lake George and the ADK Heart Lake Program Center near Lake Placid, at the head of the Van Hoevenberg Trail, offer ADK publications and other merchandise for sale, as well as backcountry and general Adirondack information, educational displays, outdoor equipment, and snacks.

Lodges and Campground

ADIRONDAK LOJ, on the shores of Heart Lake, offers year-round accommodations in private and family rooms, a coed bunkroom, and cabins. It is accessible by car, and ample trailhead parking is available.

The Adirondak Loj Wilderness Campground, located on the Heart Lake property, offers thirty-four campsites, sixteen Adirondack-style lean-tos, and three tent cabins.

JOHNS BROOK LODGE (JBL), located near Keene Valley, is a seasonal backcountry facility located in prime hiking country. It is 3.5 mi from the nearest road and is accessible only on foot. Facilities include coed bunkrooms and small family rooms. Cabins near JBL are available year-round.

Both lodges offer home-cooked meals and trail lunches.

Join Us

We are a nonprofit membership organization that brings together people with interests in recreation, conservation, and environmental education in the New York State Forest Preserve.

ADKers choose from friendly outings, for those just getting started with local chapters, to Adirondack backpacks and international treks. Learn gradually through chapter outings or attend one of our schools, workshops, or other programs.

Membership Benefits
• Discovery: ADK can broaden your horizons by introducing you to new places, people, recreational activities, and interests.
• *Adirondac* Magazine
• Member Discounts: 20% off on guidebooks, maps, and other ADK publications; discount on lodge stays; discount on educational programs
• Satisfaction: Know that you're doing your part so future generations can enjoy the wilderness as you do.
• Chapter Participation: Experience the fun of outings and other social activities and the reward of working on trails, conservation, and education projects at the local level. You can also join as a member at large.
• Volunteer Opportunities: Give something back. There are many rewarding options in trail work, conservation and advocacy, and educational projects.

For more information
ADK Member Services Center
(Exit 21 off the Northway, I-87)
814 Goggins Road, Lake George, NY 12845-4117

ADK Heart Lake Program Center
P.O. Box 867, Lake Placid, NY 12946-0867

ADK Public Affairs Office
301 Hamilton Street, Albany, NY 12210-1738

Information: 518-668-4447
Membership: 800-395-8080
Publications and merchandise: 800-395-8080
Education: 518-523-3441
Facilities' reservations: 518-523-3441
Public affairs: 518-449-3870
E-mail: adkinfo@adk.org
Web site: www.adk.org

ADK Publications

Index

Locations are indexed by proper name with Camp, Lake, Mount, *or* Mountain *following.*